*Social History of Africa*

# POISON AND MEDICINE

**Recent Titles in**
**Social History of Africa Series**
*Series Editors: Allen Isaacman and Jean Allman*

# POISON AND MEDICINE

## ETHNICITY, POWER, AND VIOLENCE IN A NIGERIAN CITY, 1966 TO 1986

Douglas A. Anthony

HEINEMANN
Portsmouth, NH

JAMES CURREY
Oxford

DAVID PHILIP
Cape Town

**Heinemann**
A division of Reed Elsevier Inc.
361 Hanover Street
Portsmouth, NH 03801-3912
USA
www.heinemann.com

**James Currey Ltd.**
73 Botley Road
Oxford OX2 0BS
United Kingdom

**David Philip Publishers (Pty) Ltd.**
208 Werdmuller Centre
Claremont 7708
Cape Town, South Africa

Offices and agents throughout the world

ISBN 0-325-07052-0 (Heinemann cloth)
ISBN 0-325-07051-2 (Heinemann paper)
ISBN 0-85255-959-3 (James Currey cloth)
ISBN 0-85255-954-2 (James Currey paper)

**British Library Cataloguing in Publication Data**

Anthony, Douglas A.
    Poison and medicine : ethnicity, power, and violence in a Nigerian city, 1966 to 1986.—
    (Social history of Africa) 1. Igbo (African people)—Nigeria—Kano—Politics and
    government—20th century 2. Igbo (African people)—Nigeria—Kano—Social conditions—
    20th century 3. Igbo (African people)—Ethnic Identity—Nigeria—Kano—History—20th
    century 4. Ethnicity—Political aspects—Nigeria—Kano—History—20th century 5. Ethnic
    conflict—Nigeria—Kano—History—20th century 6. Kano (Nigeria)—Ethnic relations 7.
    Nigeria—History—Civil War, 1967-1970—Social aspects I. Title
    966.9'78

    ISBN 0-85255-959-3 (James Currey cloth)
    ISBN 0-85255-954-2 (James Currey paper)

**Library of Congress Cataloging-in-Publication Data**

Anthony, Douglas A., 1965–
    Poison and medicine : ethnicity, power, and violence in a Nigerian city, 1966 to 1986 /
    Douglas A. Anthony.
        p.   cm.—(Social history of Africa, ISSN 1099-8098)
    Includes bibliographical references and index.
    ISBN 0-325-07052-0 (acid-free paper)—ISBN 0-325-07051-2 (pbk. : acid-free paper)
    1. Kano (Nigeria)—Ethnic relations.   2. Igbo (African people)—Nigeria—Kano—
Politics and government—20th century.   3. Igbo (African people)—Nigeria—Kano—
Social conditions—20th century.   4. Igbo (African people)—Ethnic identity—Nigeria—
Kano—History—20th century.   5. Ethnicity—Political aspects—Nigeria—Kano—
History—20th century.   6. Ethnic conflict—Nigeria—Kano—History—20th century.
7. Nigeria—History—Civil War, 1967-1970—Social aspects. I. Title. II. Series.
DT515.9.K3 A58 2002
966.9'78—dc21       2001057765

Paperback cover photo: One of Sabon Gari's many churches. Courtesy of Alan Frishman.

Printed in the United States of America on acid-free paper.

06 05 04 03 02 SB 1 2 3 4 5 6 7 8 9

To Amanda

# CONTENTS

*A photographic essay follows page 140.*

# ACKNOWLEDGMENTS

In beginning this project, I set out to understand the process of reconciliation that followed the Nigerian Civil War. I would not, I told myself, write about conflict. Rather, I would focus on the forces that brought communities together. With that in mind, I made my second visit to Nigeria in 1992, flush with assurances from Nigerians of many ethnic affiliations that I, as an outsider presumably untainted by partisanship, would be able to ask questions that Nigerian scholars had not. "People will tell you their stories," I heard. "They will be glad someone is asking."

In writing this book, I have accumulated enormous debts of gratitude to friends, colleagues, and institutions in several countries. Any such list must begin with Humphrey Umeh and Auwalu Kawu, who were invaluable in helping me find my way through what were, initially, the mazes of Kano's Igbo and Hausa communities. Their time, patience, and friendship were the best gifts for which I could have asked. In turn, I owe my acquaintance to both of them to the farsightedness and generosity of Priscilla Starratt-Galadanci. This book began as a Northwestern University doctoral dissertation conceived under the guidance of Ivor Wilks, helped through the mud by Jonathan Glassman, and brought to fruition by John Hunwick. While not much of the original remains, their stamps do.

Many Nigerian colleagues have earned my thanks as well. The staff of the Kano State History and Culture Bureau, especially its former deputy director, Auwalu Hamza, were dependable and resourceful friends and bureaucratic allies. Professor Abdullahi Mahadi and the staff of Arewa House in Kaduna provided a home away from Kano. I also thank the staffs of the Nigerian National Archives in Kaduna and Enugu. The Sociology Department of Bayero University provided an important intellectual community. And, closer to home, the staff of the Northwestern University Library's Africana collection, and particularly Pat Ogedengbe, were extremely helpful.

My wife Amanda Kemp has been sincere in her support, without which this book might never have been completed. Muhammad Sani Umar and Musa Dudu Ilu were generous with their input through the early stages, Jean Allman with her longstanding support and professional insights, and Jonathan Reynolds with the time he has spent batting so many of these ideas back and forth. I also thank Alhaji Uba Adamu, Tom Adeoye, Ahmed Bako, Alhaji Aminu Sharif Bappa, Andrew Barnes, Sandra Barnes, Misty Bastian, Malam A.U. Dan Asabe, Tom Forrest, Alan Frishman, Pius Gbasha, Phillip Jaggar, Sandra Greene, Anthony Kirk-Greene, Murray Last, Sindi Mader-Gould, Robert Montgomery, Don Ohadike, Phillip Onyebujoh, John Oriji, Ted Tarkow, Chidozie and Chimaroke Umeh, Robert Vinson, and Ado Yahuza. I also thank Walter C. Daniel, who was my first intellectual mentor, Constance Isikwemegbu, and my mother, Caroline Griswell, and hope that this book honors each of their memories.

Much of the research upon which this book is based was funded with generous Fulbright-Hays and Social Science Research Council Africa Program fellowships; other financial support, at various times, came from Northwestern's Program of African Studies, the Committee for Institutional Cooperation, Franklin & Marshall College, and the Lindback Foundation.

No set of acknowledgments would be complete without a sincere expression of gratitude to the men and women who have trusted me enough to share their stories and experiences. I can only hope that the spirit of true and generous goodwill shown by so many Nigerian citizens toward other Nigerian citizens during the disturbances of 1966 and in the postwar period continues to find expression in a new Nigeria no less challenging than the old.

# ABBREVIATIONS AND A NOTE ON CURRENCY

| | |
|---|---|
| ABC | Abdullahi Bayero College (Kano) |
| ABU | Ahmadu Bello University (Zaria) |
| AG | Action Group (political party) |
| APC | Abandoned Property Committee |
| DO | District Officer |
| ECS | East Central State |
| GRA | Government Reserved Area |
| ICA | Igbo Community Association |
| NA | Native Authority |
| NCNC | National Council of Nigerian Citizens (political party; until 1961, National Council for Nigeria and the Cameroons) |
| NEPU | Northern Elements Progressive Union (political party) |
| NPC | Northern People's Congress (political party) |
| NPF | Nigeria Police Force |
| NPN | National Party of Nigeria (political party) |
| PRP | People's Redemption Party (political party) |
| SDP | Social Democratic Party (political party) |
| UMBC | United Middle Belt Congress (political party) |

In 1973 Nigeria changed its unit of currency from the pound (made up of 20 shillings, each of 12 pennies) to the naira (made up of 100 kobo).

# INTRODUCTION

In early 1970, a young Igbo[1] man, literally penniless, boarded a north-bound Nigeria Railway train headed for the city of Kano. It had been forty-three months since he had left his teaching job there. Unlike most Igbos resident in Northern Nigeria in 1966, the young man's departure from the North had been a leisurely one. He had gone south with the intention of spending several weeks of leave in the country's Eastern Region, which encompassed most of Igboland. Within weeks of the young man's trip, the majority of the Igbos he left behind also found their way to Igboland, but only after attacks by armed mobs and soldiers left thousands of men, women, and children dead and others horribly injured. In the time between his departure and return, the young man and others like him fought and lost a grueling war in which well over a million people, most of them Igbos, died. The majority of their adversaries in the forests of Biafra were Northern Nigerians. During that war many outsiders doubted that Igbos—having experienced such enmity—would ever return to Northern Nigeria in anything approaching their former numbers. Yet, within weeks of the fighting's end, the young man so recently a Biafran soldier stood empty-handed in front of the ticket collector on a northbound train and told her "I am from the war area and I need to get to Kano."[2]

According to proverb, Kano is an elephant's belly, and as such contains a little bit of everything. For decades, that everything has included Northern Nigeria's largest Igbo community. For Igbos living and working there and elsewhere in Northern Nigeria in 1966, ethnicity was a poison that polluted relations between them and local populations, as it had done on a national level for more than a gen-

eration. After a military coup in January of that year, displaced politicians and anxious civil servants, among others, vilified Igbos as never
before. In the process they equated Igbo ethnic identity with a host of
evils, and later used negative images of Igbos to generate support for
war. By the time that the Civil War ended in 1970, however, official
discourses had helped to rehabilitate the meaning of Igbo ethnicity in
Nigeria, and the long war had led many Northerners to develop a degree of grudging respect for Igbos' resourcefulness and tenacity. More
importantly, the political party and ethnic associations that had, in
Northern eyes, defined Igbo political and economic aspirations in ethnically specific terms were defunct, and the post-war poverty of most
Igbos removed lingering fears of an economic threat. According to
officials, Igbos had not been the losers in the war; rather, they were
the unfortunate victims of sinister leadership. In that climate, Igbos
were, as an ethnic group, welcomed back into Nigerian life. As some
Igbos made their way to the North, most traveling individually rather
than in groups, they too were welcomed back. There, individually and
collectively, they carefully managed how they conducted and presented
themselves, and made their ethnic identity a resource for healing
whenever they could. Later, as they became more secure, they began
to reestablish organizations centered on ethnic and sub-ethnic identities, and used those organizations to further the task of carving out
new places for themselves and, increasingly, for their community.

The metaphor of poison and medicine, then, is intended to suggest
dual possiblitities for ethnicity. Depending on who mobilizes it and
how, ethnic identities and membership in ethnic groups can be turned
to destructive or constructive purposes. Evidence of the former is
abundant and fairly transparent; to see evidence of the toxic effects
ethnicity has had on Nigeria's body politic, one need only examine
the destructive results of colonial policies of indirect rule, the emergence of ethnic politics during the colonial period, or its flowering
during Nigeria's First Republic. Ethnicity has also been manipulated
to unsavory ends in other African countries, as recent struggles in
central Africa demonstrate, and around the world, displayed most recently in the former Yugoslavia and Soviet Union. Yet ethnicity—
membership by birth or ascription in a group based on language,
culture, or belief in common origin—does not contribute only to destructive social processes. It can be a source of order, of community,
and of security in times of uncertainty. In the context of a multi-ethnic state like Nigeria, with a history saturated with highly ethnicized
politics, the power of ethnicity in public discourses appears, for the

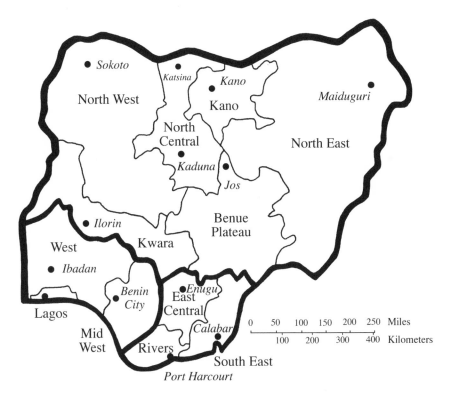

**Map I.1** Nigeria (c. 1970). (Bold lines show colonial-era regions, thin lines show 12-state boundaries).

foreseeable future, to be secure. Despite coexisting in a multi-dimensional web of affiliations based on class, gender, religion, region, and other criteria, ethnicity has remained a powerful force in formal and informal public discourses.

While the post-war reintegration of Igbos into the fabric of Nigerian society has been, in many ways, dreadfully imperfect,[3] it also demonstrates that just as leaders of thought can use ethnicity to divide, they can turn it to constructive ends. After the war, in an environment of relative political stability and economic expansion, a degree of balance between the toxic and recuperative potential of ethnicity was achieved. This happened in part because of efforts by the state, in part through the actions of non-Igbo Nigerians, and most importantly through the actions of Igbos themselves, including members of the resurgent Igbo community in Kano.

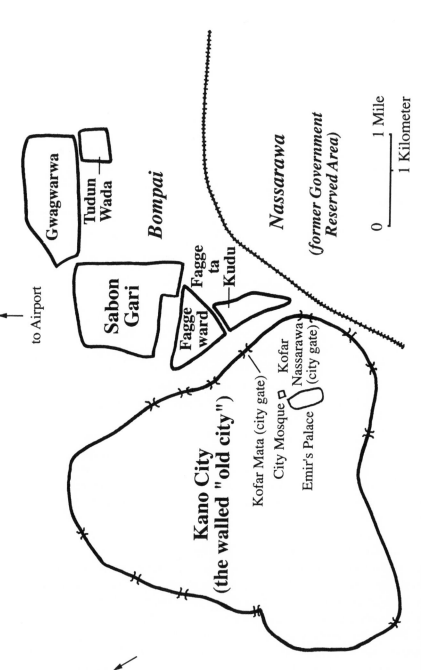

**Map 1.2** Metropolitan Kano (c. 1970).
*(Adapted from John N. Paden, Religion and Political Culture in Kano [Berkeley: University of California Press, 1971].)*

## THEORY AND PRACTICE

This work of social history has at its core three goals. The first, like any work of history, is to capture and relate a story, in this case, the story of Kano's Igbo community as it passed through an extraordinary series of historical moments. The second goal is closely allied with the first. This study attempts to locate within a single stream of history parts of a story that, by any conventional method of periodization, fall in different chapters of Nigeria's national narrative. When broken into pieces, the story's complexities slip into all-too-neat historical clichés, and its insights on the interrelatedness of ethnicity and power, and of amity and violence become obscure. The cataclysm of Nigeria's Civil War is, like all cataclysms, an invitation to politicians, historians, and ordinary Nigerians to close one era and begin another. And, indeed, such periodization makes a good deal of sense in many analyses of Nigeria's internal and external lives. Van den Bersselaar's recent study on Igbo identity, for example, argues that the war focused Igbo identity in a manner sufficient to require separation from the post-war period.[4] And he is correct, since his goal is to understand the slow development of an acceptance of common ethnicity among the Igbo. Gradual processes and cataclysmic moments make odd bedfellows. Yet to appreciate the continuities and transformations that surround Igbo communities in Northern Nigeria, we must see not only links in a chain, but also a single thread, tattered though it may be.

The book is also an attempt to bring together competing visions of ethnicity. It is, in scope and style, a work of instrumentalism, an approach to the study of ethnicity that treats group members' belief in ethnic identities as a form of social capital, and seeks to understand the ways in which ethnicity is manipulated in the service of political or economic goals.[5] My first interest here, therefore, is in the mechanisms that influence the operation of ethnic identities, and may bear some similarity to recent work on central Africa, which has exploded myths of transhistorical ethnic identites locked in permanent, inevitable struggle by making explicit the cultivation and harnessing of ethnic sentiments to accomplish political goals.[6] Ethnicity is, we know, not static, but profoundly malleable, and to manipulate a thing is, inescapably, to change it. This happens by amplifying certain parts of its meaning and suppressing others, in the process imbuing it with new historical and symbolic associations. This is precisely what happened to Igbo ethnic identity in a profound way during the crises of 1966, the Nigerian Civil War, and the years that followed the war.

The war is both the beginning and the end of Igbo identity. It was the end of a long and gradual process of becoming Igbo that had been going on since the beginning of the twentieth century. As the Civil War was perceived in ethnic terms, the Igbo identity that had resulted from this process provided one of the main lines along which people's loyalties were mobilized. However, the war also transformed this Igbo identity. To many Igbo, as we have seen, the conflict represents the climax of Igbo identity, the ultimate celebration of Igbo-ness where Igbo virtues came to the front in the shared battle for a future for the Igbo nation. In this sense, the war was the beginning of an Igbo identity that carries with it the bitterness of the lost war and the complaints of still being second class citizens; an identity that emphasizes the need to retain and strengthen [its] own language and culture as a way to defend [itself] against other Nigerian groups.[7]

In recognizing the truth of this transformation, this study moves beyond instrumentalism and toward constructivism, an approach that concentrates on how ethnic identities are made, by whom, and why.[8] This school of analysis, most often associated with studies of southern Africa, has been criticized for rendering Africans passive in the face of European agency.[9] In dealing with the creation and manipulation of Igbo ethnicity, however, the insights constructivism offers are invaluable. Identifying and documenting all the transformations in what it meant to be Igbo during and after the war could fill a book much longer than this one. Instead, what I have done is to look first at one city (Kano) and to use that city as a window on an ethnic subregion (Hausaland), and a geopolitical region (Northern Nigeria). By arguing that the war transformed how other Nigerians related to Igbos, and how Igbos, in turn, related to them, this study takes a page from the constructivist's handbook without abandoning its instrumentalism. The war reconfigured some of the meanings of being Igbo but not others; I look through the window of Kano and attempt to demonstrate what was different, what was the same, and to explain why. In so doing, I have tried to balance the agency of ordinary Africans with the power of elites.

Finally, I also nod to the oldest of the major schools of ethnicity studies, the problematic notion of primordialism. Primordialist thinkers, many in the service of colonial agendas and operating under the yoke of racist ideologies, treated African identities as ahistorical, static, and irrational. Primordialism also naively avoids questions of manipulation by assuming that membership in an ethnic group is itself sufficient motivation to act on behalf of that group. I share Young's desire to look at the "affective tie" of ethnicity—that is, its irrational, emotional side.[10] As other scholars have noted, despite ethnicity's material and constructed aspects, much of its power to motivate and unify originates in the realm of the emotional, and finds elaboration in myth, symbols, and cultural forms. In Bravman's words, "historicity does not diminish the reality" of ethnicity.[11] It is at this juncture that Bravman locates a false dichotomy between "primordial" and "constructed" ethnicity. However careful the manipulation of ethnicity, and however deliberate its management, the exploitation of ethnicity is predicated on the existence of a reservoir of ethnic sentiments that can be tapped, and it is here where primordialism's willingness to speak the language of passion is useful. According to Young, primordialism "helps make comprehensible the emotionally latent in ethnic conflict, its disposition to arouse deep-seated fears, and insecurities, or to trigger a degree of aggressiveness not explicable in purely material interest terms."[12] Like ethnic identity itself, on a certain level these emotive ties need not pass historical muster; they need only resonate with those whose sentiments are being appealed to or manipulated, and need only articulate with them at that historical moment. In this sense, what feels true, *or can be made to feel true*, often works.[13] And, in the circular alchemy of ethnicity, those apparent truths can become part of future notions of ethnic identity.

Lonsdale has offered a further explanation for the emotional power of ethnicity. In his study on Kikuyu ethnicity in colonial Kenya, he argued that ethnicity "gives the identity that makes social behavior possible."[14] It accomplishes this by simultaneously fulfilling two functions. On one side is the inward-looking manifestation of ethnicity (Lonsdale's moral ethnicity) that defines membership in an ethnic community in terms of values and cultural practices specific to the group, and which carry moral overtones. On the other side is the outward-looking face of ethnicity (political tribalism), the face that confronts those bound by different codes and contracts, often in competition for power and resources. By speaking to both sets of needs, ethnicity remains a salient political and moral force, one that is as adaptable as it is persistent. In understanding Northern Nigeria's 1966 riots, the material and the affective are inseparable, just as the inward face of ethnicity (Lonsdale's moral ethnicity) is inseparable from its political aspects. When anger and fear were mobilized to generate and sustain anti-Igbo violence, it was in large part to advance the material interests of Northern elites, and those elites succeeded because ordinary Northerners, driven by their own material concerns, participated. But material interests alone do not explain elites' success in generating and sustaining support. Their appeals succeeded because they could also tap into an established vocabulary of fears and insecurities, emotions that had been imbued over preceeding decades with ethnic overtones. How big a part ethnically framed fears played depended on a range of factors, many of which—particularly media representations— elites could control. Since to "illuminate what is 'our own' darkens the shadow of 'the other,'" the project of vilifying Igbos was accompanied by appeals to Northern virtue.[15]

Just as the actions of colonial administrators had given political reality to otherwise misguided notions of primordial ethnicity, in 1966 widely shared—and often dubious—assumptions about Igbos' universal and unquestioning loyalty to their ethnic group contributed to political upheaval and humanitarian disaster. In fact, Northern elites had carefully nurtured those same notions through years of political discourse, and Igbo elites had played the same game. Yet Northern elites' emotional appeals were not targeted only to arouse the basest emotions. As Nigeria's national balance of power changed, new elite agendas displaced older ones, bringing with them new appeals. As a result, the emotions Northerners attached to Igbo ethnicity changed during and after the war.

## POISON AND MEDICINE

In integrating these schools of thought around a core of historical materialism, the story of Kano's Igbo community unfolds as a narrative of poison and medicine. Northern elites manipulated the content and meaning of Igbo ethnicity for a Northern audience to serve their own ends, material and otherwise. Their manipulation of Igbo ethnicity shifted from negative to positive in response to changes in their perceptions of their own best interests. It is this shift that constitutes the first case in which poison was transformed into medicine. When it served their interests to represent Igbos as toxic, displaced Northern elites conjured and circulated rhetorical venom as well as physical violence. Then, in a masterful act of political alchemy, a new regime pioneered the use of many of the same essentialisms to create a salve for the wounds of dislocation and war.

The other participants in the process of changing the meaning of Igbo ethnicity were Igbos themselves. Ordinary Igbos' embrace of an ethnic identity was part of the glue that allowed Northerners to generalize about them. Within that identity, however, there was a great deal of variation around the very characteristics Northerners seemed so willing to ascribe to Igbos as a group. And for their part, Igbos in Kano altered how they embodied their ethnic identities in response to new conditions. In 1966 some manipulated superficial characteristics to save themselves, and after the war, most adopted public dispositions markedly different from those associated with Igbos before the war. At the same time, just as government propaganda had turned liabilities into assets, so many former Biafrans exploited persistent beliefs about Igbos to help themselves. This, I argue, is the second manifestation of making medicine from poison. While Igbos were reacting to a context largely shaped by elite politics, the particular adaptations they made were the product of careful decisions reached individually, within households, and through ethnic networks. With time, as Kano's Igbos felt the constraints on them lessen, they restored institutional manifestations of their pre-war ethnic identity even as their own ethnic consciousness had been profoundly changed by 1966 and the war. In appealing to the same ethnically based institutions that had been lightning rods only a few years before, they again turned poison into medicine.

## SOCIAL HISTORY, MASTER NARRATIVES, AND POWER

This book is also the story of a community that underwent tremendous change, a community that was caught within a national storm and paid a terrible price for it. Some of its former members then set about making a new community, and, in a sense, did so with help from some of the same people who had dismantled the old one. I interpret the task of the social historian to be to illuminate the experiences of ordinary people, the texture of whose lives can slip between the cracks of national, regional, and even local histories. I believe that the story of Kano's Igbos is far too important to allow to vanish, but in fact, it has already begun to do so. While conducting fieldwork in Kano, and interviewing Igbo men and women about their experiences before and after the war, their children, including adult children, would sometimes gather to listen. One young man, not much younger than me, said afterward that it was the first time he had heard his father talk about "the crisis and the war." Another young man, the son of a man proud of his military service to Biafra, worked as a research assistant for me, conducting interviews on my behalf with older women whom I alone would have been unable to interview. He told me again and again how much the things he was learning from the interviews differed from the little he had learned of the war in secondary school. Rather, the stories he was hearing were similar to things he had heard his father discuss with men his own age, but which he had not talked about with his sons. The young man was also surprised to learn of the changes to Igbo life in Kano. It seemed that talking of changes in the town came dangerously close to the subject of the dicey times surrounding the war. Another Igbo friend, a Mid-Western woman, was fascinated as she checked the spelling of proper nouns in my field notes, since in so doing she read testimony about the 1966 riots. Those years were, she said, a taboo subject in her home, and she remained unsuccessful in getting the older members of her household to discuss 1966 or the war.

Further, by the time that I began in 1992 the fieldwork that has become this book, the number of Igbos in Kano with first-hand experience of the pre-war period had suffered a sharp reduction. During the 1970s and '80s, those Igbos who had come to Kano before the war and returned were known as "Kano One," and those who arrived for the first time after the war were called "Kano Two." In late 1991 a local dispute between Christians and Muslims led to fighting. Most of the city's Muslims were Hausa and most of its Christians Igbos, and, on the surface, the similarities with 1966 were striking. For many of the "Kano One," men and women who had survived 1966, this new violence was more than enough to make them abandon Kano for good. Some turned their business interests in Kano over to apprentices or partners and returned to their home towns and villages; others moved to Lagos, Onitsha, Aba, or other southern commercial cities. A few relocated to Jos, the new national capital of Abuja, or other parts of Nigeria's religiously balanced Middle Belt. Very few chose to go to other predominantly Muslim far Northern cities. This dispersal made them difficult to track, and the fuel scarcities of 1993–1994 made it impractical to search them out. Fortunately, in their absence, the "Kano One" who remained were enthusiastic interview subjects. Many of them, however, left Kano after another religious clash in 1995.[16]

Without an opportunity to set down their motives, priorities, and strategies in their own words, the experiences of Kano's Igbos appear at risk of being collapsed into competing narratives that force lived experience into narrow, preconceived molds. Kano's Igbos might survive in the literature of the "Igbo Diaspora," where they will appear in conjunction with the failure of nationalism in Nigeria, the origins of the Civil War, the post-war return of abandoned property, and retellings of violent conflicts such as the religious disturbances of 1991 and 1995. Understandably, this already appears to be the case in a number of recent publications.[17] The community might also be absorbed into the hungry discourse of "ethnic conflict," where they are constructed as a natural foe for the city's Hausa majority.[18] Or, as appeared likely during the late 1990s, as tensions between Yoruba and Hausa communities deepened, the narrative of Igbo-Hausa symbiosis (the dialectical twin of Igbo-Hausa conflict) might prevail for a time. Each of these conceptual homes for Kano's Igbos also has the power to obliterate the three-dimensional grey zones of real life in favor of black and white in two dimensions. In place of these apparently irreconcilable models, I instead propose a narrative strategy that is at once broader and less comprehensive, one that works not in opposition to the existing narratives, but rather around and through them.

Future historians will not have to depend entirely on the oral accounts that are already becoming difficult to gather. There is a paper trail, in Nigerian and foreign archives, and in government publications and newspapers. I have made liberal use of these sources, to round out the story, and to tie it to events that were shaping the rest of Northern Nigeria and the country. On their own, however, the written sources tell only a fraction of the story and, I found, were riddled with inaccuracies that could be exposed only by appealing to other sources. Bozzoli has confronted this difficulty. She challenged a model of oral history in which "the experiences of the poor are validated by their accordance with other sources of information and interpretation."[19] I agree with Bozzoli; with much of the material with which I am concerned, it is the official accounts, particularly of moments charged with political and ethnic antagonism, that must pass muster with lived experience.[20] As a result, the various accounts hardly form a seamless whole. They do, however, fit together in ways that illuminate more than they obfuscate.

As any work of history does, this study privileges some sources over others. It inevitably embraces some subjective readings of events and their consequences to the detriment of competing interpretations. Terminology alone has provided enormous challenges. I have, for example, declined to refer to the anti-Igbo violence of May-June and September-October 1966 as "pogroms," even though many Igbo informants insisted on using the term precisely because they recognized its power. I have, instead, used the less specific terms "disturbance" and "riot," which, not surprisingly, were the terms, almost without exception, that Northern informants preferred when speaking in English. I have utilized the latter after considering Brass' definition of pogroms as "attacks upon the persons and property of a particular ethnic, racial, or communal group in which the state and/or its agents are implicated to a significant degree, but which are given the appearance, by design of the authorities or otherwise, of a riot."[21] The first problem here is to define "the state" in a context where federal and regional governments with military and civilian components coexisted with provincial and local authorities. These groups shared sometimes overlapping jurisdictions and resources. For the sake of labeling, I contain this problem by arbitrarily defining the state as a chain of the above authorities, which Nigeria's national governments sought to control, directly or indirectly, during the major outbreaks of anti-Igbo violence. To the extent that local authorities, for example, failed to follow instructions from above, I treat them as acting without the legitimacy of the state. At the same time, I present evidence, both direct and indirect, that local, regional, and federal government employees were involved in episodes of violence. This is most striking in the case of the Kano mutiny, when soldiers attacked civilians. In each case, however, it is difficult to demonstrate that these government employees were acting as agents of official policy, and in many cases it is clear that they were explicitly in violation of policy. Generally, they appear to have operated in support of agendas at odds with those of the state, and did so even as other agents of the state worked to contain violence. While it is clear that the state did not always act as expeditiously or decisively as situations warranted, it did act, and federal forces like the Nigeria Police Force and the military were, in the end, more instrumental in protecting Igbo *civilians* than in menacing them. Similarly, just as some civil servants clearly played a central role in organizing anti-Igbo activities, they did so not in their capacity as government employees, but rather in spite of the obligations their positions made incumbent on them. This disaggregation of "the state" reveals a complexity that vanishes in the overwhelming shadow of "pogrom." For those who lived through the violence of 1966, however, the points of slippage around which I construct parts of my argument pale in comparison to memories of violence that, even now, can appear monolithic. That monolith, however, does not subsume the entire apparatus of state.

I might instead have argued that the conditions for Brass' definition of pogrom were met. By extending the definition of the state to include those same civil servants and the displaced politicians from the First Republic who used patronage networks and even state resources to manipulate public sentiment, the criteria would be met in many of the worst disturbances. My decision not to follow this line of argumentation will, I suspect, generate disapproval in some quarters, and approval in others. Clearly, the distinction is open to debate, and has deeply political ramifications. As Brass reminds us, "The winning side is not only the one which inflicts the most damage and suffers the least from crowd violence, but which succeeds in labeling it a riot. The losing side may gain sympathy and political support if it succeeds in demonstrating that what in fact occurred was a pogrom."[22] The fact that both terms survive in the spoken and written words of both Nigerian and outside analysts attests to the liveliness of that debate.

While the label that I have applied might arguably represent a Northern "success" in defining the violence as riots and not as pogroms, the narratives that follow draw from multiple perspectives, including those of Igbos, Northern officials, and outside observers. Conspicuously absent in any transparent way are the views of Northern rioters. The task of representing the points of view of rioters in Kano must, I am afraid, fall to someone able to move much less conspicuously in Hausa society than I. The question of defining the book's narrative goes deeper, however, and penetrates pre-war, wartime, and post-war periods, and transcends the violence itself. Representing the riots requires the scholar to "explain them satisfactorily, to establish politically as well as scientifically their causes." However,

> this very search for causes is in no way free from the struggle to represent riots properly, thus it is not possible to present a causal theory of riots that is neutral to the interests of those seeking to capture its meaning. Most important, it is also questionable whether it is possible to develop a causal theory of ethnic riots separate from the discourses which encompass them, free from the prevailing . . . paradigms and master narratives into which they are so often placed.[23]

The unfortunate master narrative that has tended to guide discussions of Igbo and Hausa is one of irreconcilable cultural difference, of political and economic competition, and of violence that emerges as a reasonable, and often inevitable result. Cultural difference is consistent with the model of cultural pluralism introduced by Furnivall and reformulated by Kuper and Smith. Within Kuper and Smith's model, colonial rule brought together in a single political and economic order groups culturally distinct from one another, with incompatible institutions. This facilitated a mutual recognition of a meaningful boundary between groups.[24] In Nigeria's case, the boundaries were first and foremost ethnic, and the colonial state both exacerbated and exploited those boundaries. Largely within the model of pluralism, scholars of Nigeria have correctly argued that political and economic competition between groups reinscribed those boundaries.[25] As Diamond has put it, Nigerians have seen the "deliberate, systematic effort of a rising class to accumulate private wealth and to establish concentrated private control over the means of production at public expense." Members of this new class of closely aligned political and economic elites have manipulated cultural difference in their struggles against one another over power and state resources. In their efforts to control the state, the fountain from which both wealth and power flowed, "no electoral strategy seemed more assured of success than the manipulation of ethnic pride and prejudice."[26] When played out in this context, the story of Nigeria's periods of decolonization (roughly, the decade of the 1950s) and early independence (1960–1966) appear to lead, almost teleologically, to a showdown, in a general sense, between North and south.[27] Within this unfortunate dichotomy, much of Nigeria's national history has been written, often at the expense of elements that require a more nuanced analysis than competition models allow. Often this regional divide has appeared most starkly in the form of conflict between Hausa and Igbo, the two major ethnic groups that have often represented the polar extremes of Nigeria's cultural pluralism. This apparent telelogy of Igbo-Hausa conflict is but one limitation of the competition model. If the relationship between Igbo and Hausa is emblematic of anything, I believe, it is representative of the profound slippages that surround ethnicity and its manipulation.

## "IGBO," "HAUSA," AND "THE NORTH"

This study is predicated on the reality of ethnic groups, and on accepting ethnic labels unless given reason to interrogate them. This was not a step taken lightly. There are literatures that historicize both Igbo and Hausa ethnic labels, and which present the considerable limitations of both. Readers familiar with Nigeria, for example, have undoubtedly noticed my use of the simple "Hausa" label instead of the more nuanced and more common "Hausa-Fulani." I have done this because it was as "Hausas" and not as "Hausa-Fulanis" that my Igbo informants dealt with their hosts. Similarly, my view on Igbo ethnicity is limited. My view is, first of all, centered not in Igboland, where I spent little time, but rather in Kano and other Northern cities, where I have spent nearly two years working on this topic. As a result, I have a window on what it means to be Igbo that is probably more similar to that of a Kano Hausa man than that of an Igbo. Hausa eyes make little effort to see the differences between and within the many sub-groups that constitute Igbo society. I was aware of the distinctions Igbos drew, for example, between Mid-Western Igbos and Eastern Igbos, or between Eastern Igbos from old Imo State and those from Anambra, or, most importantly, between the many towns and villages to which most Igbos looked for their most reliable affiliation above the lineage. In his recent study on the Maasai, Bravman cautions us not to fall prey to assumptions of "intragroup sameness" at the expense of recognizing processes of "differentiation and struggle" within groups.[28] However, despite being aware that these distinctions existed and colored the interactions between the Igbos around me, I did not try to penetrate those identities as the anthropologist might have. While I agree with the Comaroffs that the historian must possess and exercise ethnographic sensibilities, my focus was not on the internal operation of Igbo networks, but rather on their external operation—that is, the way those networks facilitated, buffered, or biased interactions with Kano's Hausa community.[29] This study is, therefore, not an ethnography, though it may be of some small use to ethnographers, particularly as they explore changes in articulations and meanings of Igbo identity. The Igbo community I saw was, in more ways than not, resolutely aware of itself as both an amalgam and as an island, and its external frontier with the surrounding ocean of Hausa society exerted a defining influence on each perception.

### The Interplay of Igbo and Hausa

In a broader sense, Igbo and Hausa ethnic identities have each reflected a great deal of dynamism, and each has, to a degree, exerted influence on the shape of the other. Barth's seminal description of ethnicity as relational and dependent on the construction of boundaries between groups reverberates in this argument.[30] Igbo ethnic identity has changed profoundly during the twentieth century, and events in Northern Nigeria played no small part in those changes. In van den Bersselaar's words, "Igbo identity emerged very rapidly between 1900 and 1966. While around 1900 most people now considered Igbo denied that they were Igbo, by 1967 many Igbo were literally prepared to die for their own independent Igbo state."[31] In a symbolic sense, it had been the Kano massacres, more than any other single manifestation of anti-Igbo violence, that moved Igbos to militancy. Long before that, however, the presence of Igbos had helped to shape ethnic identities in the North. According to Paden, the presence of Igbos had a significant impact on the way that Hausa society defined itself by pro-

viding a foil upon which Hausas could gaze and see what they believed themselves not to be. "The rise of the southern Nigerian (mainly
Ibo) community in Kano gave major impetus to the amalgamation of
the Hausa-Fulani identity. This we-they distinction was based on religious, cultural, linguistic, and economic factors. The Ibo community
was 'different' from the Hausa-Fulani with respect to these criteria."[32]
British colonial rule in Nigeria was predicated on the relevance and
exclusivity of ethnic affiliations, and British policies reinforced the
salience of ethnicity in Nigerian lives. During the colonial period, the
country was organized by regions, of which there were three. Each
region, in turn, was centered on one of the three major ethnic groups
the British identified. In the Western Region, Yoruba-speakers predominated.[33] In the Eastern Region the British identified an Igbo majority, and in the landlocked Northern Region, the residents of
Hausaland made up the majority. In each case, however, the majority
group shared its respective region with a number of smaller groups.
As will become clear in chapter one, the close association of each
region with one of the colony's largest ethnic groups would exert a
tremendous influence on the political development of Nigeria, and help
to reinforce and even magnify cultural differences and the importance
Northerners assigned to them.

Igbos and Hausas came into regular, sustained contact with one another early in the twentieth century in the context of British colonial rule.
We can only speculate as to how members of the same societies would
have identified themselves and one another under different circumstances.
As colonial subjects, however, members of each group bore ethnic labels
that were of tremendous importance in defining how, where, and under
what conditions they would relate to one another. Under colonial rule,
officials and European-led Christian missions in Igboland created administrative and linguistic infrastructures to bind together what they saw as
Igboland.[34]

## Igbo Ethnicity and Migration

In fact, the sort of chain migration that led to the gradual rise of an
Igbo population across Nigeria was one of two central factors in helping colonial notions of Igbo identity gain acceptance among those the
colonial government placed under the blanket of Igbo ethnicity. The
other was party politics in the 1940s, '50s and '60s, and the
regionalization—and ethnicization—of the major parties. Both migration and political parties forced individuals whose affiliations had cen-

tered on lineage, village, town, and clan, to think of themselves as part of a larger, broader group. Horowitz has called this process "sub-group amalgamation."[35] According to Smock, for Igbos "a common acceptance of the wider frame of reference probably occurred only in the 1950's."[36] The process was faster for those who emigrated from Igboland to colonial cities like Lagos, Port Harcourt, or Jos, where their similarities bound them together amid much larger populations of non-Igbos.[37] They drew first on village and town affiliations to build support networks, and ultimately the town unions described in chapter one. In time, however, it was they who created umbrella organizations to link the various unions, a process which led to the formation of the national Ibo Union, later the Ibo State Union, a forward-looking organization that built secondary schools in Igboland, founded an Igbo national bank, and commissioned an Igbo national anthem.[38] Even at its peak, the Ibo State Union exercised only extremely limited power in the lives of ordinary Igbos. Yet, in Northern imaginations it became emblematic of ethnic unity within an Igbo society where, in truth, sub-ethnic affiliations retained a great deal of salience. As van den Bersselaar has noted, the Ibo State Union, an Igbo-led political party (the National Council of Nigerian Citizens), religious organizations, members of the Igbo intelligentsia, and, of course, ordinary Igbo men and women all exerted influence on how Igbo identity took shape in the pre-war years.[39]

### Hausa Ethnicity and "The North"

Talking about Hausa ethnicity also presents a number of conceptual and historical challenges. In present-day Nigeria the word "Hausa" can be applied conversationally to very different effects. For example, in the vocabulary of many southern Nigerians, the term in its least precise usage can refer to any Muslim Northerner, including non-Hausa speakers.[40] In a different context, "Hausa" identifies a Hausa speaker, particularly a native speaker, despite the possibility that that individual might claim non-Hausa ancestry.[41] In its most restrictive sense, the term distinguishes someone of Hausa ancestry from someone with Fulani, Kanuri (Beriberi), Tuareg, or other ancestry, but who may in fact speak Hausa as his or her first language, and who may be culturally indistinguishable from someone claiming to be "pure" Hausa.

Particularly in this last sense, Hausa ethnic identity has been responsive to historical forces both internal and external. In the early years of the nineteenth century, Hausaland was transformed by the rise of the Sokoto Caliphate under the Fulani Islamic reformer Usman ɗan Fodio.[42] Nearly a century later, European invaders divided Hausaland between Nigeria and the French colony of Niger.[43] Despite these most profound of political changes, one of the most important forces in Hausa society has been what scholars have referred to as its assimilative tendencies. This pattern of absorbing outsiders and making them Hausa has resulted, almost literally, in continuous infusions of new blood, a process dubbed "Hausanization."[44] In Hiskett's words, "The Hausa nation has been built up, over many generations, of different peoples of many different bloodlines who have migrated to Hausaland and joined the original stock. What unites them is a common language and, to an ever increasing extent over the course of their history, common adherence to Islam."[45] The most obvious example of Hausa society's tendency to absorb outsiders is the assimilation that followed the introduction of a Fulani aristocracy to the conquered Hausa states during the creation of the Caliphate. This has led some scholars to write of Hausa-Fulani society, and others to historicize distinctions between the two groups.[46] The Fulani of Usman dan Fodio's *jihad*, however, were neither the earliest nor most recent to become part of Hausa society.[47] For these reasons,

> It is impossible to give a simple definition of a Hausa person because different criteria were, and still are, used by different people at different times and places to define who was or should be defined as Hausa. To decide who was Hausa and who was not, some people used purely historical claims to Hausa ethnicity, others used cultural traits and social values as their yardstick, while still others used religion plus language.[48]

In this study, I have used the term "Hausa" where others might have chosen "Hausa-Fulani." Each refers to people who, though they may derive from various ethnic groups, speak Hausa as a first language, and have become part of urban Hausa culture. The vast majority of them are Muslims, and Islam, though historically insufficient to seal many social fissures within the society, has provided an important measure of unity in their relations with outsiders. I prefer the less cumbersome term "Hausa" to the amalgam "Hausa-Fulani" for two reasons. First, while Hausanized Fulani make up the largest identifiable group that has become part of modern Hausa society, they are far from the only such presence. Any number of other groups have also become part of the mix, and the process continues today. More importantly, it is as this amalgam of Hausa, Fulani, Kanuri, and other groups that my Igbo informants related to Hausa society. Only rarely did distinctions emerge in their accounts, and where they did the distinctions were largely speculative. For example, some informants used "Hausa" and "Fulani" as a shorthand to mark what was, in fact, a form of class differentiation, and not necessarily one based on ethnic origins. Those Igbos who spoke Hausa often used the Hausa terms *sarauta* (titled aristocracy) and *talakawa* (commoners), and equated the former with Fulani and the latter with Hausa, an association that has utility in a broad historical sense, but which is extremely limited in practice.

Another term requires illumination. I follow the lead of both my Hausa informants and John Paden's invaluable *Religion and Political Culture in Kano* in my use of the Hausa term *Kanawa* (literally, people of Kano; masculine singular = *Bakane*) to refer to members of the city's Hausa population. The term serves here to distinguish the actions and opinions of Kano's Hausas from 1) those of Hausas in other cities or 2) those from other areas but living in Kano. *Kanawa*, therefore, excludes any who were not part of Kano's Hausa society. These groups include, among others, Fulani and Kanuri who had not Hausanized, Yoruba Muslims from the North and other Middle Belters, as well as Hausas who identified themselves with other parts of Hausaland.

This leads to the question of how to handle the relationship between Kano and Northern Nigeria. Any attempt to treat Kano as a microcosm of the North is doomed to failure, since no such microcosm exists. Even within Hausaland, the city is as likely a candidate for exceptionalism as it is for representativeness. Further, when one steps beyond Hausaland and the Sokoto Caliphate to consider Bornu and the expanse of the Middle Belt, generalizing about "the North" becomes, at times, almost absurd. Still, the Northern Region existed, as a geopolitical entity, and at times in spirit. While its political center was the regional capital of Kaduna, and Sokoto its religious nucleus, its center of gravity by any other measure was Kano. As a result, for Nigeria's Igbos, Kano was the symbolic center of the North. Events there more than anywhere else helped to set the tone of relations between Igbos and Northern Nigerians.

## A NOTE ON ETHNICITY AND CLASS

A great deal has been written about the relationship between ethnicity and class in Nigeria. Nnoli and Diamond, respectively, have demonstrated how Nigerian elites have successfully presented their in-

terests as those of the entire ethnic group, and in the process reinforced a climate in which ethnic appeals tend to trump class interests.[49] This study offers little to challenge their conclusions. The
Northern elites to whom I refer throughout the study are members of
the intermingled "patrimonial aristocracy" (*sarauta*), mercantile capitalists, and politicians Lubeck has described.[50] In a broader sense, they
are members of the national elite Nnoli identified when he described
a comprador bourgeoisie in power not because of its control of economic resources, but rather over political resources, which it uses to
channel state resources through ethnicized channels.[51]

On the other hand, at the time I conducted this study, Kano's Igbos
represented a fairly narrow slice of Igbo society in terms of socioeco-
nomic class; most were traders, entrepreneurs, technically skilled
workers, or professionals. Historically, few of the Igbo elite have
maintained residence in Kano. Though some have had business interests there, they have never capitalized large-scale enterprises in Kano
or employed large numbers of workers there. At the other end of the
spectrum, the very poor were also largely absent. Men and unmarried
women without regular employment were likely to be pressured by
other Igbos into leaving town, for fear that their presence or their actions would reflect poorly on the community. By the 1990s, there were
very few Igbos in Kano's shrinking industrial labor force. Wages had
declined to a point where, I was told, most semiskilled Igbo workers
had taken up trading or gone into other sorts of business. The few
Igbos employed in those industrial firms were usually highly educated
people who occupied administrative and technical positions, often in
supervisory capacities. Since few *Kanawa* held these positions, the
presence of Igbos in them was often a source of tension, and was
usually expressed in ethnic terms.

There was also a fairly sharp ethnic division in the market place with
members of different ethnic groups tending to concentrate on different
types of goods. In part this is because patterns of apprenticeship have
tended to keep access to suppliers concentrated within ethnic networks.
While this might be expected to limit the sense of rivalry across ethnic
lines between traders by eliminating direct competition, this has not been
the case. The informants themselves reinforced the centrality of ethnicity
in their lives, at the expense of class. The Igbo traders I interviewed had
little contact with Hausa traders beyond casual market relations; they were
more likely to bemoan how their own access to local markets was limited by what they felt was preferential treatment for *Kanawa* by the state
and local governments.

Kano's Igbo traders and professionals have relied on connections with local traders, politicians, and bureaucrats, and worked to maintain those relationships. At the same time, however, they have done so with the knowledge that, as citizens not of Kano State, but rather the various states of Igboland, they were, in all likelihood, permanently excluded from the patrimony that characterizes relations between *Kanawa*.[52] They have been, therefore, politically impotent and economically expendable in ways that locals are less likely to be. In one sense, this has been empowering, since it has enabled them to move between opportunities relatively unencumbered by patrimonial obligations. On the other hand, they have operated without the protection patrimony affords, though they have suffered disproportionately from the corruption it engenders. Further, many have grown alienated from patronage networks in Igboland, which has left them doubly exposed to both political and economic pressure.

## METHODOLOGY AND SOURCES

This study is based on a variety of oral and written sources. First and foremost are 122 formal interviews, most conducted in Kano with Igbo and Hausa residents and especially Igbo migrants.[53] The other informants were Nigerians of other ethnic backgrounds and long-term expatriates (Lebanese, Irish, and American). Two British informants formerly resident in Northern Nigeria were interviewed in the United States. These formal interviews are cited in footnotes with the notation "FN" and a number that corresponds to the list of interviews appearing at the end of this book. The interviews were usually between one and two hours in length, and proceeded from a core set of questions, but not a formal questionnaire. Most were conducted without the use of a tape recorder, which proved to inhibit many informants' willingness to speak. After encountering great difficulties in gaining access to older women informants, I relied on an Igbo research assistant, Chidozie Umeh, to conduct interviews with twenty-six Igbo women. He operated from a similar list of questions. The fieldwork on which the project rests was conducted between December 1992 and October 1994, and during June and July 1998. The subject matter of this study, associated as it is with a period of violent conflict and also with ongoing tensions, was (and is) sensitive, particularly from Igbo perspectives. As a result, I have cited some references to field notes as anonymous ("FN-Anonymous"). In most cases this is in accordance with the wishes of the informant; in several cases I have done so myself in cases where I believe the informant would be compromised by the way in which I have used information he or she provided. In addition to formal interviews, I engaged in a more or less constant process of informal interviewing in markets and other public spaces, in many parts of Kano and in several other Nigerian cities. These hundreds of informal interviews were essentially unstructured conversations, never under false pretenses, but usually without the protocol or disclosure of a formal interview. They led me to informants, helped me to formulate questions, and to understand the broader context in which I was operating. They also inform many of the generalizations I have attributed to only one or two informants.

While I had the help of the Kano State History and Culture Bureau (HCB) in gaining access to Hausa informants, the networks through which I gained access to Igbo informants are best described as opportunistic. Though formal community structures provided a set of starting places, many of the most prominent voices in those organizations were comparatively new immigrants, with limited first-hand exposure to the matters under scrutiny here. In contrast, through a series of person-to-person contacts, I was able to meet individuals who had participated in the events of 1966 and the immediate post-war period. Being passed hand-to-hand has distinct advantages for a researcher. At the same time, it also has the inevitable consequence of giving disproportional representation to a slice of the larger community. In the case of this study, fully half of the Igbos I interviewed in Kano had origins in a single extended community in Igboland, represented in Kano by the Orlu Wayfarers Association. While I doubt this has resulted in any meaningful distortion in my conclusions, communities of equal or greater size, such as those from Nnewi, Aba, or Owerri are not represented proportionally.

The book also draws on archival sources. I relied a great deal on the archive of the Kano State HCB. Most of the Nigerian government documents that I have cited originated there, including security and intelligence reports, and Kano State publications. Other Nigerian government documents originated with the Kaduna branch of the Nigerian National Archive (NAK). I have also made use of United States consular documents from the United States National Archives II, particularly in the second and third chapters. These documents track events in May-June and September-October 1966, periods when the Nigerian records are unfortunately limited. Many of the periodical materials I have drawn on are held in the library of Arewa House in Kaduna and the Africana collection of the Northwestern University

Library in the United States. I have made substantial use of two: the *New Nigerian* and *West Africa*. The first, like its earlier incarnation as the *Nigerian Citizen* and its Hausa-language sibling *Gaskiya ta fi Kwabo*, was a semi-official publication of the Northern Regional government, and since 1968 has been owned by a consortium of Northern states. It has long been recognized as a mouthpiece for the Northern elite, and during the First Republic was a virtual party organ of the Northern Peoples Congress. *West Africa* also has a long relationship with the Nigerian officialdom; even before the Nigerian government acquired a stake in its parent company, Nigerian parastatals purchased a large share of its advertising. I have tried to use these publications critically and with due consideration of their likely limitations. Miscellaneous written sources include an undergraduate thesis written by an Igbo in Kano on her community in 1973, and a set of questionnaires gathered in the early 1970s by student researchers from the Economics Department of Ahmadu Bello University-Zaria and currently in the care of Professor Alan Frishman.

One of the largest limitations of the study is its androcentrism. While women's experiences appear alongside those of men in several chapters, particularly chapter six, they are not represented proportionately. In part this is because it was largely within historically male domains that the manipulation of regional and ethnic identities can be most visibly detailed, particularly in official materials; as a result women's roles are filtered through male gazes that minimized their relevance. There is also a male bias in the selection of informants, heavy in the case of Igbo, and total in the case of Hausa. This is for several reasons, first and foremost that of access. Islamic wife seclusion is widely practiced in Hausaland, and even supervised access to Hausa women was unusual. The question of what insights might be gained from Hausa women remains completely unexplored. The problem of access to Igbo women, who were overwhelmingly Christian, while less acute than in the case of the Hausa, was still substantial. I was routinely denied access to the wives of male informants, frequently with the explanation that the patriarch spoke for the family; gaining independent access to spaces inhabited by females proved difficult. Second, language was a problem. While I was able to conduct interviews with Hausa-speaking informants with a minimum of difficulty, and was able to speak to male Igbo informants in English, I had no command of conversational Igbo. Many Igbo women in Kano had only limited use of English. The imperfect solution to the dual problems of access and language was to have an Igbo research assistant, a mature undergraduate, conduct oral interviews with female informants. The assistant, though male, was able to enter spaces inaccessible to me and conduct interviews in Igbo. Follow-up questioning, however, was extremely limited in these cases. A deeper exploration of women's worlds than I was able to achieve will doubtlessly reveal patterns that both fit within and diverge from those I have detailed.

The political climate also affected the oral material I was able to gather. During the period in which I conducted most of the fieldwork that led to this book, Nigeria experienced a series of political crises. The most important of these unfolded when the regime of General Ibrahim Babangida, a Northerner, ended amid controversy. At its center was Babangida's annulment of the apparent election of a Yoruba, M.K.O. Abiola, to be Nigeria's new civilian president. Abiola never assumed office, and General Sani Abacha, a Hausanized Kanuri from Kano, seized power from an interim government. Nationally, considerable tension developed between opponents of Abiola and his supporters, many of the most vocal of whom were Yorubas. In Kano, this tension manifested itself in sentiments within both the Hausa and Igbo communities that, in many quarters, took on a disturbingly anti-Yoruba timbre. While these sentiments were far from pervasive, they were a constant, powerful presence. Conducting formal and informal interviews on the history of Igbo-Hausa relations meant, in many cases, listening to informants make comparisons to recent events, comparisons that often seemed strained. In those conversations, Igbos and Hausas often spoke with admiring tones of one another's ethnic groups, which they usually contrasted with "the Yorubas." Ironically, this was the case despite the fact that many Igbos saw Abiola's apparent election as an important step forward for southern political aspirations at the national level. The same Igbos and Hausas talked of a relationship between their groups that was, despite its difficulties, ultimately symbiotic, and which had been strengthened by the struggles of 1966 and the civil war. Their remarks echoed Paden's 1973 observation that *Kanawa* felt that Hausas generally liked Igbos, and had Igbos not killed Northern leaders, the trouble of the late 1960s could have been avoided. His Hausa informants anticipated a future alliance between Igbo and Hausa driven by both groups' fears of "Yoruba domination."[54] As I conducted fieldwork, many Igbos and Hausas alike were eager to dismiss 1991's religious disturbances between Muslims and Christians in Kano as the product of extremist agitation for which most members of their groups had little use. In fact, I heard again and again, it was the lessons of the 1960s and 1970s that had helped to quickly restore confidence between Igbos and Hausas in 1991.

Yorubas, their argument often went, had not yet learned those lessons. And the Igbos and Hausas who made such remarks said them in remarkably similar language, which was not surprising given the tone of much press coverage of the political crisis. Without the Abiola crisis to polarize Nigerian political sentiments, this tendency to romanticize the Igbo-Hausa relationship would certainly have been tempered. Unfortunately, as I complete this manuscript, the general timbre of Hausa-Yoruba relations in the city and elsewhere in Nigeria appears little improved.

## THE STRUCTURE OF THE STUDY

The structure of the book is in equal measures chronological and thematic. The dynamism of ethnicity has remained constant, though the ways in which that dynamism has been most visible has changed as events unfolded. This study shifts its gaze to detail the formation of ethnically polarized communities in colonial Nigeria, the politics of intercommunal violence, official discourses of ethnicity, abandoned property, and then individual and community reconstruction after the war. In so doing, the story of Kano's Igbos engages with broader narratives of Nigerian political and social history without, I hope, becoming absorbed by them. And, as much as possible, the book treats historical developments as lived experience as well as political metaphor.

The first chapter draws directly on a fairly conventional national historical narrative to contextualize the chapters that follow. It briefly describes the motives and mechanics behind the creation of a highly ethnicized socio-political frontier in Northern Nigeria. Igbos, outsiders to the region, appeared as a cultural, political, and economic antithesis of Northern Nigerians, despite the enormous cultural diversity contained within the latter. Religious and cultural differences, educational disparities, patterns of residential segregation, and insular community institutions all contributed to the maintenance of a barrier between communities in far Northern cities. Ethnicity and party politics became entwined, and in the climate of suspicion and distrust that Nigerian politicians created, Igbos came to embody a political and cultural threat to the North. Chapter one explores the construction of that perceived threat, and responses of the Northern government to it. Chapter two, which addresses the anti-Igbo violence of May and June, 1966, begins the process of filtering this narrative of competition through contemporaneous voices. Most of those voices belong to Nigerian officials, and reproduce with great fidelity elements of the master narrative, particularly as they recount the reasons

Northerners had for attacking Igbos. Even the expatriate accounts of violence in Katsina reproduce in microcosm an entirely conventional vision of Igbo-Hausa relations. What is often missing from the master narrative is attention to inconsistencies and contradictions within the conceptual fabric of Northern Nigeria. Ironically, it was the death of Northern Premier Sir Ahmadu Bello and the elimination of anti-southern policies he created that helped to bring about the type of regional unity his government had been unsuccessful in creating during his lifetime. In chapter three, we begin to step away from the master narrative and explore the contradictions of anti-Igbo violence. In addition to detailing the riots that occured in September and October, the chapter explores how Igbos' dispositions and self-representation impacted their experiences during the riots. The chapter also looks at both warnings to Igbos and the targeting of victims before and during the attacks, and concludes with brief descriptions of how two individuals used dual ethnic heritage to their advantage.

Chapters four and five extend the narrative into the war years. In the process they expose some of the contradictory actions of state agents such as civil servants, local authorities, police, and soldiers during a tumultuous period made up of many conflicted moments. The contradictions surrounding official discourses (chapter four) and the handling of abandoned property (chapter five) reveal some of the slippage contained in the master narrative itself, as the relationship between Igbos and the rest of Nigeria—at least in official terms—changed from bitterly contentious to fraternal. Chapter four explores how government propaganda carefully repackaged its interpretation of what it meant to be Igbo. Chapter five reveals some of the slippage within the new fraternal vision of Nigeria as it pertained to the handling of property Igbos abandoned in Northern Nigeria.

The riots of 1966 were cataclysmic in both political and individual terms. Cataclysmic moments create heroes, martyrs, and myth. At the same time, these moments force ordinary people to navigate between on the one hand, processes, agendas, and events over which they have little control, and on the other hand, those in which they are key actors. Unlike heroes and martyrs, ordinary people who survive the mythic moment must somehow make their way into a series of subsequent moments, perhaps less dramatic and less memorable, but in the end, just as revealing. It is these moments that chapters six and seven use to foreground the thread of continuity that links 1966 to 1970 and beyond. Chapter six focuses on returning Igbos' motives in leaving Igboland for the North, and looks at their strategies for reestablishing themselves economically, which often involved building or renewing relationships with Hausas. Chapter seven turns its gaze to the recreation of formal networks and community institutions among Kano's Igbos, and uses them as a measure of a return to some degree of "normalcy" after a long period of crisis and rehabilitation. The book concludes with a note on the changing dynamics between religion and ethnicity in today's Nigeria.

## NOTES

1. I have used the current preferred spelling throughout, except in places where the old spelling, "Ibo," appears in a proper noun or as part of a quotation.

2. Felix Agwuenu's story is told at length in chapter six.

3. The post-war "marginalization" of Igbos in public life, and in terms of access to government resources, was a staple of political discourse in Nigeria during the 1980s and '90s.

4. Dmitri van den Bersselaar, *In Search of Igbo Identity: Language, Culture and Politics in Nigeria, 1900–1966* (Leiden: University of Leiden Press, 1998).

5. Recent works that apply instrumental approaches include Bill Bravman, *Making Ethnic Ways: Communities and Their Transformations in Taita, Kenya, 1800–1950* (Portsmouth: Heinemann, 1998).

6. I have in mind here Gérard Prunier, *The Rwanda Crisis: History of a Genocide* (New York: Columbia University Press, 1995); René Lemarchand, *Burundi: Ethnic Conflict and Genocide* (Cambridge: Cambridge University Press, 1995); and Catharine Newbury, "Ethnicity and the Politics of History in Rwanda," *Africa Today* 45, 1 (1998).

7. van den Bersselaar, *In Search of Igbo Identity*, 12.

8. See Crawford Young, ed., *The Rising Tide of Cultural Pluralism: The Nation State at Bay?* (Madison: University of Wisconsin Press, 1993), 24.

9. See, for example, Bravman's note on Leroy Vail, ed., *The Creation of Tribalism in Southern Africa* (Berkeley: University of California Press, 1989). Bravman, *Making Ethnic Ways*, 11.

10. Young, *Rising Tide of Cultural Pluralism*, 23.

11. Bravman, *Making Ethnic Ways*, 14. See also Tom Spear's introduction to Spear and Richard Waller, eds., *Being Maasai: Ethnicity and Identity in East Africa* (Athens: Ohio University Press, 1993); Harvey Glickman, ed., *Ethnic Conflict and Democratization in Africa* (Atlanta: African Studies Association Press, 1995), particularly Glickman, "Issues in the Analysis of Ethnic Conflict and Democratization Processes in Africa Today."

12. Young, *Rising Tide of Cultural Pluralism*, 23.

13. One is reminded here of Anderson's insights into nationalism: "Ultimately it is this fraternity that makes it possible . . . for so many millions of people, not so much to kill, as willingly to die for such limited imaginings." Benedict Anderson, *Imagined Communities: Reflections on the Origin and Spread of Nationalism* (London: Verso Editions, 1983), 16.

14. John Lonsdale, "The Moral Economy of Mau-Mau: Wealth, Poverty and Civic Virtue in Kikuyu Political Thought," in Bruce Berman and John Lonsdale, *Unhappy*

*Valley: Conflict in Kenya and Africa, Book Two: Violence and Ethnicity* (Athens: Ohio University Press, 1992), 328.

15. Lonsdale, "The Moral Economy of Mau-Mau: The Problem," in Berman and Lonsdale, *Unhappy Valley*, 267.

16. The clashes of 1991 and 1995 are discussed in the conclusion.

17. Joe Igbokwe, *Igbos: Twenty Five Years After Biafra* (Lagos, n.p., 1995); Obiwu, *Igbos of Northern Nigeria* (Lagos: Torch Publications, 1996); Eghosa Osaghae, *Trends in Migrant Political Organizations in Nigeria: The Igbo in Kano* (Ibadan: Institut Français de Recherche en Afrique, 1994); Osaghae, *et al. Urban Violence in Nigeria* (Ibadan: Institut Français de Recherche en Afrique, 1994); Onigu Otite, *Ethnic Pluralism and Ethnicity in Nigeria* (Ibadan: Shaneson C.I. Limited, 1990).

18. Nnoli, for example, has described the perpetuation of "the image of the Igbo as the traditional and 'natural' victims of Northern hostility" as a consequence of intercommunal clashes. Okwudiba Nnoli, *Ethnic Politics in Nigeria* (Enugu: Fourth Dimension Publishers, 1978), 237.

19. Belinda Bozzoli, *Women of Phokeng: Consciousness, Life Strategy, and Migrancy in South Africa, 1900–1983* (Portsmouth: Heinemann, 1991), 3.

20. One such example is a security report from Kano written during the Ironsi period. It records Igbos wearing a "tiger tail cap," and displaying paper models of the same cap in their vehicles. According to the recording officer,

> Both the cap and the paper cut are coloured like tiger skin and it is described by the source, who is experienced in Ibo social behavior, to mean that a tiger has been killed and is being exhibited by the hunters. It is believed to have a bearing on the January 15th incident whereby it is said they are celebrating the death of all the reactionary Northern leaders killed during the encounter.

I could find no reference in ethnographic literature to any such symbol, which was not surprising since the tiger is not indigenous to southern Nigeria, or, in fact, the African continent. Similarly, no Igbos I contacted, including several historians, had knowledge of such a symbol or any similar. Nonetheless, the presence of such confident testimony in government records bespeaks the power of officials to inscribe partial truths or even falsehoods as fact, and to allow those "facts" to influence the thinking of others. HCB R.56, Vol. III, 527, Intelligence Report, April 1966.

21. Paul Brass, *Riots and Pogroms* (New York: New York University Press, 1996), 33.

22. Brass, *Riots and Pogroms*, 33–34.

23. Brass, *Riots and Pogroms*, 2.

24. Leo Kuper and M.G. Smith, eds., *Pluralism in Africa* (Berkeley: University of California Press, 1969), particularly Kuper, "Plural Societies: Perspectives and Problems," and Smith, "Institutional and Political Conditions of Pluralism." J.S. Furnivall, *Colonial Policy and Practice: A Comparative Study of Burma and Netherlands India* (Cambridge: Cambridge University Press, 1948).

25. Scholarly accounts of the process in Kano include, most notably the work of John Paden. See Paden, *Religion and Political Culture in Kano* (Berkeley: University of California Press, 1973), and "Communal Competition, Conflict and Violence in Kano," in Robert Melson and Howard Wolpe, eds., *Nigeria: Modernization and*

*the Politics of Communalism* (East Lansing: Michigan State University, 1971), 113–144. A number of more recent studies have touched superficially on the question.

26. Larry Diamond, "Class, Ethnicity, and the Democratic State: Nigeria, 1950–1966," *Comparative Studies in Society and History* 25, 3, (1983), 468. See also Nnoli, *Ethnic Politics* and *Ethnicity and Development in Nigeria* (Brookfield: Ashgate Publishing Company, 1995).

27. I capitalize the term "North" since, for much of Nigeria's history, there was a single Northern Region. There was no analogous "Southern Region," or after 1914, a single "South." The capitalized term refers to the Northern Region of Nigeria, or after 1968, to the states carved out of the region. The "south" refers collectively to the former Eastern Region, Western Region, and after 1964 to the Mid-West Region, and to the states they became.

28. Bravman, *Making Ethnic Ways*, 10.

29. John Comaroff and Jean Comaroff, *Ethnography and the Historical Imagination* (Boulder: Westview Press, 1992).

30. Fredrik Barth, ed., *Ethnic Groups and Boundaries: The Social Origin of Cultural Difference* (London: George Allen and Unwin Press, 1969), Introduction.

31. van den Bersselaar, *In Search of Igbo Identity*, 7.

32. Paden, *Religion and Political Culture*, 379. Elsewhere he wrote that "certain Ibo cultural traits seemed to take on special importance within a Hausa context, especially those traits which resisted assimilation: endogamy, maintenance of obligations in the Eastern Region, and the persistence of certain traditional religious customs among the lower classes." Paden, "Communal Competition," 141.

33. For a discussion of the transformations surrounding Yoruba ethnicity during the colonial period, see David Laitin, *Hegemony and Culture: Politics and Religious Change Among the Yoruba* (Chicago: University of Chicago Press, 1986).

34. See Felix Ekechi, *Tradition and Transformation in Eastern Nigeria: A Sociopolitical History of Owerri and its Hinterland, 1902–1947* (Kent: Kent State University Press, 1989), and van den Bersselaar, *In Search of Igbo Identity*. Other important works include A.E. Afigbo, *Ropes of Sand: Studies in Igbo History and Culture* (London: Longman, 1981), and Elizabeth Isichei, *A History of the Igbo People* (New York: St. Martin's Press, 1976).

35. Donald Horowitz, *Ethnic Groups in Conflict* (Berkeley: University of California Press, 1985), 66.

36. Audrey Smock, *Ibo Politics: The Role of Ethnic Unions in Eastern Nigeria* (Cambridge: Harvard University Press, 1971), 7.

37. For a discussion of this process in colonial African cities, see Kuper and Smith, *Pluralism in Africa*.

38. James S. Coleman, "The Ibo and Yoruba Strands in Nigerian Nationalism," in Melson and Wolpe, *Nigeria: Modernization and the Politics of Communalism*, 78. For more on the Ibo State Union, see chapter one.

39. van den Bersselaar, *In Search of Igbo Identity*.

40. Similarly, for Northerners, "Igbo" sometimes becomes a generic term for southern Christians.

41. The tendency for southerners to blur the line between Hausa ethnicity and Northern regional identity is, in part, a reflection of the special status the Hausa language enjoyed in the region during the colonial period, and to a lesser degree,

continues to enjoy in most of the region's successor states. In the North, where the penetration of English was more limited than in the south, the regional government promoted Hausa as a *lingua franca*, and encouraged its administrative use in much of the region. British officers in the North were more likely to speak the language well than were officers in the south likely to speak southern languages.

42. D.M. Last, *The Sokoto Caliphate* (London: Longmans, 1967).

43. William F. S. Miles, *Hausaland Divided* (Ithaca: Cornell University Press, 1994).

44. I have Americanized Mahdi Adamu's term "Hausanisation." Mahdi Adamu, *The Hausa Factor in West African History* (Zaria: Ahmadu Bello University Press, 1978), 2–3.

45. Mervyn Hiskett, *The Development of Islam in West Africa* (New York: Longman, 1984), 68.

46. Paden, for example, detailed patterns of occupancy of emirate political offices in terms of lineage and ethnic affiliation. Paden, *Religion and Political Culture*.

47. For example, see Frank Salamone, "Becoming Hausa: Ethnic Identity Change and Its Implications for the Study of Ethnic Pluralism and Stratification, *Africa* 45, 4 (1975), 410–423.

48. Mahdi Adamu, *The Hausa Factor*, 3.

49. Nnoli, *Ethnic Politics in Nigeria* and *Ethnicity and Development in Nigeria;* Diamond, *Class, Ethnicity and Democracy in Nigeria: The Failure of the First Republic* (London: Macmillan Press, 1988).

50. Paul Lubeck, *Islam and Urban Labor in Northern Nigeria: The Making of a Muslim Working Class* (Cambridge: Cambridge University Press, 1986), 79.

51. Nnoli, *Ethnicity and Development in Nigeria*, 6–7.

52. State citizenship in Nigeria is, generally, a matter of patrilineal descent, irrespective of one's place of residency or birth.

53. Interview notes and transcriptions are on deposit with the author.

54. Paden, *Religion and Political Culture*, 357.

# 1

# ETHNICITY ENSHRINED:
# IGBOS IN HAUSALAND

## INTRODUCTION

At the close of the twentieth century, a walk from the walled "old city" that is the heart of Kano's Hausa community to the Sabon Gari ward, with its Igbo majority, was a striking experience. In a very short time one could, in a sense, pass from the heart of Nigeria's far North to a microcosm of urban southern life. During the colonial period, the differences were equally pronounced, perhaps more so, since the boundaries between the city's wards were less permeable than they were in the late 1990s. Though separated by only a few thousand meters, Sabon Gari and the old city could hardly have made more different impressions. Sabon Gari's streets were laid out in a modified grid, as opposed to the winding footpaths that characterized the old city beyond its main thoroughfares. Most of the buildings in Sabon Gari used wooden planks and tin sheets to approximate, at least superficially, European architectural styles. This constrasted sharply with the less angular earthen structures that predominated in old Kano, and which bore comparison with North African and Middle Eastern conventions. Sabon Gari was home not only to most of greater Kano's Christians, but also its churches, which were unthinkable in the old city. Beer and spirits—strictly banned under Islamic law—were available at any number of Sabon Gari bars and hotels. The absence of Islamic wife seclusion, which expanded among Kano's Muslims during the colonial period, meant that adult women were more visible in the streets and markets of Sabon Gari than in those of the city. The denizens of Sabon Gari, both male and female, favored western dress, and those who wore African garb tended toward southern varieties distinct from Middle Eastern-inspired Hausa styles. And where Hausa, and to a lesser degree Arabic, were the languages of life in the city, Igbo, English, and Nigeria's distinctive English-based pidgin were the tongues of Sabon Gari.

Then and now it is clear to even casual observers that cultural differences between the two groups were significant. What is more important, and what requires a nuanced analysis, is the way in which structural features of the colonial state exacerbated the impact of those differences. Like other southerners in the far North, most of the Igbos who ventured to colonial Kano did so as participants in the political and economic order Britain had imposed through force of arms. Most Igbos wore the clothing of the invader and spoke the invader's language; some took great pride in doing so. Economically, most were fairly affluent by local standards, but, as Easterners who could never become citizens of the North, they sent large chunks of their earnings home rather than circulate it in the local economy. They consumed liquor, often publicly, and they ate different foods, including some Islam prohibited. Further, many made great show of practicing the colonizer's faith. While Kano's Muslims—including internationally recognized Islamic scholars—accepted Christians as fellow believers in God and "people of the book," the comparatively recent arrival of Christianity in Igboland left Igbos bearing some of the stigma of "paganism." For example, in a thinly veiled reference to Igbos, the Grand Qadi of Northern Nigeria, Sheikh Abubakar Gumi, wrote that the British "built schools to teach destructive western culture and they began by teaching the children of idolatrous infidels whose fathers walked the land naked, unaware of what morals, manly virtue and humanity might be. They placed them in sensitive government positions and they came to lord it over Muslims whose brains had fallen asleep amid fantasies of superstition."[1] Worse still, in Muslim eyes, many Igbo Christians allowed "pagan" religious practices to linger, and to infiltrate their Christianity.[2]

On the other hand, most of Kano's Igbos were there because they, or members of their households, had clerical, technical, or professional skills that were the result of years of study, skills that *Kanawa* had not acquired in significant measure. They and other migrants, in some cases quite literally, made possible the operation of much of the infrastructure that the British had imposed. They had acquired the colonizer's knowledge, and their leaders agitated for the invaders to go, so that skilled Africans could take Europeans' places within the apparata of government and commerce. Already many Igbos held positions of influence, if not outright authority, over local Muslims. Some made no effort to hide the fact that they regarded most locals as unskilled and—since most could not read or write in English—illiterate. Furthermore, very few Igbos answered to Hausa superiors. In the market, Igbo merchants had access to commercial networks that local traders and entrepreneurs did not. These factors combined so that to the extent that the British government positioned itself as a force for "modernization," Igbos and other southerners represented—to themselves and the British, if not necessarily to most Northerners—Africans at an intermediate stage in the process of adopting European values and practices, and who were eager to take the next step.[3]

That Igbos could be perceived as an embodiment of "otherness" in Kano or other far Northern cities is neither mysterious nor novel. British colonial rule consistently exploited ethnicity, class, and religion for its own purposes. Just as Igbo workers had helped to extend the infrastucture of British imperialism into the North, so Hausa soldiers had helped to complete the military conquest of Igboland. It is important, however, to remember two things. First, any generalized depiction of the gulf between groups fails to take into account the ability of individuals to build bridges. As will become clear, friendship, marriage, commercial and political cooperation, and simple civility played key roles in connecting individuals and, sometimes, communities. More importantly, we must avoid the trap of linking the potential for conflict across ethnic frontiers with a belief in that conflict's inevitability. This chapter and those that follow argue that ethnic difference is not sufficient to engender antagonism; nor does the presence of antagonism necessarily lead to violence. The forced departure of Igbos from Northern Nigeria in 1966 was first and foremost a product of political and economic competition between elites. As is so often the case with ethnic conflict, Nigerians at all socio-economic levels contributed to the cycle of suspicion and misunderstanding that made violence possible. It was, however, within Nigeria's political class and military forces that the cataclysm of 1966 was born. Left to their own devices, ordinary Nigerians would not—*could* not—have accomplished the horrors that they did under the influence of some of their leaders and the infrastructure that those leaders commanded.

Still, the political and economic relations that governed the growth of Igbo communities in the North created a situation ripe for manipulation and exploitation. Colonial rule created a set of circumstances where distrust between groups flowed easily, and too many Nigerian leaders chose to exploit those cleavages rather than to bridge them. In that sense, the groundwork for the violence of 1966 lay in colonial polices that created enormous educational disparities between the south and the far Northern Region, enforced patterns of residential segregation based on religion and ethnicity, and relied on ethnic and regional identities to divide Nigerians politically. Broad questions of regional and ethnic divisions are beyond the scope of this study, and have been addressed in great detail elsewhere.[4] Instead, this chapter addresses Igbo migration to Northern Nigeria during the colonial period, the ethnic and regional politics of decolonization during the 1950s, and the rising tensions of Nigeria's First Republic between 1960 and 1966. It begins by tracing the genesis of Igbo communities in the North, giving particular attention to the system of town unions that permeated Igbo life in migration and which linked migrants with home. A different manifestation of this system of Igbo unions was the Ibo State Union, which was an important symbol in the anti-Igbo disturbances of 1966. Further, the significance of unions extends beyond 1966; as I argue in chapter seven, the creation of a new umbrella organization for Igbo town unions was an important marker in the reestablishment of Kano's post-war Igbo community. The second section of this chapter turns to the last decade of the colonial period and looks at the Kano riot of 1953 and the Northernization policies of the Northern Peoples' Congress as turning points in relationship between the far North and its Igbo communities. The chapter concludes with a brief look at the role of ethnic politics in the First Republic, and the rising currency of "Igbo domination" in the vocabulary of Northern politicians.

## IGBO MIGRATION TO NORTHERN NIGERIA

Igbo migration to Northern Nigeria was a direct result of colonial policies. According to Mamdani, "The great crime of colonialism went beyond expropriating the native, the name it gave the indigenous population. The greater crime was to politicize indigeneity in the first place: First negatively, as a settler libel of the native; but then positively, as a native response, as a self-assertion."[5] By constructing legal apparata that "legally inscribed and enforced" ethnic identities, the relationships of individuals and groups with one another and with the state were reconfigured in terms set by the invader and given explicitly political ramifications.[6] The courts and body of law to which one answered, the authority to whom one paid taxes, to say nothing of one's access to employment, land, and state resources were all filtered through one's membership in state-recognized groups. Such categorization had the further effect of instilling "a binary preoccupation that was as compelling as it was confining."[7] This preoccupation with discreet, inflexible affiliations which one was either included in or excluded from survived the demise of the colonial state embedded in political institutions and in a politicized system of ethnic classification. It is hard to imagine a clearer laboratory for these concerns than colonial Nigeria, or a place with as cogent a post-colonial legacy.

The origins of an Igbo presence in the North lie with the thousands of Igbos who worked on the construction of rail lines during the 1910s and 1920s. As British activity in the North increased, however, a larger and more permanent Igbo presence followed. Elegalam has detailed both "push" and "pull" factors behind Igbo migration. They include unprecedented pressure on finite agricultural resources in Igboland because of population growth, the demand for cash that colonial taxation and a changing economy produced, and the presence of more mission-educated Igbos than the Eastern region's largely agricultural economy could absorb. Most early migrants went to the colonial capital of Lagos, though, with time, the North claimed an increasing share. The main factors "pulling" Igbos toward Northern Nigeria were opportunities for trade, and more significantly, skilled employment.[8] The British were reluctant to allow the introduction of mission schools in the emirates of the far North, since the Islamic authority structures of the emirates worked neatly with British techniques of indirect rule. This fueled stunning disparities in western education between the southern regions and the North. Primary school enrollment in the East in 1947 was 320,000; in the North, despite a much larger total population, enrollment was 66,000.[9] By 1950 the Eastern Region had trained 17,000 primary and 900 secondary school teachers; during the same period the North produced 4,500 primary and only 100 secondary teachers.[10] Compounding the problem for the far North was the fact that a disproportionate share of the Northern Region's teachers and students were in the Middle Belt, an area where Islam had a limited presence, and where Christianity had expanded rapidly during the colonial period. These factors combined to create opportunities in private enterprise and the public services as clerks, technicians, skilled workers, and teachers for southerners willing to relocate to the far North.

In fact, one of the great ironies of Nigerian history is that five of the Igbos who figured most prominently in Nigeria's crisis years—and in Nigerian history more generally—had strong connections to

Northern Nigeria. The country's first indigenous head of state, Nnamdi
Azikiwe, was born in 1904 in Zungeru, where his father was a civilian clerk with the colonial West African Frontier Force. Chukwuemeka
Odumegwu Ojukwu, who would become military governor of Eastern
Nigeria and later the president of Biafra, was also born in Zungeru,
and spent much of his childhood in Zaria, where his mother had business interests. The leader of Nigeria's first military coup, Chukwuma
Kaduna Nzeogwu, the son a Mid-Western Igbo civil servant, was born
and raised in Kaduna, the Northern capital. Nigeria's first military
ruler, J.T.U. Aguiyi-Ironsi, attended school in Kano. Like Ojukwu and
Nzeogwu, Ironsi spoke fluent Hausa. And Ukpabi Asika, the civilian
administrator of federally controlled Igboland during the war, and later
of East Central State, was born in Jos and worked for the regional
government in Kano.

While many migrants spent large portions of their lives in their host
communities, migration was almost always considered temporary. Even
long-term migrants expected at some point to return home. "Home,"
for most Igbos, referred, then and now, to the patrilineal village. As
Onwubu has written, "any change in residence in the form of migration is viewed as a temporary event, usually predicated on economic
exigencies. As generally understood, the objective of 'migration' from
one's home-place is to earn some fortune with which eventually to
establish oneself on returning *home*, and then to settle down . . . "[11]
Frequent communication and the repatriation of money and goods
characterized the relationship between migrants and home. The most
mobile participants in such networks were traders, who traveled home
more frequently than civil servants or company employees, in some
cases every two to three weeks, and almost always several times a
year. For other migrants, annual visits home were the norm, usually
during Christmas holidays. Also furthering links with home was the
fact that much Igbo migration was chain migration, in which established migrants hosted new arrivals from the same home community,
and in many cases from the same lineage.

Igbo migrants in the North were predominantly city and town dwellers. In 1931, for example, despite making up less than one percent of
the region's total population, Igbos constituted 14.6 percent of its urban dwellers.[12] Igbo migration increased with the heightened level of
economic exploitation of Nigeria by Britain after World War II. By
1953 Igbos constituted an important minority in cities like Zaria,
Kaduna, and the Middle Belt city of Jos, which, because of its mining
industry, had the North's largest Igbo population until the 1950s, when

Kano overtook it. On the other hand, some Igbos lived in rural areas where they worked as roadside mechanics, government clerks or technicians, or produce buyers. Census data from 1963 recorded that a quarter of the Igbos in Kano Province lived outside of cities and major towns.[13]

## RESIDENTIAL SEGREGATION: THE *SABON GARI* SYSTEM

In predominantly Muslim urban areas, colonial policies segregated non-Muslim Africans from Muslims. In Kano this meant preserving the practice of restricting residence within the walled "old city" to Muslims, most of whom were Hausa, but also included Fulani, Arabs, Kanuri, and members of other groups, many of whom were in various stages of Hausanization. The British encouraged Lebanese and other non-Nigerian Muslim merchants to settle adjacent to the walled city, in the largely Hausa Fagge ward, an area historically associated with Muslim long-distance traders. Since all land within the emirates was designated "crown land," and local officials had the right to grant or refuse usufructuary rights, it was fairly simple to contain and concentrate the southern population by granting them rights of occupancy only in certain areas.[14] Beginning with the arrival of southern railway workers in 1913, the colonial government in Kano settled them in *Sabon Gari* (Hausa = "New Town"; usually translated as "strangers' quarters"). The government created similar settlements in cities such as Zaria and Sokoto. Kano's Sabon Gari grew quickly, and the completion of a rail link between Kano and the southeastern coastal city of Port Harcourt in 1932 saw a sharp rise in Kano's Igbo population. By the 1950s Sabon Gari had become predominantly Igbo; second were Yorubas who had been the ward's first majority, followed by other southern groups.[15]

The most important distinction between the old city and Sabon Gari was a degree of administrative separation. While nominally under the Native Authority (NA) that governed the old city, Sabon Gari had its own courts and administrators. Sabon Gari was administratively linked with two smaller wards that housed a population comprising mostly Northern Muslim immigrants. The three wards were collectively referred to as Waje (literally, in Hausa, "outside." Also outside the old city, beyond the jurisdiction of the Native Authority was still another area, the Government Reserved Area, or GRA, where European and eventually African civil servants lodged).[16] After World War II, it became increasingly difficult for the British to keep members of Kano's

rapidly expanding Hausa population out of Sabon Gari. This was particularly true of men arriving from other parts of Hausaland in search
of work. While Yoruba Muslims from the southwestern portion of the
Northern Region were allowed to reside in Sabon Gari, there were a
number of efforts by British authorities to remove Hausas from the
ward and place them in the old city, where they would live under the
direct jurisdiction of the Native Authority and the city's Islamic institutions. Allowing Yoruba Muslims to remain in Sabon Gari while removing Hausa Muslims is evidence of residential policies that had less
to do with "preserving Islamic culture" than with using residential
segregation predicated on ethnic distinctions as an instrument of political control. As Bako has argued, the strong correlation of ethnicity
and occupational categories served the regime's economic interests by
imprinting class stratification with the stamp of ethnicity, and vice
versa.[17] Bako's observations are on target; it is important, however, to
note that, though incomes were generally higher in Sabon Gari than
in the old city, living conditions were not necessarily better. The ward
suffered from significant overcrowding in the 1950s and 1960s. A 1963
report estimated Sabon Gari's population at just under 40,000 and
pointed out that, with seven residential occupants per room—more than
four times the average in the old city—the ward was near residential
saturation.[18]

## COMMUNITY STRUCTURE: IGBO UNIONS

Perhaps the most serious consequence of the Sabon Gari system was
the obstacles it presented to contact between groups, obstacles that persisted into the post-colonial period. While the Igbo population was inte-
gral to the economy of greater Kano, social intercourse between denizens
of Sabon Gari and the old city was more an exception than the rule.
Patricia Ogbogu, who grew up in the Kano Igbo community, wrote in
1973 of the Igbo migrant's relationship to Sabon Gari and the larger community before and after the war.

> His connections with others notwithstanding, the Ibo settler was a man
> whose moral universe was largely confined to the quarter. Most of his
> friends are Ibo, not Hausa or Yoruba. If he develops [a] relationship of
> friendship with [a] Yoruba man or with Hausa besides business friends,
> he will be looked upon with suspicion by the Ibo in [Sabon Gari]. His
> strongest moral obligations are towards people in the quarter, not in
> the rest of the town.[19]

As discussed in chapter six, where contacts between Igbo men and Hausas were limited, those between Igbo women and the Hausa community were even more so.

While commercial and professional networks and the Catholic church were part of many Igbo migrants' lives, the most pervasive institution for both men and women was the system of town unions, which blended social, economic, political, and often kinship ties.[20] Each union was based on a town or village in Igboland; men and un-married women joined with others from their home area, while mar-ried women affiliated with their husbands' unions. While unions sometimes joined to form larger clan and divisional unions, the town union was, in most cases, the fundamental unit. Each union partici-pated simultaneously in two parallel networks, one that tied it to the home town, and a second that tied it to Kano's Igbo community. A third, far less important manifestation of the union system was the national Ibo State Union.

The first network was centered on the home town, and linked the Kano branch with the main union at home and with branches in other migrant communities. As members of their home town union, migrant members could contribute to the development of their home area and participate in decisions made there. However, the most important func-tion of town unions was to act as a resource for members and their families in times of need.[21] In particular this applied, and continues to apply, in cases of the death of a family member. In such cases, the union placed a levy on its members, usually a fixed amount, to defray the costs of transporting the body of an adult to Igboland for burial, and to provide the decedent's family with a financial cushion.[22] In addition to these death benefits, town unions could be expected to financially and materially assist sick members, to help new arrivals locate employment and lodging, and to host prominent visitors from home. They were also an important force for social control. The unions enforced standards of public appearance and conduct among members, for example. On a more serious note, those guilty of criminal behav-ior might be threatened by members of their town or clan groups with being handed over to the police—a daunting prospect when the union probably represented one's most likely allies and source of financial support. And in cases where Igbos were convicted of crimes, "imme-diately after serving his sentence he was deported home."[23]

The second network in which town unions participated was cen-tered on Kano, and connected Kano's 100 or so town unions into the Kano Ibo Union. By 1966 each town union in Kano sent two or three representatives to meetings of the Kano Ibo Union, which concerned itself with the well-being of Kano's Igbos. Since broader bodies such as clan and division unions were not represented in the Ibo Union, those without town unions either went without representation or affiliated themselves formally or informally to a neighboring town's union. The primary mandate of local umbrella organizations like the Kano union was to present a single voice for local Igbo interests. In Sokoto in 1954, for example, the local Ibo Union protested to the British Resident the use of the derisive appellation "Inyamiri" by local people.[24]

> This derisive nickname "Inyamiri" which has gained a firm footing in this locality is being so disturbingly used these days as to provoke even a Reverend. That as we have no intention of falling out with the populace of this Great City . . . we would be happy if the Authority could help us to put a stop to this [insulting] word that is being used on Igbos without respect or otherwise on their feelings.[25]

The line between union activities and party politics was, to outside eyes, sometimes a thin one. For example, during the First Republic, the president of the Kano union, Felix Okonkwo, was also chairman of the Igbo-led National Council of Nigerian Citizens (NCNC) in the far North. Not surprisingly, the union cooperated informally with the NCNC. During the bitterly contested 1963 census that set the major political parties at odds with one another, Okonkwo, in his capacity as Kano union head, led a delegation "representing the entire Ibo population in the North" to Lagos where they met with the Prime Minister.[26]

The Kano Ibo Union served other functions as well, including the coordination of cultural activities or contributions on behalf of the Igbo community to local capital development projects. In addition, as in the example of the 1953 Kano riot discussed at length below, the Ibo Union provided an apparatus through which authorities could deal with community leaders in times of crisis.

Another important and ongoing activity of the Kano Ibo Union was the construction and operation of the Ibo Union Grammar School. Since, in official eyes, Kano's Igbos were citizens of the Eastern Region, even children who had spent their entire lives in the North, were, like other non-Northerners, ineligible for waivers of school fees that the regional government introduced in the 1950s. In most cases, this left Igbo parents who wished to educate their children beyond primary school with the choice of either sending their children home to the East for schooling, or entering them in one of Kano's few—and comparatively expensive—church schools. It was to these students that the school catered. The Igbo Union Grammar School accepted non-Igbo students, but most of its pupils were the children of parents who were union members.[27] The creation of the school was a highly visible undertaking. That the Kano Ibo Union successfully packaged the school as a contribution to the development of the city and region is underscored by the fact that the Premier of the Northern Region, Ahmadu Bello, and the Emir of Kano, Muhammad Sanusi, laid the building's first and second stones in 1959.[28] By 1961 the school had 150 students, of whom thirty-four were girls. According to school records, nine "Hausa and Fulani" students attended in 1961, and twelve in 1963; in 1965 there were seventy-four students identified as "Northern" out of a student body of 290. That fifty-five of these students were boarders suggests that the Kano school drew students from other parts of the North.[29]

The final important manifestation of the Igbo union system was the Ibo State Union, a national body with representatives from communities across Igboland. As a national body ostensibly concerned with issues that affected Igbos as a group, it was the union furthest removed from the everyday activities of ordinary people. Until it was banned in 1966, the Ibo State Union, as will be seen in chapter three, was for many non-Igbos a symbol of Igbo unity and national political aspirations. The reality of its existence, however, was very different than its critics imagined it. Founded as the Ibo Union in 1936 by migrants in Lagos, it changed its name as its membership grew. In the mid-1940s it became the Ibo Federal Union, and in 1948 the Ibo State Union. In common usage, however, it remained the Ibo Union.[30] By the 1950s the Ibo State Union comprised members representing, in theory, every town, clan, divisional, and provincial union in Igboland.[31] It would be incorrect, however, to interpret the existence of concentric unions—from town to clan, to division, to the Ibo State Union—as evidence of a hierarchical relationship.

Although the inauguration of the Ibo State Union preceded the establishment of most of the rural ethnic unions in the Eastern Region, the Ibo State Union did not call forth a sudden proliferation of these associations. The formation of all of the unions about which information is available occurred in response to specific needs or goals in the community, not as a result of the organizational activities of the Ibo State Union or its predecessors. Consequently, the local ethnic unions remained autonomous and resisted the superficial efforts of the Ibo State

Union to coordinate their undertakings. In fact, the very success of the parochial ethnic unions made superfluous most of the planned programs of the Ibo State Union.[32]

The Ibo State Union, however, used the perception that it could exercise control over Igbos to intervene on their behalf in times of difficulty. In 1959, for example, complaints by the Igbo community in the Middle Belt city of Bida led the Ibo State Union to issue an ultimatum to the Emir of Bida.

> Of late, disturbing news of maltreatments, threats and molestations of Igbos in Bida by your indigenous subjects have reached the Ibo State Union Secretariat and I have been directed to communicate with you on same.
>
> The Ibo State Union had always impressed on all Ibo to eschew lawlessness and respect the customs of the land in which they sojourn. So far there has not been any complaint that the Ibo in Bida are going against the customs of the land[.] [I]nstead, as is alleged, your subjects use one excuse or another to attack and insult them.
>
> The Ibo State Union could order all the Ibo to quit your emirate but it will not produce good results for either party.[33]

The matter was resolved, and the Union issued no quit order. The line between the Ibo State Union and the NCNC, however, was often a thin one. During a series of crises in 1964, the Ibo State Union and the NCNC jointly lodged written protests in response to suggestions in the Northern legislature that Igbo public service employees in the region be "deported" and their property seized. Eventually officials from the NCNC and the union met with the prime minister, and Northern leaders denied the allegations.[34]

## DECOLONIZATION AND
## THE APPEAL OF NORTHERNIZATION

The 1964 controversy is closely related to others that are collectively emblematic of how the presence of a highly visible Igbo population in the North impacted regional and national politics during decolonization and the early years of independence. The 1950s in Nigeria were characterized by struggles between the Northern Region and the south over the timetable for decolonization. While the two major southern political parties pushed for internal self-government in

1956 as a prelude to full independence, the dominant Northern party, the Northern Peoples Congress (NPC), worked to slow the process, largely on the grounds that the North lagged behind the south in commercial infrastructure and human resources, and required time to close the gap. A letter to the editors of *Gaskiya ta fi Kwabo* warned that independence, when it came, would bring with it new dangers of "oppression and injustice." According to the reader, "We shall escape from the domination of the white man only to be enslaved by the black man. We were conquered by the white man, but he did not enslave us, and now those who did not conquer us will enslave us."[35] In response to fears like these, the NPC developed a series of policies known collectively as "Northernization." Northernization was designed to prepare the North for self-government and the coming end of colonial rule. Northernization was specifically intended to protect the North from administrative and economic domination by southerners, and the policies remained in place after Nigeria became independent in 1960. Not surprisingly, in much of the political discourse surrounding Northernization, the face of the south was Igbo, and the condition the North had to avoid at all cost was "Ibo domination." The high degree of visibility Igbos enjoyed in Northern Nigeria helps to explain a major outbreak of politically inspired violence between Igbos and Hausas in Kano in 1953, a riot that was closely linked to the same issues that surrounded Northernization.

It is difficult to overstate the significance of Northernization policies on both the Northern Region, and, in time, on the position of Igbos in the North. After World War II, lobbying by southern politicians for self government and eventual independence from Britain reached new levels. In order to help each of the colony's three regions to prepare for self-government, the Littleton Constitution of 1954 divided Nigeria's single Public Service into three regional branches while preserving a separate federal civil service. Under the guidance of their ruling parties, the Eastern and Western Regions took steps to "Nigerianize" (or "indigenize") their public services by replacing Europeans and other expatriates with Nigerians. The North, however, had a different set of priorities. Since World War II, colonial administration in the North had relied heavily on skilled southerners to sustain Britain's increased demands on the region's resources. Therefore, indigenization would have meant, in large measure, replacing foreigners with southerners. This was politically unacceptable in the North.[36] In 1952, NPC leader Ahmadu Bello unveiled a broad plan that called for the region's public service to train, employ, and promote Northerners whenever possible. It also gave explicit preference to expatriates over southern Nigerians. This plan for Northernization also included provisions to limit the influence of southerners by restricting land use, access to government contracts and other economic opportunities to Northerners. While Northernization did not affect federal services, such as the railway, postal service, military, or federal ministries, it did lead to the dismissal of thousands of non-Northerners in the regional service who were replaced in the years following its implementation in 1954.[37] "Aside from engendering bitter southern resentments, this policy worked almost precisely as intended, purging the [Northern regional] bureaucracy of all but one southerner by 1959, heavily disposing it toward manipulation and domination by the ruling NPC, and so further concentrating administrative and political power in the narrow dominant class of the North."[38] As we will see, Northernization had two profound and far-reaching effects. First, it was important as mortar in the edifice of Northern regional identity, and strengthened class solidarity among the North's western-educated elites and those who aspired to join them. In so doing, Northernization also reinscribed the dichotomy of southerners as modern, and Northerners as lagging behind in the race to acquire the skills necessary to manage the region's administrative and economic institutions. The second major consequence of Northernization was to present a clear target for those who felt discriminated against by its provisions, or who felt that it contradicted the spirit of a unified country. Southern resentments over Northernization lingered until an Igbo-led government in 1966 dismantled Northernization policies, with disastrous repercussions.

## "IT COULD HAPPEN AGAIN":
## ETHNIC POLITICS AND THE 1953 KANO RIOT

If Northernization policies exposed the North's understandable feelings of vulnerability vis-à-vis the south during a period of profound change, then the 1953 Kano riot demonstrated how easily ethnic politics could translate into intercommunal violence. The riot was not the first instance of intercommunal violence between Igbos and Hausas in Northern Nigeria; a market dispute had grown to a major riot in Jos in 1945.[39] By 1953, however, the prospect of Nigerian self-rule had transformed the political climate. Many of the core issues underpinning the 1953 Kano riot were the same as those behind Northernization. In April of that year, Northern representatives attending a federal budget meeting in Lagos were harassed by crowds protesting the NPC's opposition to self-rule. The NCNC and the dominant party in Western Nigeria, the Action Group (AG), favored rapid decolonization, and saw self-rule as an important step in that direction. The Lagos demonstration was a major embarrassment to the NPC, and led to a wave of anti-southern sentiment in the North. When Chief Samuel Akintola, a Yoruba politician representing the AG planned a visit to Kano the following month, NPC politicians organized a march in protest. The British Resident canceled Akintola's visit after getting reports suggesting southerners in Kano feared reprisals against them for the treatment the Northern delegation had received in Lagos. According to one report, a dealer had sold 172 machetes to southerners. Further, there had been "a considerable theft of scrap iron," and a large commercial firm's grindstone "had been worn right down overnight by being used for sharpening matchets and scrap iron." The Kano Ibo Union went so far as to appeal to the District Officer for "protection against Northerners who were stated to be coming into the town from nearby villages, many carrying weapons."[40]

An AG delegation did visit Kano, however, and Northerners, apparently NPC supporters, rallied in protest on Saturday, 16 May. Violence ensued when members of the crowd attacked southerners. A government report identified the attackers as "mostly of the hooligan and casual labour type." The same report determined that the protesters who had initially gathered to hear NPC representatives outside the Sabon Gari hotel where the AG delegation was lodged included members of other socio-economic classes, but that they had not joined in the attacks. NPC politician Inuwa Wada succeeded in dispersing some of the crowd, and the report suggested that those who remained were responsible for starting the violence. Fighting continued for four days, until the government brought in police reinforcements and established a Reconciliation Committee of community leaders, including top Kano Ibo Union representatives.

The most troubling question behind the 1953 riot, which Paden has pursued, is why a political dispute between the NPC and the AG, a party with few Igbo members, led to violence against Igbos, most of whom were NCNC supporters. The AG was a predominantly Yoruba party, yet it was primarily Igbos and not Yorubas who were targets of violence, and who fought back against their mostly Hausa attackers. Igbos made up the vast majority of the twenty-one southerners killed and seventy-one injured; no Yoruba deaths and only two injuries were reported.[41] Investigators found no evidence that Northern rioters in

1953 were either organized or paid to participate in the violence.[42] This, and the fact that Igbos were the main targets of violence, led the investigators to see "spontaneous" violence set off by longstanding economic tensions and not by any immediate political manipulation. Investigators were aware of the structural problems in the relationship between Northerners and southerners in Kano. Central to their analysis was the "relationship existing between the average Northerner and Southern petty officialdom, and the Southern staff of the commercial firms." The resulting "underlying feeling of resentment" among Northerners was sparked by the AG visit.[43] About the riot they wrote that

*It could happen again*, and only a realisation and acceptance of the underlying causes can remove the danger of recurrence.

The disturbances and the reactions that they provoked were so spontaneous, so violent and so wide spread that no thinking person could assign to them short-term causes, such as the jealousies of rival nationalist parties or the desire for loot on the part of the criminal sections of the populace. The root causes go far deeper than that. Everyone who has lived for any length of time in the North is well aware that, for a long period of years, there has been something radically wrong with the relationships between the inhabitants of the Region on the one hand and the Southern communities now settled there. This generalization does not apply to many hundreds, possibly thousands, of individual cases but is of sufficiently general application to carry crucial significance in periods of tension and crisis.[44]

Paden, who has written the only sustained analysis of the riot, agreed with the government's arguments. Nnoli, however, disagreed, instead arguing that the NPC "masterminded" the riot as part of its efforts to delay the push for independence in 1956.[45] In as much as Nnoli also identified political organizers at work, his assertion is largely in keeping with my conclusions about the 1966 riots. Given the available body of information, however, it remains difficult to prove or disprove either Paden or Nnoli's interpretation of the 1953 incident. It is equally clear, however, that the elements of intercommunal competition that Paden identified were present, and were very much part of the public consciousness at the time of the disturbance. The colonial officers who reported on the incident were, perhaps, understandably reluctant to explore the "root causes" of the relationship gone "radically wrong." Among "root causes" of violence in 1953, both Nnoli and Paden agree on intense economic competition, economic inequalities, a national climate of escalating political tension set against ambient religious and cultural differences. More importantly, both emphasize the limited opportunities for residential, social, and political integration under the colonial *sabon gari* system. What remains uncertain is whether the Lagos incident was sufficient provocation to catalyze otherwise "spontaneous"—meaning unplanned—violence.

Several characteristics of the 1966 riots were present in 1953. Not only did many Northerners choose not to participate in the violence, but some actively worked to protect potential Igbo victims. According to the government report, some unnamed NPC leaders helped southerners to escape the first attack, in the process "being hit by stones in the melee." On the other side of the same coin, the next day police rescued a Hausa man after two Igbos reported to police that other Igbos had attacked him.[46] Incidents such as these, in which hundreds were protected, led the writers of the report to comment that

> While irresponsible mobs on either side were attacking their opponents indiscriminately wherever they could be found, it is a great relief to record that sober and decent citizens of all races afforded shelter or protection to those of other races than themselves during the point of danger.

and

> One of the few gleams of sunshine in the gloomy picture of the recent rioting has been the way in which Northerners sheltered Southerners in Fagge and Southerners sheltered Northerners in Sabon Gari, frequently at risk of personal injury to themselves.[47]

Despite this bit of optimism, the authors of the report were, on the whole, pessimistic. Kano, however, would remain free from major outbreaks of intercommunal violence for more than a decade, during which time Northernization policies would lead to a sharp decrease in the number of Igbos in regional and local public service positions. Those who remained were hired on short-term contracts, and not on a permanent basis. Kano's Igbo population, however, continued to grow. A cadre of Igbo federal employees remained, and the number of Igbo traders dealing in southern produce and imported manufactured goods in Kano grew as the Sabon Gari market became an increasingly vital part of the regional economy.

## INDEPENDENCE: THE FIRST REPUBLIC

The issues that polarized relations between Igbos and Hausas during the 1950s persisted after Nigeria became independent on 1 October 1960. Party politics provided a dizzying terrain for intergroup relations. Since the early 1950s, an alliance between the NCNC and the Kano-based Northern Elements Progressive Union (NEPU) provided an important bridge between communities. As part of its search for allies in the North, the NCNC lent its financial and material support to the NEPU, and the NEPU consistently outpolled the NPC in Kano city, but was unable to dislodge the NPC as the region's ruling party. Through its control over Native Authorities, which answered to the regional government, the NPC worked to undermine NEPU's effectiveness in Kano and its other strongholds of Kaduna and Jos.[48] In Kano, NEPU was strongest among the working and lower-classes (*talakawa*; commoners), many of whom sometimes distinguished themselves as "pure" Hausa in contradistinction to the Fulani heritage common within the precolonial ruling class (*sarauta*). Many of the leaders of Kano's Ibo Union were also prominent in the local NCNC, and they worked closely with their NEPU counterparts. NCNC-NEPU cooperation would have important ramifications in years to come. Despite the longstanding alliance, however, the NCNC's national leadership formed an uneasy governing coalition with the NPC. The Igbo NCNC leader, Dr. Nnamdi Azikiwe, became Nigeria's first head of state, while Sir Abubakar Tafawa Balewa of the NPC became the country's first Prime Minister. The AG, which controlled the Western Region, led the opposition in Parliament. To the degree that it is possible to speak of Igbo and Hausa political interests, for a time it seemed that they were to some degree parallel, or at least overlapped.

Still, the politics of the First Republic were stormy, and the on-again, off-again relationship between the NCNC and the NPC was no exception. In part this was because of what Kirk-Greene has called the "hairspring delicacy and complexity of the Nigerian political system."[49] The vicissitudes of the First Republic are well documented and need not be pursued in depth here.[50] Ethnicity, though, remained an unfortunate staple of political discourse. According to Diamond, party leaders and publications "never failed to keep the local elites and candidates amply supplied with ethnic accusations and suspicions, however hysterical or malicious[.] Farfetched to the extreme, such tactics nevertheless successfully transformed people's basest prejudices and wildest fears into resounding electoral mandates."[51] Similarly, Nnoli has pointed out that political leaders created "the false impression that the various political parties were the champions of the interests of the various ethnic groups, and that struggles of these parties for political dominance in the country represented the struggles of the various ethnic groups for political ascendency. . . . They covertly and even openly used emotive ethnic symbols and played on alleged ethnic conflicts of interests as a means of mobilising mass support" for their own purposes.[52] Political cartoons featuring ethnic caricatures, editorials in which ethnic stereotypes substituted for argumentary evidence, and fear-mongering were part and parcel of political life. The NPC, for example, used real and amplified threats of southern domination to downplay the internal fissures in the North, and as leverage against NEPU and other sub-regional rivals like the Bornu Youth Movement and the United Middle Belt Congress.[53] And, in their interactions with one another, the presence of Igbos in the North provided both the NPC and the NCNC with fodder for their rhetorical cannons. The NPC's policy of Northernization, for example, remained an open sore for the NCNC and national Ibo State Union during the First Republic. In the face of discussions in the Northern House of Assembly about restricting non-Northerners access to land in the region, some of which singled out Igbos, the Ibo Union protested.

Now that the Ibos are being victimised merely because they are Ibos; now that Nigeria is considered in many quarters as four or more countries; now that Ibos in Northern Nigeria have no protection under the law nor are their lives and property safe; now that the Constitution can freely be violated at the whims and caprice of a section of the community with impunity; in so far as such violation is aimed at victimising the Ibos; the Union demands a revision of the present constitution which has proved unworkable.[54]

All of the major parties, including the NCNC and the NPC, had been implicated in corruption ranging from electoral malfeasance to misuse of public funds, nepotism, and manipulation of critical census data. These factors contributed to an erosion of public confidence in elected officials. The most volatile and destructive politics, however, were in Western Nigeria, where pressure from the other major parties contributed to a split within the AG. In the West, by the end of 1964

party thuggery and political gerrymandering reached new heights. Each of the parties was prepared to use all and every means at its disposal to ensure victory at the elections: setting fire to the cars and houses of political opponents, attacks by thugs and the use of police force to intimidate prospective candidates became common-place.

In the prevailing atmosphere of tense, cut-throat competition, Regional and ethnic chauvinism developed apace, and accusations of an alleged attempt at "Ibo domination" or "Hausa-Fulani domination" were freely exchanged.[55]

Federal elections such as those of 1964 featured "virulent anti-Iboism" in the government-controlled newspapers of the West and North. Speeches on assembly floors by members of the NPC and its allies in the West used the specter of Igbo commercial and political domination to rally support.[56] In the process, "in an alarmingly open fashion . . . the election was declared to be a battle of the Ibo against the rest."[57] This was just one element of an increasingly desperate political situation. The last weeks of the First Republic featured widespread civil disturbances in the West. It was in what Balogun called "this atmosphere of chaos and the near-collapse of the country's political institutions" that a group of junior military officers staged Nigeria's first coup d'état.[58]

## NOTES

1. Sheikh Abubakar Mahmud Gumi, *al-'Aqida al-sahiha* (Beirut, 1972), 79; cited in Mervyn Hiskett, *The Sword of Truth: The Life and Times of the Shehu Usman Dan Fodio*, 2nd ed. (Evanston: Northwestern University Press, 1994), fn. xix.

2. According to Paden, "Despite the association of persons in the Sabon Gari with Christian religious ideas, the Northern perception of the Igbo was that they were only nominal Christians and thus in reality were pagans." Paden, *Religion and Political Culture*, 314.

3. The reality, of course, was far more complex, with each group utilizing both new and old tools in pursuit of a range of goals. In the context of Kano, "Many Ibos . . . were traditional in their sense of adherence to ethnic cultural values, and many Hausa traders in Kano City (some of whom were literate in Hausa and many in Arabic as well) were modern in their aspirations and organization." Paden, *Religion and Political Culture*, 320.

4. See, for example, Diamond, *Class, Ethnicity and Democracy in Nigeria*; Nnoli, *Ethnic Politics in Nigeria*; Kenneth Post and Michael Vickers, *Structure and Conflict in Nigeria 1960–1966* (London: Heinemann, 1973); Richard Sklar and C.S. Whitaker, *African Politics and Problems in Development* (Boulder: Lynne Rienner, 1991). For a comparative perspective, see Donald Horowitz, *Ethnic Groups in Conflict* (Berkeley: University of California Press, 1985).

5. Mahmood Mamdani, *When Victims Become Killers: Colonialism, Nativism, and the Genocide in Rwanda* (Princeton: Princeton University Press, 2001), 14.

6. Mamdani, *When Victims Become Killers*, 22. See also p. 15.

7. Mamdani, *When Victims Become Killers*, 14.

8. Charles Elegalam, *The Causes and Consequences of Igbo Migration to Northern Nigeria, 1900–1960* (Ph.D. dissertation, Howard University, 1988).

9. A. Babs Fafunwa, *History of Education in Nigeria* (London: George Allen and Unwin, 1974), 174.

10. K.M. Buchanan and J.C. Pugh, *Land and Peoples in Nigeria* (London: University of London Press, 1958), 233, cited in Elegalam, *Causes and Consequences of Igbo Migration.*

11. Chukwuemeka Onwubu, "Ethnic Identity, Political Integration, and National Development: The Igbo Diaspora in Nigeria," *Journal of Modern African Studies* 13, 3 (1975), 406. [Original emphasis.]

12. Nigeria, *Population Census of the Northern Region of Nigeria, 1931* (Lagos: Government Printing Office, 1931), cited in Elegalam, *Causes and Consequences of Igbo Migration,* 80. An important exception to the pattern of urban residence is the significant population of Igbo farmers in the Idoma-speaking areas of Benue Province in the Middle Belt, where they constituted more than 13 percent of residents in 1952 (82, 85).

13. Nigeria, *Nigeria Population Census: Northern Region, Vol. II* (Lagos: Government Printer, 1963), cited in *Kano State Statistical Yearbook, 1972* (Kano: Military Governor's Office, 1972), 21. The census counted a total of 11,474 Igbos in Kano and surrounding areas. Like other Nigerians, most Igbos had returned to their home areas to be enumerated, so the totals represent only a fraction of the normal population.

14. In exchange for certificates of occupancy, which guaranteed rights of occupancy for up to 99 years, Sabon Gari tenants paid annual land dues to the local government.

15. See Paden, *Religion and Political Culture*, 315.

16. See Paden, *Religion and Political Culture*, 17–19.

17. Ahmed Bako, *A Socio-economic History of Sabon Gari Kano, 1913–1989* (Ph.D. Dissertation, Bayero University-Kano, 1990), 27, 39.

18. B.A.W. Trevallion, *Metropolitan Kano: Report on the Twenty Year Development Plan, 1963–83* (Oxford, Pergamon Press, 1963), 50–51.

19. Patricia Ogbogu, "Ibo Integration in Kano After the War" (unpublished undergraduate thesis, Ahmadu Bello University, 1973), 45. I am grateful to Alhaji Uba Adamu for sharing this document with me.

20. Smock's study of Igbo unions in pre-war Nigeria outlines the structural characteristics of the unions. Smock, *Ibo Politics: The Role of Ethnic Unions in Eastern Nigeria*, 13. See also Austin M. Ahanotu, "The Role of Ethnic Unions in the Development of Southern Nigeria: 1916–1966," in *Studies in Southern Nigerian History*, B.I. Obichere, ed. (London: Frank Cass, 1982).

21. In addition, the women's wings of town and division unions frequently assisted members with grants or loans of business capital. This phenomenon and the parallel structure of men's and women's wings are discussed in chapter seven.

22. In most cases the benefit paid a widower is less than that paid a widow. Similarly, in most cases death benefits for children under 18 are less than adult benefits, as it is likely the child will be buried in a Christian cemetery in Kano; if the

family should choose to transport the child home, it would be expected to absorb most of the cost.

23. FN 35: Interview with Mr. Donatus Ezemwata, 16 April 1994, Kano.

24. *Inyamiri* derives from the Igbo imperative "bring water," and probably originates from early contact between Igbos and Hausa-speaking workers during construction of railway lines linking Eastern and Northern Nigeria in the 1920s. This explanation turns on a division of labor wherein Igbo workers requested water from Hausa porters, who then used the Igbos' utterances as a term of reference for them. The phrase, frequently heard among Hausa speakers, is generally offensive to most Igbos.

25. NAK Sokoto Prof 798/4789, letter, O. Ijeh (president, Sokoto Ibo Union) to Resident, 14 October 1954. An addition by the investigating officer noted that "Inyamiri" was often coupled with "*kare*," Hausa for "dog."

26. "The Census Issue Hots Up: Ibo Leaders Storm PM's Office," *New Nigerian*, 28 March 1964. M.A. Agbamuche, another prominent Kano Igbo, was legal advisor to the delegation.

27. HCB 1429/SCH 221, n.p., n.d.

28. "Premier and Emir to Lay Foundation Stones of Ibo School," *Daily Comet*, 21 January 1959. The school was taken over by the state during the Civil War.

29. HCB 1429/SCH 221, n.p., n.d. A second institution, the Ibo Union Secondary School was operated by the Ibo Union in Kafanchan, and among some members of the Kano Ibo Union there were aspirations to expand the Kano school to include post-secondary levels.

30. Nnoli, *Ethnic Politics*, 106, 156, and 230. Hereafter, the national body will be referred to only as the "Ibo State Union." This is to avoid confusion with the Kano Ibo Union.

31. Smock pointed out, however, that in practice, only a small proportion of the smaller unions actually registered and paid the dues required to participate in the activities of the Ibo State Union. See Smock, *Ibo Politics*, 17.

32. Smock, *Ibo Politics*, 18.

33. NAK ASI/115, letter, V.C.I. Anene to Emir of Bida, 27 October 1959.

34. Smock, *Ibo Politics*, 20–21 and "No Quit Order on Igbos," *Daily Mail*, 28 March 1964.

35. Letter from Muhammad Tafoki, *Gaskiya ta fi Kwabo*, 8 February 1950.

36. Nnoli, *Ethnic Politics*, 188–89. See also Nigeria, *The Northernization of the Civil Service: A Review of Policy and Machinery* (Lagos: Government Printer, 1954), 63–65. The report was authored by Sir Sydney Phillipson and Mr. S.O. Adebo.

37. For example, between January 1954 and August 1958, 2,148 southerners were dismissed from the Northern Nigeria Public Service. See Nnoli, "The Dynamics of Ethnic Politics in Nigeria," *Journal of West African Studies,* 13–14, (1976), 20.

38. Diamond, "Class, Ethnicity, and the Democratic State: Nigeria, 1950–1966," 473–4.

39. See Leonard Plotnicov, *Strangers to the City: Urban Man in Jos, Nigeria* (Pittsburgh: University of Pittsburgh Press, 1967).

40. Northern Region (Nigeria), *Report on the Kano Disturbances, 16–19 May, 1953* (Kaduna: Government Printer, 1953), 9–10. See also Paden, *Religion and Political Culture*, 321–22.

41. John N. Paden, "Communal Competition, Conflict and Violence in Kano," in *Nigeria: Modernization and the Politics of Communalism*, Robert Melson and Howard Wolpe, eds. (East Lansing: Michigan State University Press, 1971), 132–33. Fifteen Northerners were killed, and 170 reported injured.

42. *Report on the Kano Disturbances*, 35.

43. *Report on the Kano Disturbances*, 2.

44. *Report on the Kano Disturbances*, 39. [Original emphasis.]

45. Nnoli, *Ethnic Politics*, 162.

46. *Report on the Kano Disturbances*, 14.

47. *Report on the Kano Disturbances*, 23.

48. See Jonathan T. Reynolds, *The Time of Politics (Zamanin Siyasa): Islam and the Politics of Legitimacy in Northern Nigeria 1950–1966* (San Francisco: International Scholars Publications, 1999).

49. A.H.M Kirk-Greene, *The Genesis of the Nigerian Civil War and the Theory of Fear* (Uppsala: Nordiska afrikainstitutet, 1975), 3.

50. Important scholarly works include John de St. Jorre, *The Brothers War; Biafra and Nigeria* (Boston: Houghton Mifflin, 1972); Diamond, *Class, Ethnicity and Democracy*; Okechukwu Ikejiani and Odinchezo Ikejiani, *Nigeria: Political Imperatives* (Enugu: Fourth Dimension Publishers, 1986); Wayne Nafziger, *The Economics of Political Instability: The Biafran War* (Boulder: Westview Press, 1983); Post and Vickers, *Structure and Conflict*; Sklar and Whitaker, *African Politics*; Auberon Waugh and Suzanne Cronje, *Biafra: Britain's Shame* (London: Joseph, 1969).

Important works on the Civil War, some offering competing versions of events, include Adewale Ademoyega, *Why We Struck* (Ibadan: Evans Brothers, 1981); Ntieyong U. Akpan, *The Struggle for Secession, 1966–70* (London: Frank Cass, 1972); Frederick Forsyth, *The Making of an African Legend: The Biafra Story* (New York: Penguin, 1977); Ben Gbulie, *Nigeria's Five Majors* (Onitsha: African Educational Publishers, 1981); Alexander A. Madiebo, *The Nigerian Revolution and the Biafran War* (Enugu: Fourth Dimension Publishers, 1980); A.M. Mainasara, *The Five Majors: Why They Struck* (Zaria: Hudahuda Publishers, 1982); D.J.M. Muffett, *Let Truth Be Told: The Coups D'Etat of 1966* (Zaria: Hudahuda Publishing, 1982); Arthur A. Nwankwo and Samuel U. Ifejika, *Biafra: The Making of a Nation* (New York: Praeger, 1970); and Olusegun Obasanjo, *My Command* (London: Heinemann, 1981). There are numerous others.

An outstanding and well-balanced detailing of the events of 1966 and 1967 is A.H.M. Kirk-Greene, *Crisis and Conflict in Nigeria: A Documentary Sourcebook, Vol. 1* (London: Oxford University Press, 1971). A concise and equally balanced account of the war is Zdenek Cervenka, *The Nigerian War 1967–1970: History of the War, Selected Bibliography and Documents* (Frankfurt am Main: Bernard and Graef Verlag für Wehrwesen, 1971).

51. Diamond, "Class, Ethnicity, and the Democratic State," 469.

52. Nnoli, *Ethnic Politics*, 158.

53. B.J. Takaya, *The Middle Belt in Nigerian Politics* (Jos: ASA Publishers, 1991), 38, 42.

54. Ibo State Union, *Nigerian Disunity: The Guilty Ones* (Enugu, n.d.), 14, cited in Nwankwo and Ifekeja, *The Making of a Nation*, 104. Nwankwo quotes, among others, a 17 March 1964 statement by Assembly member Busar Umari, who said " . . . The Hon. Premier should from today empower the Minster of Land and Survey to confiscate all the houses and farms belonging to Ibos. We have finished with them and finished with them finally." (102) See also Post and Michael Vickers, *Structure and Conflict*, 119–21.

55. Ola Balogun, *The Tragic Years: Nigeria in Crisis, 1966–1970* (Benin City: Ethiope Publishing Corporation, 1973), 20. Balogun's account is concise and useful; a more detailed treatment is Diamond, *Class, Ethnicity and Democracy*.

56. Post and Vickers, *Structure and Conflict*, 123–5.

57. Post and Vickers, *Structure and Conflict*, 119.

58. Balogun, *The Tragic Years*, 20.

# 2

# THE IRONSI REGIME AND THE SPECTER OF "IGBO DOMINATION": JANUARY–JULY 1966

## INTRODUCTION

The collapse of the First Republic did not signal an end to ethnic politics. Indeed, Nigeria's first, short-lived military government presided over a period of heightened interregional tensions, and a sharpening of ethnic sensibilities. Transformed by the sudden shift in power at the center, ethnic and regional polarization not only persisted, but intensified. It is during this period between January and July of 1966 that we see most clearly the malleability of ethnicity as an instrument of politics. Northern elites positioned Igbo ethnicity and Northern regional identity in opposition to one another, in the process carefully focusing existing anti-Igbo sentiments and nurturing new resentments. Northern leaders did these things because the 15 January 1966 coup inaugurated a period in which Igbo power in Nigeria appeared ascendant, and Northern influence stifled. The coup plotters were mostly Igbos, and the coup's civilian and military casualties mostly Northerners. Further, the military ruler who emerged, General J.T.U. Aguiyi-Ironsi, was an Igbo who surrounded himself with Igbo advisers. In his brief tenure, Ironsi would leave an indelible print on Nigeria's body politic and on the fabric of intercommunal relations. His government pursued policies that, from a Northern vantage point, advanced the collective interests of Igbos and other southerners at the expense of

Northerners, and particularly Northern elites. Compounding matters at the local level, some ordinary Igbos in Northern cities gloated over the apparent reversals for the NPC and the North. Things came to a head when the Ironsi government announced in May an end to the regional administrative structure of Nigeria. In response, a loose coalition of Northern elites and aspiring elites acted to protect their interests, and in so doing achieved an unprecedented degree of political unity. Far from a spontaneous outpouring of long-simmering public sentiment, the anti-Igbo violence of May 1966 was the product of careful planning. Then, in late July, Northern officers toppled the Ironsi regime itself in a second coup, this one much more violent than the one which had brought Ironsi to power. Throughout it all, elements of the inherited discourses of ethnicity remained at the surface.

## THE JANUARY COUP AND
## THE SLOW EROSION OF CONFIDENCE

The path to violence in the North was gradual, and was driven by developments in Lagos. The coup of 15 January was organized by junior army officers. Its leader, Major Chukwuma Kaduna Nzeogwu, was a Northern-born Igbo;[1] the remaining organizers included three Igbos and one Yoruba, all at or below the rank of major. Soldiers assassinated the NPC's two most prominent figures, Federal Prime Minister Sir Abubakar Tafawa-Balewa, and the party's leader, Premier of the Northern Region Sir Ahmadu Bello. In addition, federal Finance Minister Festus Okotie-Eboh, a non-Igbo Mid-Westerner, and the Yoruba Premier of the Western Region, Chief Samuel Akintola, were also murdered. President Azikiwe was out of the country. Among the seven senior army officers killed in the coup were the four highest-ranking Northerners. The coup-plotters' vision of a country-wide uprising failed to materialize, and after a two-day standoff, Nzeogwu surrendered to then-Brigadier Ironsi, the ranking army officer. Later the same day the remnants of the civilian regime officially handed over power to the military.

Given the ferocity of the anti-Ironsi demonstrations that began in Kano a few months later, it is important to remember that, at the time it happened, the coup was popular among Kano's Hausa population (*Kanawa*), as it was elsewhere in the country. In large part the initially favorable response across Nigeria was a reflection of public disillusionment with political corruption, the increasingly vitriolic politics inside the federal government, and politically inspired thuggery in the streets of Lagos and Western Nigeria. In Kano, there was the additional fact of the longstanding political rivalry between Kano and Sokoto.[2] During the years of decolonization and the First Republic, the intraregional rivalry had played out most vividly in sometimes violent competition between the NPC and the Kano-based NEPU. Further, during the First Republic, the NPC government had directed much of the regional government's support for industrial development away from Kano and toward Kaduna.[3] The shift in economic support, combined with the NPC-engineered ouster of Emir Muhammad Sanusi in 1963, had served to fuel support in Kano for the creation of a separate Kano State. And religious politics, never entirely disconnected from party politics, played a part as well, as the strong presence of the Tijaniyya sufi order in Kano stood in contrast to the predominance of the Qadiriyya in Sokoto and in the NPC establishment. While the accomplishments of the NPC, particularly Northernization, were not lost on the people of Kano, in early 1966 most *Kanawa* held ideas about Ahmadu Bello and the NPC that ranged from ambivalence to hostility.

As news of the coup reached Kano, initial reaction was restrained. People fled the Sabon Gari Market as the news circulated the morning of 16 January, but by the next day "the public became normal and very many people were generally talking in appreciation of the happening." In the weeks that followed, local officials reported that "the only incident [about] which the public still talk and regret, was the death of Sir Abubakar, the former Prime Minister, but feelings are dying out now."[4] The national Nigeria Police Force (NPF), on the lookout for signs of trouble, took the pulse of the city's southern population and noted that while initially fearful of reprisals directed against them, the presence of the Fifth Army Battalion only a few kilometers from Sabon Gari led Kano's southerners to be less anxious than those in other Northern cities.[5] Among the Hausa population, however, class affected what meaning individuals assigned the coup. The words of the police commissioner, writing on 28 January, show that far from seeing the military government as a threat, many ordinary citizens saw the change as potentially positive. "The uninformed public in Kano, and I suppose elsewhere, have regarded this affair with an air of indifference[;] all they know is that the Army has taken over and they are sure this is going to improve their lot more than did the politicians."[6] On the other hand, the District Officer in Hadejia, a small emirate near Kano, focused his assessment not on the "uninformed public" but rather on "enlightened elements," an expression that appears periodically in such reports as code for those who were western educated and/or were well-connected in political networks. For the intelligentsia, ethnic and regional origin were immediately relevant in understanding the coup.

> [T]he greatest flaw in the coup d'état had been lack of PROPAGANDA. The omission of this has given room for speculation by some enlight-ened elements that the Revolution was directed, especially against Northern Nigeria. The following are examples of the many questions which are being asked:—
>
> (i) If Sir AHMADU BELLO and Sir ABUBAKAR TAFAWA BALEWA should be killed, why [should Igbo premiers of the Eastern and Mid-Western Re-gions] CHIEF OSADEBE and DR. OKPARA be spared?
> (ii) Why did the Revolution have the greatest impact on the North at the ini-tial state?[7]

The Ironsi government's handling of relations between Lagos and the regions was a source of both speculation and tension in the North, and fueled the rise in ethnic sentiments there. Ironsi's initial decision to main-tain the existing regional structure was generally reassuring in the North, as was the selection of an indigenous military governor for each region. Significantly, Major Hassan Usman Katsina, whose father was the Emir of Katsina, became the Military Governor of the North. After speculation that the post might have gone to an Igbo, Lieutenant Colonel Chuk-wuemeka Odumegwu Ojukwu, Katsina's appointment came as a relief to most Northerners. Ojukwu, who had commanded the army's Fifth Battal-ion, garrisoned in Kano, and had briefly detained Emir Ado Bayero dur-ing the uncertain period immediately following the coup, became governor of the Eastern Region, to the apparent disappointment of Igbos in the North.

In February, however, Ironsi generated great angst in the North when he created a commission to explore the feasibility of a unitary form of government that would replace the regional structure. The change would entail abandoning the regions and the constitutional protections of regional autonomy that had been painstakingly negotiated in the 1950s. Support-ers of unitary government argued it was consistent with a military com-mand structure. More importantly, they argued that after power was eventually restored to elected civilians, the change would address the dis-proportionate electoral power that the Northern Region, with half of the country's population, enjoyed in national politics. A unitary structure would make it extremely difficult for a dominant Northern party like the NPC to hold sway in Lagos.

For Northern elites, the ramifications of unification, should it happen, were profound. Despite the efforts of the NPC to close the "development gap" with the south, the Northern Region lagged far behind in western education, and in commercial and industrial infrastructure. Further, the number of Northerners in federal bureaucracies was tiny, since the overwhelming majority of civil servants and technocrats from the North were employed in the region's services. There, of course, Northernization policies sheltered them from competition with southerners. As discussions within the government continued, it became clear that unification would mean an end to the regional public services, and by extension, to any such protections for Northern civil servants. In addition, the preferences that Northern contractors, entrepreneurs, and property owners enjoyed as a result of Northernization would end.

The official record documents the first murmurs of ethnic sentiments among non-elites in February and March, the same time as the question of unification became part of the national conversation. In March, Kano authorities noted that "Unification of the civil service will be watched very closely. There is a general fear—not confined to the ranks of the civil service alone—that an attempt will be made to inject officers of Southern origin into posts in the Northern Provinces and that it will not be possible, in the circumstances, for reciprocal action to be taken."[8] "Reciprocal action," of course, meant the appointment of Northerners to southern postings. Such interpretations of unification apparently lent credibility to the idea that the coup had been part of a broader Igbo conspiracy to use military force to seize the political power that ballots had failed to secure. Kano's Provincial Secretary wrote to officials in Kaduna that "There is a firm belief, held by most Northerners, that the Coup was a purely Ibo affair and was carried out to bring them into political prominence and power. Until this is effectively refuted there is sure to remain an underlying antagonism between Northerners and Ibos."[9] And, in March, he noted a feeling that the coup had been inspired by the NCNC, and that the party had succeeded in "using Ibo officers in the Army as the means of furthering its ends."[10]

Unification became linked with other grievances. By late April, the Assistant Commissioner of Police noted that "whereas every Southerner" seemed to welcome the prospect of unification, opposition among Northerners was linked to "a revival of feelings on the incident of January 15th." Northerners, he reported, wanted to protect the old constitution, with its safeguards for regional autonomy.[11] He also took note of the failure of the Ironsi regime to court-martial the coup plotters. "What the Northerners would like to see done first is the punishment of those army mutineers."[12] Further, other developments in Lagos suggested that the North was being marginalized in the federal bureaucracy. Ironsi had promised to eventually return power to civilians, and many Northerners feared that in the meantime his government was stacking the deck against the North. In April, for example, local authorities noted that *Kanawa* identified an apparent ethnic bias in appointments to federal parastatal corporations. "People, Northerners to be exact, are becoming suspicious of the way the Federal Government is appointing Chairmen of Statutory Corporations in this Country. There have been a lot of talks in town of alleged plans to prepare favourable grounds for complete Ibo domination after the present Military Government should have handed over to a Civilian Government."[13] And by May, posters naming Ironsi's executive advisers were circulating in the city. According to Paden, that most of these advisers were Igbo was made clear to viewers.[14]

The words of Kano's Provincial Secretary, written in early May, show how these various issues—the increasing likelihood of unification, the apparent marginalization of the North in Lagos, and the assassination of Northern leaders—had become solidly linked in the minds of Kano's elites. Further, they had coalesced into a generalized anti-Igbo sentiment.

> The comment and thinking of the intelligentsia and the politically conscious has been directed towards the future constitutional arrangements of the country and the proposed unification of the civil service. There have been many expressions of dissatisfaction at the apparent anti-Northern activities of the Federal Military Government and the lack of information as to how the Northern Regional Government intends to deal with these activities. Anti-Ibo feeling has increased in the urban areas—particularly in Kano—and there is considerable mistrust of the intentions of the F[ederal] M[ilitary] G[overnment] and increasing resentment of the loss of only Northern politicians and army officers during the coup. There is general agreement that the proposed unitary form of government and the proposed unified civil service must be resisted at all costs; the extreme opinion has advocated [secession] should the Military Government endeavor to impose its will with regard to these two matters.[15]

About the same time, the British High Commission, drawing on an intelligence network dating back to the colonial period, laid blame for in-

flamed public opinion squarely at the feet of former politicians and political party operatives. A secret report dated 14 May by British High
Commissioner Francis Cumming-Bruce concluded that a "threat is emerging in the form of [a] growth of public restlessness encouraged by former
politicians and party agents."[16]

With party politics sidetracked, and the prospect of unification looming, unresolved NEPU-NPC divisions and calls for a separate Kano State
became secondary. In a broader sense, "there was a revival of the idea of
Northernism as a counterbalance" to the Ironsi regime and its purport-
edly pro-Igbo agenda.[17] If the alliance between the NEPU and the NCNC
had represented an opportunistic bridge across ethnic and regional di-
vides, then the threat of unification sorely tested its strength. In the later
words of Tanko Yakasai, a NEPU leader, Northerners feared unification
as "another silent move to impose Igbo domination upon them."[18] As the
intraregional fissures of the First Republic lost their currency and
"Northernism" gained relevance, the image of Ahmadu Bello, the father
of Northernism, was rehabilitated. By May, the Sardauna had once again
become a hero, a multi-faceted symbol of Northern self-determination,
and of resistance to Igbo domination. His vision of a monolithic North
and his murder would become focal points in the coming struggle against
unification, and would help to justify the anti-Igbo violence that accompanied it. Along with Tafawa-Balewa, he had become in many eyes a
martyr.

As the North's slain leaders grew in stature, derisive references to
them by ordinary Igbos ate at what was left of confidence between
communities. For example, some *Kanawa* pointed to Igbo traders who
tauntingly referenced Ahmadu Bello's death during marketplace hag-
gling. Another informant described Igbos in the market saying to
Northerners, in reference to Sir Ahmadu, "your father is dead," then
adding "This is your father now" while indicating a photograph of
Nzeogwu.[19] Displays of arrogance took on other forms as well. A civil
servant cited the example of an Igbo who aroused the ire of local
officials by threatening to petition the head of state after not receiving a liquor license.[20] While members of both communities recalled
such incidents, Igbo informants remembered them as indiscreet remarks usually uttered by young men who should not have been taken
seriously. Non-Igbos, including other southerners, however, recalled
derisive tones, and said they were uttered by men and women of all
ages, though some were clear to point out that many Igbos maintained
decorous, civil relations with *Kanawa*. It is impossible, more than
thirty years after the fact, to reconstruct such exchanges. What is clear,
though, is that whatever the tone and frequency of such comments,

and however many or few Igbos uttered them, they made lasting impressions on those Northerners who heard them, and were a topic of general conversation among *Kanawa*. The District Officer for Kano Township recorded that "The attitude of the Igbos in Kano today is that of pride. They see themselves as a big nation, [with a] bright future for their trade and [as] masters in all fields. They jeer at angry Northerners saying 'You said you didn't want us in the past, what do you say today?'"[21] Similar sorts of teasing also took place in the south, where the wives of Igbo soldiers reportedly taunted Northern wives at barracks in Apapa, Ikeja, and elsewhere. Word of such treatment traveled to Northern cities, where it spread. Just as the actions of Igbo civilians insulted their counterparts, there were concerns in political circles that such comparatively small provocations compounded an already explosive situation in military quarters.[22]

Scholars have noted similar patterns. Elegalam concluded that, across the region, some Igbos "helped to provide opportunity for their massacre by ridiculing publicly the deaths of the Northern leaders and by boasting openly that the leadership of the country was in the hands of the Igbos."[23] Paden limited his conclusions to Kano, writing that "the prevailing interpretation of the new military regime by the Kano Sabon Gari was that it represented an 'Ibo' victory over the Hausa. The relief and pride felt by the Igbos at this status reversal was evident."[24] And, according to Kirk-Greene, in the weeks before the May disturbances, there was "arrogant flaunting of wall photographs of a smiling Nzeogwu and the circulation of an article accompanied by a picture depicting the late Sardauna stretched out at the feet of an Ibo."[25] The article in question appeared in the June edition of *Drum* magazine, which circulated in May. The publication was staffed largely by southern Nigerians and owned by South Africans. The article—attributed to an author whose name was Yoruba—centered on a fictionalized interview with Ahmadu Bello who was "in Limbo," provocatively suggesting that the Sardauna, a major religious figure, had not passed on to heaven after his death.[26] The article was not the magazine's first; the March *Drum* included a piece entitled "Why Blame the Sardauna" that struck readers in Kano as "most embarrassing, disgraceful and cheeky to the people of Northern origin."[27]

## THE UNIFICATION DECREE AND THE RIOTS OF MAY 1966

When Northern opposition to unification manifested itself in communal action, it did so powerfully. On 24 May 1966, the government promulgated Decree 34, commonly referred to as the Unification Decree. The decree abolished the regions, though the four military governors were to remain as governors of "groups of provinces" corresponding to the former regions. The regional public services, however, were to be merged into a single Nigerian service. The threat to the political and administrative classes in the North did not end there, however; a second edict, the Public Order Decree, abolished political parties. It also banned several dozen semi-political organizations, including ethnically specific groups like the Ibo State Union.[28]

The Unification Decree proved so unpopular in the North that it was not only unworkable but utterly disastrous in its consequences. The decree set in motion a series of protests across the region, many of which led directly to looting, arson and lethal street violence directed against Igbos. As a result, the period between 28 May and 6 June was a bloody one, with major demonstrations in Kano, Kaduna, Katsina, Sokoto, Zaria, Bauchi, Gombe, Gumel, Had'ejia, Jos, and Bukuru. There were also lesser disturbances in at least a dozen other cities and towns. During and after the disturbances thousands of Igbos left the North.

The first protests happened simultaneously on Saturday, 28 May in Kano, Kaduna, and Bukuru, near Jos, and offer important clues about the organization of demonstrations across the region. In Kaduna, junior civil servants were the driving force, and in Jos, observers credited former NPC operatives. In Kano, university students staged a demonstration with the support of local political elites. Unification represented a major blow to members of each of these groups, and its specter became a catalyst for an informal coalition that mobilized around the theme of Northern self-determination, and against Igbo economic and political participation in the North. There is no question that the military government in Kaduna expected trouble, and expected it to involve civilians. In the Military Governor's later words, "I knew very well there was going to be those riots." In fact, during the national debate over unification, Governor Katsina had functioned as an intermediary between traditional rulers in the North and Ironsi. "The emirs and chiefs sent me to Ironsi saying that there would be secession unless something [was] done. They were provoked. I told [Ironsi] people were being urged to go and fight against the Igbos."[29]

The section that follows chronicles the disturbances in Kano and the neighboring emirates of Had'ejia and Gumel, and in the urban centers of Kaduna and Jos-Bukuru, where the first demonstrations happened. Also discussed is Katsina, where the most vicious of the May-June violence took place, and for which we have a degree of documentation unavailable for other cities.[30] There are brief summaries of disturbances in a number of other cities included in Appendix A. Nigerian records of events during May and June of 1966 are incomplete, in large part because of the administrative discontinuities that were endemic between 1966 and 1968, during which time the country underwent two sudden changes of government, experienced the breakup of its four regions into twelve states, and began a civil war. I have, I believe, exhausted available official records on Kano Province, and on Kaduna.[31] For other parts of the region I have relied on a mixture of Nigerian sources and information recorded in recently declassified United States State Department Records. Three important themes emerge from the data.[32]

First, while Northerners referenced Igbos primarily in monolithic ethnic terms, they set Igbos in opposition not to any analogous ethnic grouping, but rather, to Northerners. According to a former assistant to Ahmadu Bello, "What the Sardauna and his colleagues tried to do was to create a new tribe of 'the Northerner.'"[33] Ironically, the political alchemy of the January assassinations and the Unification Decree arguably led to a stronger manifestation of that "tribe" than at any time during decolonization or the First Republic. Igbos had long been constructed as the embodiment of alien-ness in the North, but the apparent rise in Igbo power elevated them, in the hands of an astute political class, to the level of nemesis. The remedies protesters insisted on ranged from a return to regional autonomy and the expulsion of Igbos to calls for Northern secession from Nigeria. In any case, "disparate elements within the North found that an appeal to ethnicity was the easiest bond of unity."[34] The ethnicity to which these Northerners appealed, however, was not their own, but rather one against which they could best construct a working coalition.

The second theme that surfaces is the uniformity with which such sentiments found violent expression. It is easy to understand that, by the end of May, tensions between Northerners and Igbos were high. Still, the pattern of demonstrations begs the question of organization. There is an orthodoxy of opinion among Nigerians of many ethnic stripes that former politicians encouraged violence through methods that ranged from floating unsubstantiated and inflammatory rumors[35] to having their operatives pay unemployed urban "ruffians" to attend demonstrations with the expectation that those "ruffians" would catalyze violence. The motives of these former politicians supposedly ranged from the obvious goal of negating unification to the more subtle objective of destabilizing the military government in the furtherance of a return to civilian rule. Accounts of the riots in Kano and other cities describe or suggest that Qur'anic school children, members of the lower classes, and "hooligans" or "thugs" joined organized protests, and introduced violence to them. These accounts echo Brass' description of "institutional riot systems" in some multi-ethnic cities. "The kinds of violence that are committed in ethnic, communal, and racial 'riots' are . . . undertaken mostly by 'specialists' who are ready to be called out on such occasions, who profit from it, and whose activities profit others who may or may not actually be paying for the violence carried out."[36] He argues that the participation of such "specialists" is usually required for a full-scale riot to take place. These specialists also include organizers who, not surprisingly, are drawn from the ranks of politicians, businessmen, religious leaders, and intellectuals. They rely on the participation of youth gang members, criminals, and, more importantly, ordinary citizens from all strata of society. Unfortunately, it remains extremely difficult to do more than speculate as to the identity of individuals in Kano responsible for either organizing violence, or carrying it out. Nonetheless, the available data are consistent with both Brass' model and the opinions of virtually all of my informants.

The third theme that emerges in the accounts is perhaps the most unsettling. There was a substantial gulf between the efforts of different branches of government to restore public order. In a general sense, federal and regional authorities were much more effective than local ones in protecting the lives and property of Igbos. Unlike Native Authority (NA) police, who were recruited locally, and tended to have strong roots there, the men of the NPF served in ethnically mixed units and changed postings on a regular basis. This meant that most had limited connections to the communities in which they served; further, the force was disproportionately southern. NPF and army units, often acting in cooperation with regional authorities, contained and in some cases prevented disturbances. In contrast, there were cases where NA personnel not only failed to stop violence and looting, but actively participated in it.[37] The Emirs, however, retained enough religious and moral authority and personal prestige that those who chose to were able to intervene with some effectiveness, in some cases by using NA police. The former Secretary to the Military Governor recalled being with Governor Katsina in Okene when news of the first riots first reached them. Upon returning to Kaduna the next day and realizing the seriousness of the situation, "We appealed to the Emirs because it was beyond us."[38] In that sense, the interventions by Emirs such as those of Katsina, Gumel, and Hadejia were, to varying degrees, reflections of regional government agency.[39]

In large part, however, it was senior civil servants who stepped into the political void the coup had left and provided what continuity there was at the regional and provincial levels.[40] In that sense, these senior civil servants, as a group, enjoyed unprecedented influence and appear to have used it, by and large, to protect lives and property. This they did through organizing protective escorts, evacuations, and law enforcement. On the other hand, many party members who had held elected or appointed offices in regional or federal government had returned to their respective cities and towns where they had taken up positions in local government and/or commerce, in either case outside of the regional administrative apparatus. In this sense, civil servants and former politicians who had been colleagues in the past found themselves, perhaps reluctantly, on opposite sides during the disturbances. Governor Katsina, who like all of the regional governors had reportedly opposed unification, worked to restore order. "But underneath, I was happy it had happened because I knew the decree [would] soon be demolished, and this was what happened."[41]

## REACTION: METROPOLITAN KANO

Anti-unification protests in Kano presented grievances entirely in keeping with the established discourse on the dangers of unification. Local political elites and university students led the way. On 27 May a group of prominent local men calling itself "Kano Citizens" presented Emir Ado Bayero with a letter addressed to the Military Governor in Kaduna alleging the Ironsi government was advancing an NCNC agenda.[42] Students at Abdullahi Bayero College (ABC) in Kano were also quick to protest the decree. On Saturday, 28 May the students joined pupils from the Provincial Secondary School, the School for Arabic Studies, and the Technical Training College in a demonstration at the Emir's palace at about 8 a.m. The ABC Students Union presented a letter of protest to the Emir, which argued that "the south, being educationally numerically superior, will dominate the Northern Civil Service and render a large proportion of Northerners jobless."[43]

According to the regional government-owned *New Nigerian*, the demonstration was "highly organized and carefully coordinated."

Some organisation had obviously been carried out during preceding days as details of the proposed demonstrations were common knowledge by early on Saturday morning. Those responsible did not, however, appear to be present to lead the demonstration.

There were several reports of former prominent politicians being involved in the planning of the demonstrations—some of whom are still without jobs since being removed from power.[44]

Police estimated the number of demonstrators at 6,000 "students and citizens," some carrying placards in English and Hausa.[45] Others carried pictures of slain leaders Ahmadu Bello and Abubakar Tafawa-Balewa.[46] Foreign observers reported that the demonstrators were mostly young men, and estimated their average age to be thirty.[47] The Emir received the protesters, and promised to deliver their petitions to the governor. He then warned the crowd against lawlessness, and, at about 10:30 a.m., asked its members to disperse. By that time, however, the crowd had swollen with young men and boys. Local government observers described how "school children from neighboring schools, more out of curiosity than full understanding of the situation, jumped out of the class rooms and joined the demonstration." Among them were a large number of Qur'anic school students. In the process, police reports note, the crowd "had now turned into a large gang of hooligans who had joined and out-numbered the original peaceful demonstrators."[48] According to the *New Nigerian*, "Many of those caught up in the demonstrations, they told reporters, had joined in out of curiosity."[49]

Much of the crowd dispersed as the Emir had asked, but some carried their message to the office of the Provincial Secretary, and to the home of Colonel Muhammadu Shuwa, an army officer, in the GRA. Significantly, others went to businesses where Igbos worked. As protesters left the walled city, violence began. Crowd members began to stone vehicles, houses, and people.[50] The NPF noted that "this situation was brought about by acts of hooligans who infiltrated into a peaceful demonstration" and took advantage of the situation to loot.[51] Word of the demonstration "went round the town like wildfire and hooligans took the advantage to stone cars and beat up passers-by."[52] Police spent the day breaking up the crowds at Kofar Mata and Fagge, and, according to the report, restored order by the end of the day.[53] Meanwhile, the Army moved in to protect Sabon Gari, where some demonstrators threw rocks at soldiers.[54]

NPF and soldiers worked to keep the two sides apart, with limited success. During the night, rumors circulated in the city, Fagge, and Sabon Gari that "Igbo planned to attack Hausa and vice versa. Each side prepared itself." About 8 A.M. on Sunday the 29th trouble began anew when "about 500 armed Ibo men" left Sabon Gari for Fagge, apparently believing attack imminent. "This sparked off panic within the Hausa at Fagge who also gathered and started to march toward the Ibo group." By 11 A.M. there were wildly exaggerated rumors circulated in the old city that Igbos had killed all the Hausas in Sabon Gari before heading for Fagge. Police positioned at the Sabon Gari market tried to stop the confrontation, but rioters from the city entered Sabon Gari. According to NPF, "the Hausas descended in thousands in readiness to defend their brothers and as they came they killed and destroyed any Ibo man and property," including setting fire to large sections of the Sabon Gari Market.[55] Both Igbo and Hausa stalls burned, but Igbo traders suffered most of the losses. A complaint filed by a group of Igbo lawyers is consistent with other accounts. "On the 29th of May the Northern elements of Fagge, City and Gwagwarwa areas of Kano without any excuse or provocation, attacked the inhabitants of Sabon Gari with guns, machetes, bows and arrows, sticks, and stones *in Sabon Gari*. This attack resulted in loss of lives, arson, looting and damage to property."[56] The lawyers also accused Native Authority police of assisting the Hausa mob. They said NA police used tear gas not on the attackers, but rather on Igbos "in front of their homes" in Sabon Gari. It was, they said, the army who established control of the situation.[57] A group of Igbos identifying itself as "Kano Traders" concurred. In a letter to the military governor, they described "law enforcing agencies in Kano who stood by and allow[ed] rioters to loot and destroy by fire our goods in Sabon Gari market Kano."[58]

Inside Sabon Gari, Igbos fought back. Distinguishing between defensive actions and counter attacks, however, is impossible. According to police: "At Sabon Gari, all houses belonging to Hausa (Northerners) were either burnt down or demolished and it is believed that a number of Hausa men were killed and burnt with their property."[59] The vast majority of violence, however, was directed against Igbos. Over the next three days rioting continued, largely in Sabon Gari, but also in "places where Igbos were known to dominate the employment structure: the post office, the railway station, and certain commercial areas" to the south and west of Sabon Gari.[60] For example, on the 29th, a group searched for Igbos in the Central Hotel in Bompai, a commercial area adjacent to Sabon Gari.[61] And on Monday the 30th, the Bata shoe warehouse at the edge of Sabon Gari was burned, as was the Texaco office building, and most of the city's petrol stations.[62] Among the hundreds of smaller businesses looted and burned was a Sabon Gari hotel owned by the mother of Eastern Governor Ojukwu.[63]

To contain the violence, authorities imposed a 7 P.M. to 7 A.M. curfew, and trucks of police, some of them reinforcements from Lagos, circulated.[64] Soldiers patrolled as well, and on at least one occasion troops fired on Hausa rioters.[65] On 30 May officials counted fifty-one Ibos, nineteen Hausas, four Yorubas, and one "unidentified" among the dead, though it is unclear on what basis they assigned ethnic affiliation. They also counted forty-seven "seriously wounded," 156 wounded, and noted that all of the six shot by the army were Hausa.[66] Even as authorities brought the violence under control, rumors persisted.[67] By Tuesday the 31st, Kano was quiet, despite untrue rumors that Igbos—a majority of the skilled staff of the nearby Challawa waterworks—had poisoned the city's water supply.[68]

## KANO PROVINCE: HAĐEJIA & GUMEL

Shortly after violence broke out in Kano city and Sabon Gari, it spread around Kano Province, which included the emirates of Gumel, Hađejia, and Kazaure. While the army and the national police force were far more effective than the Emir or local NA police in controlling violence in metropolitan Kano, authorities in the smaller cities of Kano Province had to rely on their own resources. The Emirs of Hađejia and Gumel, together with the District Officers, played important roles in containing violence in their respective towns. In each case, they were cooperating with provincial authorities, who in turn, answered to the military government in Kaduna.

Late in the afternoon of 28 May, the day the Kano disturbances began, telephone operators and the local post master in Hađejia reported rumors of plans to kill all the Igbos in the town to the Provincial Secretary in Kano. He then contacted the District Officers and Emirs in Hađejia and Gumel and told them that there were no police reinforcements to send from Kano, and appealed to them to use Native Authority police to protect Igbos from harm. The Emir in Hađejia, in response, instructed the traditional law enforcement official, the *Wakilin Doka*, to post Native Authority police at all Igbo houses, and to patrol the city's streets. When trouble struck the next day, and rioters burned Igbo market stalls, the Emir ordered NA police to round up Igbos and bring them to the palace for protection.[69] One Igbo reported that between 50 and 60 remained there for several days.[70]

Gumel followed a similar pattern. There were peaceful demonstrations on Saturday the 28th. According to the District Officer, the next day demonstrations began anew at 10 A.M. and became violent when "thugs came from Kano and were blocking the main road to Kano.

They were joined by local ones and were beating up Ibos in protest of the Supreme Commander's announcement." News of the beatings traveled to nearby Mala-Maduri, and more trouble appeared likely. Some local Igbos decided to take refuge at the local Leventis store, but a truck loaded with their property was attacked and robbed en route. They then appealed to the District Officer for protection. He offered to transport them to the Emir's palace, but they declined in favor of the Leventis store. The District Officer posted NA police at the local post office, the bank, and at the store, where the Igbos remained until 11 o'clock that evening, when they again moved.[71] The town experienced another round of violence the night of Wednesday, 1 June, when two were injured in fights. Another group of Igbos in Gumel was "kept under the Emir's custody for some days, and were released when the tension in town came to normal."[72]

## KADUNA

Kaduna was and is a very different type of city than Kano. Situated at the northern edge of the Middle Belt, Kaduna was a colonial city, and grew by attracting people from other parts of Northern Nigeria. By 1966 the vast majority of Kaduna's population were recent migrants, and much of the city's elite maintained only part-time residency there. Where Kano was a commercial and intellectual center with ancient roots, Kaduna was a new city with a high proportion of civil servants and politicians past, present, and aspiring. It was no surprise, then, that junior civil servants—the main beneficiaries of Northernization—organized the 28 May demonstration in Kaduna, and made up the majority of the 800 to 1,000 who gathered around Sultan Bello Mosque, several hundred meters from the burned-out official residence where Ahmadu Bello had been slain in January. The demonstration took place in spite of police orders banning it, and over the objections of more senior civil servants.[73] Demonstrators chanted NPC slogans and called for Northern secession. Like demonstrators in Kano, some bore placards of the Sardauna and the Prime Minister in defiance of radio broadcasts explicitly prohibiting the display of the likeness of persons "living or dead."[74] Foreign observers reported that NPF used tear gas and clubs to disperse the crowd, members of which hurled stones at police.[75]

The worst of Kaduna's violence began the next day, Sunday 29 May, at 5 P.M., when groups of fifty to seventy young men began stoning cars as they passed near the site of the previous day's demonstration on the main road. The crowds then moved south toward Kaduna's Sabon Gari, roughly two miles away. Again police responded with tear gas.[76] On the 30th there were rumors that violence would break out again that evening, but joint patrols by soldiers and police, appeals for calm by community leaders in sound trucks, and a radio announcement from the Military Governor that looters and arsonists would be shot were effective at maintaining the peace.[77] The next day authorities turned off the electricity in Sabon Gari, and the city remained calm.[78]

## JOS-BUKURU

Jos and nearby Bukuru experienced a modest protest, but escaped the violence that plagued Kaduna and Kano. Like Kaduna, Jos owed its growth to the colonial economy. The leading city of the Middle Belt, it was divided more evenly between Northern Muslims and Christians from the south and Middle Belt than other major Northern cities. There had been substantial preparation for the 28 May demonstration in Bukuru. A Hausa-language pamphlet announcing demonstrations circulated, and among the estimated 300 demonstrators, some carried placards reading "Down with Ibos." Rumors circulated that Igbos who did not leave town by the next day would face violence.[79] Later in the week rumors circulated that Igbos would burn the Central Mosque on Saturday, and that Hausas would burn churches on Sunday. Police guarded both, and Jos remained quiet.[80]

## KATSINA PROVINCE: KATSINA

Katsina, like Kano a core Hausa city, experienced some of the worst violence in the north. Officers of the NPF contained the first round of violence in the city, but after their departure there was a second outbreak that was far more serious. Both Ahmadu Bello and Abubakar Tafawa-Balewa had schooled at the Training College in Katsina, as had many of the region's first cadre of home-grown senior civil servants. Not surprisingly, the city of Katsina had been a reliable NPC stronghold.

Katsina Training College was a locus of anti-unification and anti-Igbo activity in Katsina. In addition to a number of foreign teachers at the college, there were also U.S. Catholic missionaries and Peace Corps volunteers in and around Katsina. As a result, U.S. diplomats in Kaduna generated a particularly detailed report of the May-June disturbances there. The limitations of these U.S. documents, however, are abundant and clear. First, they filter the actions and voices of Nigerians through two layers of foreign interlocutors. Second, given the general tone of official U.S. correspondence on Northern Nigeria, there is every reason to expect that the diplomats and missionaries, if not necessarily the teachers or Peace Corps volunteers, cast events in ways less sympathetic to Hausa Muslims than to Igbo Christians.[81]

Nonetheless, despite these shortcomings, the documents provide a useful window on the disturbances there, in many ways the most detailed contemporaneous accounts of the May and June disturbances in Northern Nigeria yet available. Among other things, they foreground the role of rumors in the escalation of violence in Katsina, and beg the question of the origins of those rumors.[82] It is clear that the demonstrations were the product of planning, and that the organizers anticipated violence. The documents also reveal that organizers included both NA employees and NPC members. At least one source reported to U.S. consular officers that the NA actually trucked in "ruffians." Consular officials reported that "there were numerous reports that the ex-politicians were involved in organizing the demonstration *cum* protest." For example, prior to the 29 May outbreak, a foreign teacher at the college received a visit from a village head from Bakyara who was accompanied by a man the teacher recognized as a local NPC leader. After asking the teacher's opinions on Northern secession, the NPC leader asked if the teacher owned a pistol. The teacher told him that he did not, and the man inquired if the teacher could procure a shipment of guns from the United States. As was the case in most of the North, it was national NPF forces and soldiers who successfully contained the violence, and not NA police. On the other hand, the Emir took steps to stop the killing. There is also a record of the covert warnings some local Hausas gave individual Igbos of impending trouble, and, in one case, help from a Northerner in escaping violence.

As in other anti-unification demonstrations, it was those with the most to lose who protested first. Students from Katsina Training College (KTC) protested the Unification Decree on Sunday, 29 May, a day after student demonstrations in Kano and Jos. Many carried signs that observers noted were "professionally lettered," framed, and mounted on staffs. They read "Down with the Military Government," "Regionalism or Secession," and "No United Nigeria." Teachers from the college, students from the local Government Secondary School, and "five or six well-dressed elderly people" joined the crowd of several hundred as it marched from the old city, past the Catholic church and to the house of the Provincial Secretary. Foreign observers described a festive atmosphere, and reported seeing a large group of women—whom they correctly or incorrectly identified as prostitutes— within the crowd, many of them carrying beer bottles, and some apparently intoxicated.[83] Others in the crowd also appeared to be intoxicated. When they arrived at the secretary's house, student leaders presented a prepared statement opposing military government. Protesters also demanded the expulsion of Igbos from Katsina, though it is unclear if the document included that point. When the secretary refused to sign the statement, members of the crowd tore down the secretary's flag and stoned his house, breaking windows, and then went off in search of Igbos. A contingent of NPF from out of town helped to restore order since it appeared that NA police had little interest in intervening against the disturbances.[84] For example, a foreign teacher stopped his car to take a photograph of the looted Kingsway store. NA police on the scene asked him to photograph them posed in front of the damaged building. They then invited the teacher to tour the store with them, at which point they chased looters from the building and took the teacher inside. After his tour, they allowed looters to reenter.[85] Unlike many Northern cities, Katsina had no *sabon gari*, so before the NPF left Monday for Funtua, most of the city's Igbos gathered for safety at a race course located outside of town. They remained there until Tuesday or Wednesday, when some returned to Katsina and others departed for the relative safety of Kano. Crews from the city prison cleaned the streets, but the city remained tense.

The worst, however, was yet to come. On Saturday, 4 June, the second round of violence in Katsina began when a mob burned the car belonging to the Igbo manager of the local Shell station on the parade ground in front of the Emir's palace. Rumors of an Igbo conspiracy fueled the outbreak of violence. Though any Igbos appear to have been potential victims, several prominent Igbos were targeted for death. In one case, that of Gabriel Ogbalu, no specific motives were apparent, though Ogbalu was a successful businessman and prominent Christian. He had lived in the north for twenty-seven years, and had owned a cinema in Katsina. In 1966 he operated a Mobil Oil dealership that burned on the first day of violence. Ogbalu apparently escaped Katsina on 4 June, though there is no record of how.

The other incidents in Katsina reveal the power of rumor to motivate ordinary people to violence. They also give important clues about how ordinary citizens imagined the dangers that Igbos posed to their community. The second Igbo singled out was the head of Katsina's Ibo Union, remembered as Sylvester. He sold auto parts and dealt in scrap metal. Rumors had circulated that he had been discovered in possession of a book detailing plans to overthrow the Emir of Katsina as part of an Igbo master plan for national domination. Allegedly, after national unification and the entrenchment of an Igbo elite in the north, he planned to install himself in the office of the Provincial Secretary as Igbo "king."[86] Other rumors said that he had been discovered to have, variously, a store of weapons in his home, a single gun, or simply a room in which guns might have been stored.[87] Sylvester was one of nine or ten Igbos reported to have died under protective custody when a mob entered the police station where they were held. The mob then burned the station, which was also filled with Igbo property.

The same rumors that marked Sylvester also identified one Mr. Azubuike as the man who, according to Sylvester's supposed book, would be secretary to the Igbo king. Azubuike, a KTC employee, had apparently "earned the ill-will of some of the young men in Katsina by refusing to allow them to use KTC sports equipment, and in particular, by refusing a request for sports jerseys from a hockey team composed of young government and Native Authority employees."[88] Azubuike had been the target of the only incident that occurred in the days between the arrival of NPF reinforcements and the outbreak of the second round of violence in Katsina. This happened on the afternoon of the 31st when a mob armed with machetes and cudgels went to the grounds of KTC searching for him. Azubuike received a warning that originated with an NA clerk who was reluctant to inform Azubuike directly, and asked two students to do so on his behalf. Azubuike declined an NPF offer of protective custody, and remained on the KTC campus. Authorities then closed the college and turned the mob away when it arrived at the gates. When the second round of violence broke out on 4 June, a mob again appeared and demanded Azubuike, and again Azubuike had been warned. This time the warning came from a nephew of NPC stalwart Isa Kaita, a former regional minister; again the warning passed through intermediaries. A KTC teacher relayed the message for the nephew, who had told the teacher that he could not deliver the message himself. This time the mob successfully entered the campus, chanting "The Emir says Azubuike is here." Mob members went to his house, carried his property to the yard, and burned it. Some mob members wanted to burn his house, but others pointed out that it was attached to the home of another teacher. In the search for Azubuike, several dozen others entered the house of an American teacher with whom Azubuike was friendly, and who had agreed to hold some of his property. When members of the group began to remove property belonging to the American, other members confronted them and saw that all was returned. At the time, Azubuike, his wife, and children had locked themselves in a store-room at the college, where they avoided searchers.

Events elsewhere in Katsina offer a window on the systematic nature of violence against the Igbo population in general. In the Government Reserved Area, an Igbo girl of seven or eight sheltered in the house of a Peace Corps volunteer. The volunteer, who did not speak Igbo, did not realize that the girl's sister was outside of his house, searching for her. Later, a teenage Igbo boy hotly pursued by a mob also took shelter in the same house. The mob, members of which had seen the teenager enter, lingered outside the house, then left, promising to return. Over the next two and a half hours, small groups scoured the area for Igbos in hiding. Then, in an attempt to restore order, the Emir's car drove through the GRA. From the car, the Emir shouted at crowd members, in Hausa, to "stop this, go home." The Peace Corps volunteer flagged down the car. Though he could speak Hausa, he told the Emir in English that he had two Igbos in his house and asked what to do. The Emir told him to "keep them for two or three days. I will be in touch with you." That night, however, soldiers began to patrol Katsina, and the following morning the volunteer asked soldiers to take the two young Igbos, which they did. When the volunteer later recognized members of the mob who had been outside his house, he asked them whom they had been after, and was told the "pork-eaters." Not all foreigners were as successful in sheltering Igbos, as evidenced by the clubbing death of another teenage Igbo boy on the grounds of a KTC teacher's house where he had been desperately seeking shelter.

As was the case across the region, non-Igbos were sometimes victimized, either because mobs mistook them for Igbos, or because they had associated closely with Igbos. One man, Lazarus Aseora, apparently from Benin in the Mid-West Region, was marked for violence with the three Igbo men discussed above. He had been director of the Nigerian Broadcasting Company in Katsina, and was evidently believed to be Igbo because of his Catholicism, his close personal association with prominent Igbos in the community, and because of his marriage to a woman of mixed Fulani-Igbo heritage. It was, in fact, the intervention of his Fulani mother-in-law that saved him when mobs sought him at her home during the 29–30 May violence. He remained in her house for some days. Then, after soldiers began patrolling the streets, Aseora and his mother-in-law fled to the home of the same Peace Corps volunteer. There they spent the night of 4 June, and left at five the following morning.

Others fled in the days to come. The evacuation of Katsina's surviving Igbos was probably the most dramatic that resulted from the anti-unification disturbances. By 6 June, "practically all Ibos" from Katsina had gotten themselves to Kano.[89] After three buses from Kano arrived to take Igbo residents away, the acting Provincial Secretary in Kano reported "a strong rumour" that "all Igbos" had been instructed to gather in Kano in preparation for an attack on the city and outlying towns.[90] In fact, however, some Igbos in the far North had fled north rather than south. Local authorities in predominantly Hausa communities in Niger questioned the wisdom of accepting refugees from Nigeria, but had received at least 100 Igbos by 12 June.[91] Katsina's military curfew remained in place until 12 June, by which time there appear to have been no Igbos living openly in the city.[92]

## THE AFTERMATH

As they worked to preserve the peace, regional authorities in Kaduna tried to stem the flight of Igbos. On 31 May the Governor's office announced that it opposed evacuation of anyone from the region, but that authorities were to offer protection to those who chose to leave.[93] Similarly, on 4 June the Provincial Secretary for Kano instructed the Native Authorities in Kano Province to encourage Igbos to remain.[94] Those efforts included a radio appeal on 8 June by Emir Ado Bayero of Kano assuring Waje residents of their safety. Similar actions took place in other parts of the region, including, a "Peace Committee" made up of community leaders that made similar assurances in Minna.[95]

Nonetheless, thousands of Igbos departed the region. Authorities in Enugu estimated 10,000 Igbos had arrived by train, including extra trains put into service to help with the evacuation. The early trains carried mostly women and children, but by the time violence had subsided by the second week in June, passengers included an increased number of single men and complete families, many heavily laden with their belongings.[96] Over-the-road transportation to the East was also at a premium following the disturbances, in part because of demand, but also because some drivers feared being caught in attacks on their passengers. Long-distance drivers in Kano reported that Igbos who wanted to leave had a very hard time finding transportation.[97] Across the region, provincial secretaries began to form "essential services committees" to plan alternative staffing of public services, and telephone service in

Katsina shut down completely for lack of operators.[98] On the whole, however, public service and commercial firm employees were less likely than traders to flee. Some traders and artisans returned to the south with cash and trading stock, leaving behind apprentices to maintain skeleton operations. Other parts of the country also felt shock waves from the North's troubles. By 6 June Lagos authorities noted a departure of many Igbos fearing similar disturbances there. There, like in the North, some men remained after their families left.[99]

The Ironsi government scrambled to reassert itself in the North, but its days were numbered. In mid-June, the Military Governor convened a meeting in Kaduna of Northern traditional rulers. The meeting produced exhortations for calm and peace, but its also fed the anxieties of southerners. In Kano Township, the Local Authority attributed the flight of some southerners to rumors that if a communiqué from Ironsi to the Sultan of Sokoto "was not favourable to Northern Nigerians, another bloody state of affairs would follow. Many more people, as a result, moved southwards."[100] There were potent rumors in Hausa circles as well. In Hadejia, the District Officer wrote that "Another thing generally discussed among the public is the exodus of Igbos to the East. It is generally believed that on their return to the North, they will come readily armed to face any future occurrence of disturbance. This story is really disturbing the minds of peace-loving citizens."[101] And Kano authorities noted that "Considerable anti-Ibo feeling persists and there is still a great deal of mistrust of the intentions of the National Military Government."[102]

Despite the climate of mutual suspicion, the rate of departure among Igbos slowed substantially by July. Then, amid official assurances of security from the federal government and the Military Governors of the East and North, some began to trickle back to Kano. Few returned "readily armed" and the July security report from Hadejia mentioned that "confidence amongst Hausas and Igbos is being restored gradually."[103] In Kano, however, the official assessment was less sanguine: "The apprehension by all Northerners [ . . . has] made it difficult for them and Southerners to live together without fear or bitterness."[104]

Against this shaky backdrop, the Ironsi regime made yet more false steps. First, it announced plans to begin rotating the military governors between the regions every six months. Secondly, in order to provide continuity, military prefects would monitor local affairs. While the response of southerners in Kano was muted, locals felt the proposal "premature, ill-advised and suspicious."[105] Further, "The Southerners have since the last disturbances changed their attitude by abstaining from any provocative action and careless utterances. The proposal to transfer the [ . . . ] Military Governors and the appointment of Prefects is most likely to spark off a big unrest and possibly another disturbance by the public."[106] Ironsi himself began a tour of the North during which he met with traditional rulers. Unfortunately, the cooperation of some traditional rulers with federal and regional authorities in May and June had undercut their authority with their subjects. Kano authorities reported that "The Natural Rulers have become very unpopular and are being accused of becoming a party to the National Military Government's forceful attitude towards causing changes." An appeal from the Emir was unsuccessful in stopping protests at the palace when Ironsi visited Kano.[107]

## THE END OF THE IRONSI GOVERNMENT: THE JULY COUNTER-COUP

Ironsi had alienated both civilian and military leaders in the North, and in so doing had all but sealed his fate. Even before the Unification Decree, there had been speculation inside and outside of Nigeria that Northern officers would retaliate for the loss of their comrades and political leaders in the January coup. On 28 July Northern officers staged a second coup in which they assassinated Ironsi and dozens of Igbo officers and men.[108] In addition to military officers, some civilians knew the coup was coming. Beyond common regional political interests, military officers were tied to civilian elites by ties of kinship, local origin, and sponsorship into the officer corps. Further, according to the British High Commission, there were explicit financial connections as well. The High Commission report predicting the May disturbances pointed out that many young military officers lived beyond their means, creating situations in which "an astute politician could well make use of private or party funds with the idea that officers helped out of temporary embarrassment could be useful allies in the future."[109] Governor Katsina, the son of an emir, said in 1995, "there were some civilians that we hinted to that [the second coup] might happen." He also said that officers had assured Northern traditional rulers that "in one way or the other there would be retaliation."[110]

Just as some Northerners warned Igbo friends and associates of plans for violence in May, similar warnings passed before the coup, as evidenced by the case of a well-connected Igbo trader in Haḍejia who received a warning from a Northern friend who was, in turn, the father of a high-ranking army officer. "He told me, in confidence, as a friend [to go home]. He said there was a plan for major trouble within the army. He said they could secure me, but people might come from another area. He told me there would be trouble—major one—but that when things cooled off I could come back. He advised me to take my family and go."[111] In fact, outside of the military, there was little violence associated with the second coup.[112] The civilian dependents of Igbo soldiers, by and large, were left alone. In early August drivers noted women and children carrying bundles along the road between Kano and Kaduna outside the Nigerian Military Academy, apparently awaiting transportation. There were no men among them, which led observers to conclude that they were the families of slain soldiers.[113] According to a military dentist, Igbos who served on the staff of the military hospital in Kaduna remained but were planning to leave on 1 September. In any case, Northern patients were not accepting treatment from them.[114]

## CONCLUSION

The short-lived Ironsi regime deeply polarized relations between Igbos and Northerners as groups. What is most striking about the Ironsi period is the degree to which his government's actions made it possible for Northern leaders to successfully bring Ahmadu Bello's "tribe of the Northerner" into being. Certainly, not all Northerners belonged, or wished to belong to this "tribe," yet it was in the name of regional interests that many Northerners took up arms against Igbo civilians in May and June, and Northern soldiers against their Igbo comrades in July. Igbos had been constructed for Northerners as the most foreign of Nigerians, the embodiment of fears about outsiders gaining unfettered access to the institutions of commerce and government in the North. And, as we will see, the "tribe of the Northerner" existed only long enough to dispatch with threats of "Igbo domination." It was, in that sense, a formation based on political expediency, and as such was vulnerable to the same centrifugal forces that had pulled at the North of the First Republic. Whether Ironsi's regime was a government of Igbos and for Igbos is a subject for another history.[115] What is clear—and far more important for Nigeria's future than the "reality" of the regime's agenda—were the perceptions that Ironsi's government generated in the North. Indeed, the monolithic Igbo menace that Ironsi had embodied would linger in Northern rhetoric for more than a year, even as Ojukwu supplanted Ironsi as the symbol of Igbo ambition. Ironsi's government had led Northerners to see the national government as a threat, and as long as that was the case, Northern leaders could make a persuasive case for a unified regional response. On the other hand, once that threat was no longer present, regional agendas would again give way to increasingly local ones. While a sense of Northern-ness would linger, in various forms, never again would it hold sway on the scale it did between May and July of 1966. Nigeria was changing. Unfortunately, however, the presence of Igbos in the North would continue to be a political and economic affront to the interests of Northern elites. By September, anti-Igbo violence on an unprecedented scale began to push Nigeria down the path to civil war.

## NOTES

1. Nzeogwu's middle name reflected his birth to Igbo migrants in Kaduna.

2. The rivalry dates back to the creation of the Sokoto Caliphate, and manifested itself in the Kano Civil War of 1893–1894. See Paden, *Religion and Political Culture in Kano.*

3. Kano, after World War II, had been the beneficiary of similar plans by the colonial government, which helped Kano displace Jos as the region's industrial center.

4. HCB K/SEC/38, n.p., Security Report, January 1966.

5. HCB R.56, Vol. III, 491, 493, Intelligence Report, January 1966.

6. HCB R.56, Vol. III, 491, Intelligence Report, January 1966.

7. HCB K/SEC/39, 211, Intelligence Report, January 1966. Osadebe (usually "Osadebay") and Okpara, both Igbo, were the Premiers of the Mid-West and East, respectively. [Original emphasis]

8. HCB R.62/305, 289, Intelligence Report, March 1966.

9. HCB R.62/303, 286, Intelligence Report, February 1966.

10. HCB R.62/305, 289, Intelligence Report, March 1966.

11. HCB R.56, Vol. III, 425, Intelligence Report, April 1966.

12. HCB R.56, Vol. III, 425, Intelligence Report, April 1966.

13. HCB K/SEC/38, 156, Security Report, April 1966.

14. John Paden, "Communal Competition, Conflict and Violence in Kano," 134. Many *Kanawa* informants also recalled that the names of appointees were identifiably Igbo.

15. HCB R.62/314, 306, telegram, Provincial Secretary to Secretary to Military Government and Commissioner of Police (Kaduna), 7 May 1966.

16. Report of the British High Commission. Enclosure to USNA POL 23-9/2529/ A-577, 5, 28 May 1966.

17. Paden, *Religion and Political Culture,* 333.

18. Tanko Yakasai, "The Fall of the First Republic and Nigeria's Survival of the Crisis and the Civil War of 1966–70," in Yusufu Bala Usman and George Amale Kwanashie, eds., *Inside Nigerian History 1950–1970. Proceedings of the Presidential Panel on Nigeria Since Independence History Project, 7–9 June 1995* (Zaria: Ahmadu Bello University Press, 1995), 214.

19. FN 50: Interview with Mr. Abdul R. Khatoun, 10 September 1994, Kano; FN 38: Interview with Alhaji Abdulrahman Howeidy, 18 April 1994,

Kano. Other informants related similar stories. See also Muffett, *Let Truth Be Told*, 70–71.

20. USNA POL 18/2509/A-16, 7, 25 March 1971. This was the observation of the Kano State Permanent Secretary for Local Government, an Australian expatriate.

21. HCB K/SEC/38, 158, Security Report, February 1966.

22. FN 101: Interview with Alhaji Liman Ciroma, 4 July 1998.

23. Elegalam, *Causes and Consequences of Igbo Migration to Northern Nigeria, 1900–1960*, 189.

24. Paden, *Religion and Political Culture*, 333.

25. Kirk-Greene, *Crisis and Conflict in Nigeria*, 49. On 1 June, after violence erupted, the Secretary to the Military Governor sent a telegram to provincial secretaries ordering that anyone in possession of such photographs "should be arrested immediately for conduct likely to cause breach of peace." HCB 218/R.974, telegram, Secretary to Military Governor to Provincial Secretaries, 1 June 1966. The article in question is: Coz Idapo, "Sir Ahmadu rose in his shrouds and spoke from the dead . . . ," *Drum* (June 1966).

26. In Kano Township, the Local Authority wrote that the *Drum* article and pictures sorely provoked many Hausa. HCB K/SEC/38, 163–4, Security Report, May 1966.

27. HCB R.56, Vol. III, 519, Intelligence Report, March 1966.

28. Gen. J.T.U. Aguiyi-Ironsi, "The Regions are Abolished" (Lagos: Federal Ministry of Information Press Release, 1966). National radio broadcast the speech 24 May 1966. Reprinted in A.H.M. Kirk-Greene, *Crisis and Conflict in Nigeria*, Vol. 1, 174–77.

29. Hassan Usman Katsina, quoted in Usman and Kwanashie, *Inside Nigerian History*, 118, 119.

30. Muffett has argued that the North's Ministry of Information was "anxious and willing to publish" official casualty and arrest figures, but that "Ironsi personally forbade it." The regional death total that he has quoted (306, including 73 in Kano and 55 in Katsina) seems implausibly low. Muffett, *Let Truth Be Told*, 84.

31. As of 1998, when Civil War-era security reports were declassified.

32. A fourth theme—the mechanisms through which potential victims of violence were targeted—is developed in chapter three.

33. Liman Ciroma, quoted in Usman and Kwanashie, *Inside Nigerian History*, 97.

34. Frank Salamone, "Ethnicity and the Nigerian Civil War," *L'Afrique et l'Adie Modernes* 111 (1976), 9.

35. Kukah, for example, reports rumors that were Decree 34 implemented, the traditional ruler of the Igbo city of Onitsha would be installed as the Sultan of Sokoto, or alternately, the Emir of Kano. Matthew Hassan Kukah, *Religion, Politics and Power in Northern Nigeria* (Ibadan: Spectrum Books Limited, 1993), 39.

36. Paul Brass, *Riots and Pogroms*, 12.

37. See examples from Katsina in this chapter, and Sokoto and Gombe in Appendix A.

38. FN 101: Interview with Alhaji Liman Ciroma, 4 July 1998.

39. This represents something of a reversal in the pattern of relations between regional and local authorities from the First Republic when the NPC had increased

the regional government's control over Native Authorities at the expense of traditional rulers. After the January coup, however, ties between the regional and local governments weakened, in large part because the vertical networks the NPC had so carefully cultivated had been eviscerated.

40. See Adebayo O. Olukoshi, "Bourgeois Social Movements and the Struggle for Democracy in Nigeria: An Inquiry into the 'Kaduna Mafia'," *African Studies in Social Movements and Democracy*, Council for the Development of Social Science Research in Africa (Oxford: CODESRIA, 1995), 252–4. See also A.D. Yahaya, "Experiences in Northern States" in *Nigerian Public Administration 1960–1980: Perspectives and Prospects*, 'Lapido Adamolekun, ed. (Ibadan: Heinemann Educational Publishers, 1985) and B.J. Takaya and S.G. Tyoden, *The Middle Belt in Nigerian Politics* (Jos: ASA Publishers, 1991).

41. Katsina, quoted in Usman and Kwanashie, *Inside Nigerian History* , 119.

42. The authors asked "Does the strength of a country lie only in the unitary form of government? Can it not be achieved through [a] Federal form of government? Or is it because one political party had wanted it to be so?" HCB 218/R.974, letter from "Kano Citizens" to Governor Katsina through Emir Ado Bayero of Kano, 27 May 1966.

43. HCB 218/R.974, n.p., letter, ABC Students Union to Emir of Kano, 28 May 1966.

44. Censored front page of *New Nigerian*, 30 May, 1966. The Secretary to the Military Governor of the North instructed the Provincial Secretaries to "ensure that local radio and television stations and press do not carry reports of incidents inside or outside your province." See HCB 218/R.974, n.p., telegram, 29 May 1966. The Lagos edition of 30 May was printed with several blank pages; in the North it was not distributed at all. The newspaper later printed the story on 2 January 1967.

45. Placards read *"Bamu So"* (We Don't Want It), *"Aware"* (Separation or Secession); "North is a Region not Province," "No Change without Referendum," and "No Dictatorship." Others read "Hell with Military Government," "Federation Should Return," "No Military Government without Referendum," and "Tribal Rule Should Prevail." HCB R.56, Vol. III, 533, Intelligence Report, June 1966. See also USNA POL 23-8/2529, 30 May 1966.

46. USNA POL 23-8/2529, 28 May 1966.

47. USNA POL 23-8/2529, 28 May 1966. The observers worked for the United States Information Service and NASA, which had a tracking station near Kano.

48. HCB K/SEC/38, 162, Security Report, June 1966. Also HCB R.56, Vol. III, 533, Intelligence Report, June 1966.

49. Censored *New Nigerian*, 30 May 1966, printed 2 January 1967.

50. HCB K/SEC/38, 162, Security Report, June 1966. Also HCB R.56, Vol. III, 533, Intelligence Report, June 1966.

51. HCB R.56, Vol. III, 534, Intelligence Report, June 1966.

52. HCB K/SEC/38, 162, Security Report, June 1966.

53. HCB R.56, Vol. III, 533, Intelligence Report, June 1966.

54. USNA POL 23-8/2529, 28 May 1966.

55. HCB R.56, Vol. III, 533-4, Intelligence Report, June 1966.

56. HCB 218/R.974, 22–23, letter, M.A. Agbamuche, S.E. Nwokoye, and E.U.O. Emodi, Barristers and Solicitors to the President and Military Governor, Northern

Provinces, 4 June 1966. The letter also demanded reparations from the government. [Original emphasis]

57. HCB 218/R.974, 22-23, letter M.A. Agbamuche, S.E. Nwokoye, and E.U.O. Emodi, Barristers and Solicitors to the President and Military Governor, Northern Provinces, 4 June 1966.

58. HCB K/SEC/147, 170, telegram, Sabon Gari Traders (Kano) to Military Governor, Kaduna, 6 June 1966.

59. HCB R.56, Vol. III, 534, Intelligence Report, June 1966.

60. Paden, "Communal Competition," 134.

61. USNA POL 23-9/2529/A-123, 23 June 1966.

62. USNA POL 23-8/2529, 29 May 1966.

63. Enclosure to USNA POL 23-8/2529/A-617, 2, 9 June 1966.

64. USNA POL 23-9/2529/A-123, 23 June 1966; USNA POL 23-8/2529, 30 May 1966. Other reinforcements from Enugu were dispatched to other cities.

65. USNA POL 23-9/2529/A-118, 13 June 1966.

66. HCB R.56, Vol. III, 534, Intelligence Report, June 1966.

67. Rumors presented a challenge to authorities across the region. Muhammadu and Haruna have described stories of Igbo plans to "kill every 'Northerner' of promise right down to primary school age." Turi Muhammadu and Mohmammed Haruna, "The Civil War," in *Nigerian Government and Politics Under Military Rule 1966–79*, Oyeleye Oyediran, ed. (New York: St. Martin's Press, 1979), 28.

68. USNA POL 23-8/2529, 31 May 1966.

69. HCB K/SEC/39, 222, Intelligence Report, May-June 1966.

70. FN 79A: Interview with Chief Michael Onyeador, 5 April 1994, Kano.

71. HCB K/SEC/39, 222, Intelligence Report, May-June 1966.

72. HCB K/SEC/39, 221, Intelligence Report, May-June 1966.

73. USNA POL 23-8/2529, 28 May 1966; USNA POL 23-8/2529, 29 May 1966; USNA POL 23-8/2529, 29 May 1966, 2.

74. USNA POL 23-8/2529, 28 May 1966.

75. USNA POL 23-8/2529, 28 May 1966.

76. USNA POL 23-8/2529, 29 May 1966.

77. USNA POL 23-8/2529, 31 May 1966.

78. USNA POL 23-8/2529, 31 May 1966.

79. USNA POL 23-8/2529, 28 May 1966; USNA POL 23-8/2529, 29 May 1966.

80. USNA POL 23-8/2529/A-617, 2, 9 June 1966.

81. Many of the U.S. documents generated during the crises of 1966 reveal an uncritical embrace of prevailing stereotypes of Igbos as "modern," "industrious" and, in a geopolitical sense, pro-western. Northern Muslims, on the other hand, appear as inflexibly tradition-bound. There is also, arguably, a thinly veiled religious bias against Muslims. During Nigeria's Civil War, U.S. Consul General Stokes was, in the eyes of most Northern leaders, pro-Biafran.

82. The following account of events in Katsina draws heavily from the eight-page enclosure to USNA POL 23-9/2529/A-123, 23 June 1966.

83. The limited appropriateness of "prostitute" in Hausa society is discussed in chapter six.

84. The testimony of Enoch Ejikeme before the Judicial Tribunal of Inquiry convened by Justice G.M.C. Onyiuke accuses NA police of taking part in the distur-

bances. "Some of the NA Police took active part, while others made no attempt to bring the situation under control . . . " Ejikeme, quoted in Oha-Na-Eze Ndi Igbo, *The Violations of Human and Civil Rights of Ndi Igbo in the Federation of Nigeria (1966–1999)*, (n.p. 1999), 12 (section 3.5.2). Ejikeme's testimony implicates Emir of Katsina Usman Nagogo and former federal Education Minister Isa Kaita, among others, in the violence.

85. USNA POL 23-9/2529/A-123, 2, 23 June 1966.

86. The English term "king"—the word recorded in consular documents—is probably a translation of the Hausa *sarki* which can mean king, chief, or, loosely, leader. In the sense that, as the leading spokesperson for Katsina's Igbo community, local Hausa speakers may have casually referred to Sylvester as *sarkin Inyamiri* (chief of the Igbos).

87. These rumors were among the many in circulation. Hausa domestic workers in expatriate households at KTC told their employers about rumors that the *Magajin Gari*, a high-ranking official within the royal household—and in this case a son of the Emir—gave the go-ahead for the violence of 4 June. Other rumors said that the Emir himself approved the violence. USNA POL 23-9/2529/A-123, 2, 5, 23 June 1966.

88. USNA POL 23-9/A-123, 2, 23 June 1966.

89. HCB 218/R.974, 27, 10 June 1966.

90. HCB 218/R.974, letter, Acting Provincial Secretary, Katsina, to S. Awoniyi, n.d., probably 3–4 June 1966.

91. USNA POL 23-8/2529, 16 June 1966.

92. USNA POL 23-9/2529/A-122, 23 June 1966.

93. HCB 218/R.974, telegram, Secretary to the Military Governor to Ministry of Information, 31 May 1966.

94. HCB 218/R.974, letter, Kano Provincial Secretary to Native Authorities, 4 June 1966.

95. USNA POL 23-8/2529, 8 June 1966.

96. USNA POL 23-8/2529/A-79, 25 June 1966.

97. USNA POL 23-8/2529, 9 June 1966.

98. HCB 218/R.974, telegram, Secretary to Military Governor to Provincial Secretaries and Police, 4 June 1966.

99. USNA POL 23-8/2529/A-267, 6 June 1966.

100. HCB K/SEC/38, 166, Security Report, June 1966.

101. HCB K/SEC/39, 222, Intelligence Report, May-June 1966.

102. HCB R.62/319, 314, Intelligence Report, May-June 1966.

103. HCB K/SEC/39, 223, Intelligence Report, July 1966.

104. HCB R.56, Vol. III, 542, 30 July 1966; HCB K/SEC/39, 223, Intelligence Report July 1966.

105. HCB K/SEC/39, 223, Intelligence Report, July 1966.

106. HCB R.56, Vol. III: 542, 30 July 1966.

107. HCB R.56, Vol. III: 542, 30 July 1966. Despite heavy security, placards posted on a tree along Airport Road, which Ironsi's caravan passed, asked "Ironsi ina Zakariya Maimulari? Ba Amsa!" ("Ironsi, Where is Zakariya Maimulari? There is no answer!") Colonel Maimulari had been the army's highest ranking Northern officer.

108. The most often cited tally of the dead is twenty-seven Igbo officers, 154 Eastern enlisted men, twelve non-Igbo officers (all southerners), and seventeen non-Eastern enlisted men. Nnoli, *Ethnicity and Development in Nigeria*, 133.

109. Report of the British High Commission. Enclosure to USNA POL 23-9/2529/ A-577, 5, 28 May 1966.

110. Katsina, quoted in Usman and Kwanashie, *Inside Nigerian History*, 121, 118.

111. FN-Anonymous.

112. One exception was in Kano North Division (Haďejia Emirate), where a District Head reportedly saved four Igbos from a mob. One eventually died of his injuries, and the other three were delivered to police in Kano for protection. HCB K/ SEC/39, July-August 1966, 266.

113. USNA POL 23-9/2530, 2 August 1966.

114. USNA POL 23-9/2530, 30 August 1966.

115. Muffett, for example, gives voice to theories of Igbo conspiracy. See Muffett, *Let Truth Be Told*, particularly chapter 5. See also, Nnoli, *Ethnicity and Development in Nigeria*, 130-135.

# 3

# PURGING THE NORTH: AUGUST–OCTOBER 1966

## INTRODUCTION

Had the purges of late 1966 happened thirty years later, they would have been labeled "ethnic cleansing."[1] Bell-Fialkoff reminds us that population cleansing (which includes purges based on ethnicity, race, class, or religion) is a deeply problematic euphemism. As he has used the term, it covers a continuum of actions, ranging from "genocide at one end to subtle pressure to emigrate at the other. Between these extremes lie expulsion and mass population transfers."[2] The anti-Igbo violence of late 1966 contains elements from across this spectrum, reflecting the relatively fragmented origins of the violence, and the lack of coordination among its perpetrators when compared to the anti-unification riots or the July counter-coup, which had sown the seeds of the purge. The slaughter of Igbos in the military that accompanied the second coup was first a reclamation of political power, and second retribution against Igbo officers and men for the death of the Sardauna and other Northern leaders slain in January. The sense of resolution Ironsi's assassination offered to Northerners did not, apparently, resolve resentments or anxieties surrounding Igbos' continued presence at the local level. Anti-Igbo sentiments so carefully managed during the first half of 1966 had not been directed solely at Ironsi, but rather at Igbos in general, and as late as September of that year, substantial Igbo populations remained in Northern cities. Ironsi had, after all, been constructed as a symbol of the domineering tendencies ascribed to *all* Igbos; those who remained in the North fit into an established discourse of Igbo domination. Further, their property and positions in local economies presented attractive trophies, and with Ironsi gone and the military purged, Igbos in the North were more vulnerable than ever before. Though the perceived threat that Igbos represented had ceased to have the concrete form the Ironsi regime gave it, a climate saturated with mutual suspicions was extremely vulnerable to manipulation. While the purge of the military spoke to the formal balance of political power on the national stage, Igbos ensconced in the North remained a focal point for the manipulation of ethnic sentiments. Again, ethnicity would be a tool in the hands of political agitators, again with disastrous consequences.

The months between July and October were tumultuous, characterized by an escalating crisis in confidence between Igbos and Northerners, a widening dispute over the relationship between the regions and the central government, and more violence. Again, events in Kano would play a pivotal role. There were scattered incidents of anti-Igbo violence before radio broadcasts on 29 September set off a series of disturbances across the region. The crisis reached its crescendo two days later when a mutiny by soldiers in Kano began a massacre there. It is fairly clear from the case of the Kano mutiny that participating in anti-Igbo violence had become a sort of status symbol within the military, and perhaps to a lesser extent among some civilians. Between thousands of deaths and large-scale flight to the East, the September and October disturbances purged the North of its civilian Igbo population in much the same way that the July coup had the military. The purge happened in large part because, despite an unprecedented level of political vulnerability, Igbos in the North had continued to occupy coveted positions in local economies. As a result, ordinary Igbos remained the focus not only of lingering resentments over public indiscretions during the Ironsi period, but also the actions of regime itself, and the widening dispute between the new federal government and the Eastern Region over the constitutional configuration of Nigeria. This meant that to be identified as Igbo in the North was again to potentially be a political scapegoat and, by extension, a target for violence.

The anti-Igbo violence in September and October, as much as any other set of events, set the country down the path to civil war. The abandonment of the North by Igbos that followed was on a scale far larger than those following the anti-unification disturbances or the July coup. And, unlike those evacuations, this time it would be years before Igbos returned in large numbers. This chapter concerns itself with three overlapping sets of concerns, all of which apply to varying degrees across the North, but which I approach from a Kano-centered perspective. The first section of this chapter details events that are immediately relevant to understanding the manipulation of ethnicity in pursuit of political goals in the North. The second section examines some of the mechanics involved in the anti-Igbo violence, including criteria used in the targeting of victims, and ways in which some Igbos were able to manipulate those criteria in their own interests. Finally, the third section of this chapter carries the analysis of Igbo responses into the period beyond the riots. It touches on the reasons a few Igbos were able to remain in the North, including two who used dual ethnicity as a tool for evasion. It concludes with a brief nod to the difficulties non-Igbo southerners and Middle Belters faced after the riots in Kano's ethnically charged environment.

## THE CHANGING FACE OF VIOLENCE

Several elements emerge as particularly important in understanding how the meaning of anti-Igbo violence changed after the July coup. The first major difference is the heightened role some military units played in intimidation and violence. Their participation contributed to its deadliness and to the difficulty authorities faced in containing it. It appears that the soldiers behind the Kano mutiny victimized Igbos in order to elevate their own status in the eyes of their comrades in other military units. Secondly, while rumors figured in the anti-unification riots, stories of aggression by Igbo civilians played a much larger part in inciting ordinary Northerners to participate in the September and October riots. There was a pattern of stories alleging violence against Northerners in the East, as well as a series of local rumors. The third point is the most important. The fall of Ironsi and the rise of the Yakubu Gowon government signaled a major change in Northern politics. While the threat of "Igbo domination" vanished, the rising influence of Middle Belt officers and soldiers meant that the ability of a few far Northern elites to directly influence political and economic life throughout the region appeared, at least for the time being, to be in abeyance. As a result, agendas based on sub-region, emirate, city, or even ethnic constituencies were increasingly relevant. This was particularly true as the Gowon regime appointed many former opposition politicians to administrative positions. It was no longer plausible to justify violence against Igbos as necessary for the political and economic survival of the North. Removing them, however, remained politically and economically appealing to many. Once the Igbos were gone, Northern power brokers were able to take for themselves what Igbos had possessed in property and position, which they were then able to keep for themselves or distribute among their supporters.

In pursuing their agendas, elites took advantage of existing networks, remaking them to serve new needs. According to an official of the British High Commission, "the events of the crisis days pointed to very competent organization and allegations are widely heard to the effect that the NPC were the instigators. One expatriate Northern civil servant referred to the 'old band-wagon' of the sort that used to accompany the Sardauna on his progresses."[3] The Secretary to the Military Governor also suspected the riots were not spontaneous, and that money had been used to induce participation.[4] The difference between the May-June anti-unification riots and the September-October purge was that in the first case the goals had been explicitly regional, while by September, much of the focus was on smaller constituencies. In concrete terms, the less concentrated timing of this later violence speaks to its decentralization. Having toppled the tree, Northern elites now used the same tools to dislodge what fruit they could from the branches. At the same time, they sent a message. One might be tempted to argue that that message was that "the North is for Northerners," the mantra of the May demonstrations, since in a superficial sense the purge was in keeping with goals of the anti-unification riots. The profoundly different political climate, however, underscores the limitations of this similarity. Leaders and citizens in many parts of the North had been unhappy with the NPC's rule, and for them the Gowon regime represented a chance to break with the NPC's vision of the Northern Region without the threat to their sub-regional interests that the Ironsi government had manifested. In Kano, an attitude that "Kano is for *Kanawa*" was ascendant, and analogous sentiments were present in other parts of the North. With time, the Gowon regime would give concrete form to these nativist sentiments, and give them the form of new states.

## THE GOWON REGIME:
## FORGING FEDERALISM FROM ANTI-IGBOISM

Without the Ironsi regime to focus the energies of leaders across the region into a fairly unified Northern bloc, the Gowon government would have been impossible. There have been assertions that the July coup was initially intended to facilitate Northern secession from Nigeria, and not to reestablish Northern control of the center. According to this theory, the coup plotters met with an unexpected degree of success and, finding control of the country within their reach, quickly adjusted their plans.[5] In any case, by design or by fluke, they succeeded in destroying the Ironsi government. This was the ultimate rejection of Ironsi and his administration's agenda. The coup-makers then selected Gowon to head the new government.

Based on the political calculus inherited from the First Republic and the Ironsi period, Gowon's regime was a "Northern" government to the degree it reflected a convergence of Middle Belt and far Northern interests. That convergence, however, was both limited and conditional. Significantly, Gowon was a Middle Belter and a Christian, and his selection represented both an unprecedented level of influence for the Middle Belt and a recognition of the importance of Middle Belt officers and soldiers in the Nigerian Army.[6] The Gowon regime itself presented a new beginning for intra-regional politics, as leaders from the various sub-regions of the North began to reassess and pursue their respective interests in light of the Middle Belt's new prominence. Nnoli has argued that during the Ironsi regime Middle Belt leaders aligned themselves with far Northerners not out of loyalty to the North *per se*, but in self interest. In particular Nnoli has pointed to Ironsi's refusal to create a Middle Belt state apart from the Northern Region. This alienated former United Middle Belt Congress (UMBC) supporters who during the First Republic had allied themselves with the NCNC and battled the NPC in Tivland. Middle Belt leaders, particularly those affiliated with the UMBC, wanted their own state and threw in their lot with the far North, mainly as a means of removing the obstacle—in 1966, Ironsi—to their own sub-regional interests.[7] That Ironsi thwarted Middle Belt goals explains in part why it was in former UMBC strongholds in Tivland that some of the worst anti-Igbo violence of late 1966 occurred, and Paden has contended that citizens of Benue Province, where Tivland is located, played a significant role in anti-Igbo violence in Kano.[8] Significantly, Gowon's government would, in time, pursue a policy of state creation that gave Middle Belt loyalists the autonomy both Ahmadu Bello's NPC and Ironsi had steadfastly denied them. In the end, Gowon's government was, for Northerners, a welcome change from Ironsi's, though for both the far North and the Middle Belt, it represented new opportunities and challenges.

The first months of the Gowon regime witnessed a deepening of tensions surrounding the safety of Igbos in the North. Eastern Governor Ojukwu's refusal to recognize the legitimacy of the Gowon regime lay at the center of the widening chasm. The July coup triggered the second mass departure of Igbos from the North in a two-month period, and relations between Ojukwu and the Gowon regime in Lagos worsened as new arrivals strained resources in the East, and Igbos openly questioned their safety outside of the region. In an attempt to resolve the crisis, high-ranking representatives of the four regions met in Lagos on 9 August. They agreed to abandon Ironsi's plans for unification by restoring Nigeria's federal structure.[9] They also agreed to repatriate soldiers to their regions of origin in hopes of bolstering public confidence in the military, and preventing additional barracks violence.[10] They did not, however, settle more pressing constitutional matters. A second meeting to do so began on 12 September. The stated task of the conference, dubbed the Ad Hoc Conference on the Nigerian Constitution, was to determine what type of constitution Nigeria would have, and to settle related concerns like revenue allocation and rights of secession. The presence of largely unexploited underground petroleum reserves in the East gave an added sense of urgency to the talks, and attracted international attention. It was clear to all involved that Nigeria could ill afford to allow the East, with its oil, to go.

The conference dragged on for weeks, and the sides failed to come together. Significantly, however, the conference witnessed a major shift in the positions of the regions. In light of recent events, Eastern representatives argued for a loose association of semi-autonomous regions and a weak central government. This position, historically associated with the NPC, was at odds with both the NCNC's many attempts to break down regional barriers and the Ironsi government's plans for unification. That Igbo leaders would push for confederation showed both the depth of their suspicion and fear, and their recognition that the center was, for the foreseeable future, in Northern hands. Representatives from the North initially stayed true to the conventional Northern position and accepted the proposal for strong regions and a weak center. After consultations with other Northern leaders, however, the delegation changed its positions and insisted on a strong center. The East resisted, and the resulting deadlock persisted until the conference broke down in early October, by which point conditions on the ground in the North had deteriorated precipitously. According to Nnoli, dissatisfied by the discussions, "the privileged classes of the North unleashed harrowing waves of violence."[11] In fact, the process of inciting violence began even earlier.

## SEPTEMBER AND OCTOBER: COMPLETING THE PURGE

After a comparatively quiet August, manifestations of anti-Igbo sentiment became more common in September. In part this was because deadlocked negotiations in Lagos appeared to many Northerners to be the result of Eastern intransigence, and in particular that of Ojukwu. What was more important, however, was the failure of the May-June disturbances and the second coup to dislodge Igbo civilians from the North. Following the July coup, both Gowon and Ojukwu had made public statements assuring Igbos of their safety throughout the country. Many Igbos who had fled to the East chose to remain there, but others returned to the North, with the notable exception of Katsina. While Gowon's government made efforts to restore Igbos' confidence, many Northerners remained resentful of the positions Igbo traders and artisans enjoyed in local economies, of their presence in federal public service and parastatal jobs, and of market stalls, land, and other property that Igbos held in Sabon Gari wards and elsewhere. A series of events throughout the month deepened the polarity between Igbos and the North. On 11 September, the day before the Ad-Hoc Constitutional Conference began, two bombs exploded in Lagos, including one at the Federal Palace Hotel, where delegates to the conference were to have lodged. Authorities laid blame for the explosion on an Igbo university instructor, E.O.D. Agwu, whom they said died in the explosion. Public reaction in Lagos was such that when Eastern delegates arrived, they did so under Gowon's personal pledge of safe conduct. Authorities in Kaduna, fearful of similar attacks in the North, sent hand-delivered messages to operatives in Northern centers. The messages said that it was "imperative [to] keep watch [on the] movements of stranger elements [in] your respective areas with [a] view to neutralizing risks of further attacks against vital targets." "Stranger," was a much-used code of colonial vintage for southerners, and usually referred to Igbos in particular. Kaduna recommended a highly visible police presence in the streets, and at public utilities and government offices.[12]

In this climate, the discovery of several boxes of phosphorous in Kano four days after the bombings nearly had violent repercussions. The afternoon of 15 September, a Hausa man fishing near the Plaza Cinema in Fagge, just outside the old city, found a small box. A carpenter opened the box, and was overcome by fumes, as were several bystanders. Rumors that the box had been a bomb planted by Igbos began to circulate, and an informal search for more evidence of "sabotage" ensued. The next day searchers found six similar boxes in the area. With news of the Lagos bombing fresh in people's minds, the discovery launched rumors that the boxes had also been planted as bombs. At noon the next day, Friday, an estimated 300 people marched through the area, some armed with sticks and matchets, shouting "*a raba*" ("separation", often translated as "secession").[13] In Sabon Gari, news of the march spread quickly and residents prepared for trouble. According to the Provincial Secretary, "Attack on Ibos living in Sabon Gari was narrowly prevented by prompt action taken by Administration, Army, Police and Native Authority."[14] Whether all the boxes, those found on the second day, or none at all were planted by local agitators is subject to speculation. In any case, for Kano, the reprieve was to be brief.

Additional rumors and specific threats circulated, and authorities prepared themselves for more disturbances. A secret communiqué from Kaduna to the Provincial Office in Kano dated 23 September called for recruitment of additional police in preparation for emergencies, and urged that such recruitment be "discreet."[15] Three days later the office of the Military Governor ordered that Native Authorities take steps to "prevent molestation or provocation" of the sort that set off "events in May and July."[16] That same day, 26 September, "a gang of hooligans" broke into Kano Native Authority Works Yard and threatened to kill all Igbo workers there. Police responded, but only after the workers had escaped. For authorities the incident was yet another reminder that the "present situation is highly delicate as tension mounts."[17]

As October first, Nigerian Independence Day, approached, threatening notices appeared. Authorities reported that many Igbos in Kano and the East believed that the end of September would bring trouble.

Exodus of Ibo personnel from this Province continued throughout [August and September]. Self-employed and Government servants alike resigned their posts and made their ways to the [Eastern] Region in alarming numbers. A cross section of correspondences from the Eastern Region reveals that parents and friends have been writing to their dear ones only to quit the North within the shortest possible time. In some cases, target dates have been fixed to 28th and 29th September, 1966, within which the recipients have been warned to report to the East or face the resulting consequences. This state of affairs is rather causing great embarrassment on some of the Easterners who are not ready to go back to their region and to the Northerners who feel that plans are ahead for sabotage or subversion against the North. On the other hand it may be concluded that those originating the call-back are deliberately threatening their fellows brothers only to go back as that is the only means to attract their attention back home.

A number of anonymous letters have been written to senior Government officers who are from the Southern origin, the letters threaten those concerned to quit the North or be killed. The letters

[are] usually written in English, but bear the Hausa code "Zanga Zanga." Enquiries reveal that this action is likely being carried out by a person or group of persons whose interest is to bring [confusion] into the Government Machinery. [ . . . ] Latest of such anonymous writing was a warning notice distributed on leaflets on the night of 24th September, 1966 by unknown person or persons, address[ed] to "ANY IBO ORIGINAL" and reads "Your continuous stay in Kano does not improve the peace of the inhabitants of this town, instead it constitutes such a menacing Danger. You are hereby warned to leave this town for your place of origin (The Republic of Biafra) [*sic*] as soon as you desire, but before or at the ending of the month September, 1966. This is the first warning, but do not expect another. JUSTICE."[18]

Another report suspected that "numerous anonymous letters" that threatened Igbos with violence if they did not leave Kano by the end of September were "written by either some Northerners who want to cause trouble or by Easterners who want excuse for their departure." Handwritten in the margins of the report were references to Abdullahi Bayero College, whose students had been central to the May demonstrations.[19] Among *Kanawa*, however, there is a received wisdom that many of the same former politicians believed to have contributed to the May disturbances also participated in floating threats and rumors against Igbos in September, though this remains impossible to prove or disprove.

Across the region, Independence Day provided a symbolic deadline that appeared in rumors and threats directed against Igbos. In late September, the Inspector General of Police reported widespread rumors that there would be violence come October.[20] Similarly, the sister of an Igbo employed in the household of a foreign diplomat reported being put off of a lorry headed north to Ilorin on 29 September. Passengers told her "we don't want any Ibos in the North. Return to Ibadan and we will settle accounts October first."[21]

During late September other Igbos received well-intentioned warnings from Hausa friends and associates. An Igbo employee of Nigerian Airways in Kano reported that Northern colleagues warned him and other Igbos of impending trouble. While he could not recall the exact timing of the warnings, he remembered that they were several days in advance of the massacres of 1 October. "They said things like 'tomorrow won't be a nice day,' or 'Keep indoors; don't send your children to school.'" In his case, such warnings allowed him to plan for his family's evacuation on 1 October.[22] Similarly, the father of the

Northern military officer who warned his Igbo trading partner in Hadejia of the July coup also told him in September that there would be a "major massacre" in October. The trader was able to evacuate his family and warn friends.[23] And a third Igbo man who had worked for and maintained links to the local administration was also tipped off in September by a former Native Administration official that "the time for me to leave had come."[24]

Most Igbos, however, received no warnings, though some reached the decision to leave Kano on their own. Others, despite acts of intimidation and rumors threatening their safety, felt secure enough to remain in Kano. In neighboring Hadejia, authorities made similar observations. "It is heavily circulated around Mala-Maduri Railway Station that Easterners, particularly Ibos, should do all they could to travel to the East, before the end of this month. [ . . . ] However the few Ibos that were left behind do not care much for the rumours. They are carrying on with their normal business in Mala-Maduri."[25] As authorities in and around Kano were well aware, however, during mid-September things were far from normal in parts of the Middle Belt.

Soldiers in the Tiv Division of the Middle Belt's Benue Province accounted for a great deal of that area's anti-Igbo violence. On 20 September soldiers in Makurdi launched attacks on Igbos that continued through the next morning. The outbreak coincided with the arrival of a new company of soldiers, and missionary accounts reported tension between loyal and insubordinate troops. Tiv civilians, reportedly armed with Dane guns and hand weapons, joined in at Makurdi, and mounted attacks at Gboko and Oturkpo.[26] Elements within the Nigeria Police had anticipated the violence in Tivland. Inspector General Kam Salem told U.S. diplomats in September that he had asked Gowon to disarm soldiers in Makurdi and Oturkpo and to confine them to barracks. Salem also had more general fears about the conduct of military units; he proposed to Gowon the creation of a "Provost Corps" to be drawn from the country's minority groups, the function of which would have been to police the military. He also expressed concern about reports of hooligans posing as soldiers. He reportedly told Gowon that the smallest incident could set in motion a chain reaction of violence.[27]

Outside of Tivland, other Middle Belt cities also experienced anti-Igbo violence the following week. In Minna several dozen Igbos died on 26 September, and another 600 fled. And, on 27 September, an Easterner and a soldier fought in Jos; later that evening solders attacked his house with small arms.[28] And two or three days earlier a dispute between an Igbo railway employee and a soldier was followed by attacks by soldiers.[29] As a result, by 30 September Mobil, British Petroleum and Shell Oil companies and Barclay's Bank had all begun to evacuate their Igbo staff, and mining companies on the Jos Plateau chartered planes to airlift Igbo employees to the East.[30] At the same time, fearing reprisals from locals, some tin-mining companies prohibited their employees from offering any help to Igbos.[31]

## CREATING MASSACRES:
## FROM RADIO COTONOU TO THE KANO MUTINY

Anti-Igbo violence escalated on 29 September after Radio Cotonou, in the neighboring Republic of Benin, broadcast grossly exaggerated reports that large-scale attacks on Northerners were underway in the East's commercial capital of Onitsha. The broadcast appears to have been a calculated fabrication designed to move Northerners to attack Igbo civilians, and perhaps to intimidate the East into breaking the political deadlock in Lagos. Its timing, perhaps by chance, but more likely by design, was only two days before Nigerian independence day. The Broadcasting Corporation of Nigeria repeated the report, apparently citing Radio Cotonou, and the next day the *New Nigerian* led with the story. According to the *New Nigerian* account, Igbos seized the property and money of the Hausa butchers and merchants who were the core of the Northern community in Onitsha.[32] Further, the North's Ministry of Information in Kaduna issued a press release that repeated the Radio Cotonou story.[33] There had indeed been protests of the anti-Igbo violence, some directed at Northerners resident in the East, but not on the scale described, and those that took place appear to have been peaceful. Unfortunately, no detailed accounts exist. Still, in Kano and other cities the stories spread, mostly by word of mouth.[34]

There is a consensus among Igbos and Hausas in Kano that the story was deliberately planted with the intention of inflaming passions in the North, though it is unlikely those allegations will ever be confirmed or repudiated. Most likely, the story was fabricated and fed to Radio Cotonou in order to give it the appearance of an impartial observation; then, after its broadcast abroad, authorities in the North repeated it.[35] If the story was in fact planted, as it almost certainly was, the question of who planted it remains. Unfortunately, the list of those who stood to benefit materially and politically from the expulsion of Igbos is substantial. It includes white collar workers, professionals, and civil servants eager to purge their respective ranks of Igbos; landlords and would-be landlords who coveted property Igbos held; entrepreneurs, merchants, and traders out to capture more business for themselves; and political leaders responsive to the interests of these groups, or who wished to consolidate the political gains of the July coup. Many *Kanawa* concur; several remarked privately that they believed the story was placed by disgruntled politicians who hoped to discredit the military government by creating a crisis beyond its ability to control in the hope of being invited to reassume power. In any case, the creation of an incendiary story like the one fed to Radio Cotonou could have been the work of many, or a well-placed individual.

The impact of the broadcast was immediate and severe; Northerners attacked Igbos in cities across the region. The day of the story, there were reports from Jos and Bukuru of soldiers shooting Igbos on sight, and of civilian mobs attacking Igbos.[36] Soldiers also participated in killings in Maiduguri, and in the Western city of Abeokuta.[37] Major anti-Igbo riots by civilians took place in Zaria, Minna, Kaduna, and at the Kainji Dam. In the days that followed, killings spread to Gombe, Bauchi, and other cities. Kano, interestingly, remained quiet on the 29th and 30th.

After the Radio Cotonou story broke, soldiers and mobile police had patrolled streets of Kano, keeping peace even as rumors about killings of Northerners continued to circulate. One, for example, claimed that 33,000 Northerners had been murdered in the East.[38] Broadcasts by the Emir and the Military Governor disavowing the stories had, in the eyes of the Kano District Officer, helped to prevent the rumors from sparking action.[39] Nonetheless, some Igbos, expecting trouble or having been warned to leave, continued to head south, most by train, but some by air. Events in Kano, however, would hinge on a small group of soldiers and, indirectly, the nearby village of Nguru, where the District Officer had gone missing in a violent local disturbance unrelated to the larger crisis. Police from Kano were unwilling to travel to Nguru without a military escort.[40] According to several reports, a platoon of thirty-one men assigned as an escort were issued live ammunition. The platoon mutinied. They started shooting as their commanding officer addressed them on the barracks parade ground the afternoon of Saturday, 1 October. The officer, one Major Kyari, fled, and non-commissioned officers on the scene failed to restore order.[41] According to one report, a regimental sergeant and an officer died trying to stop the mutinous troops, though Major Kyari— a Middle Belter—and other officers remained in hiding off base. The mutineers raided the barracks armory, then headed into town, where they took local "hooligans" into their vehicles and asked them to take them to where Igbos were.[42] They attacked Igbos at the railroad station and Electricity Corporation of Nigeria facilities in Bompai ward, and at the airport, located near both Sabon Gari and the barracks.[43] Others set off for the water purification and pumping station at Challawa, some miles away.[44] At the airport, mutinous soldiers fired when several dozen Igbos tried to board a VC-10. A missionary saw several people pulled out of a crowd, then shot by troops; and a Peace Corps administrator on the plane reported that soldiers boarded after twenty-five Igbos rushed aboard. The soldiers ordered "Ibos off." Some complied when the soldiers loaded rounds into the chambers of their weapons. Those who deplaned were shot. One man, wounded in the leg, made it back aboard the plane, which then flew to Lagos.[45] During the night, "the mutineers were joined by civilians, and it was simply war against the Ibos."[46] As had been the case in Katsina in June, men, women, and children alike were targets for violence, and mobs burned or looted Igbo property. As mobs entered Sabon Gari, some Igbos there defended themselves as best they could; others went into hiding, as did those caught outside of Sabon Gari.

The NPF organized an airlift to evacuate Igbos, though its men did not confront the mutinous soldiers until the next day when loyal troops under a well-respected far Northern officer, Lieutenant Colonel Muhammadu Shuwa, arrived from Kaduna by 5 A.M.[47] Governor Katsina rushed to Kano as well. The presence of Katsina and Shuwa, the District Officer reported, restored order among soldiers, who returned to barracks.[48] Years later, however, Katsina argued that he relied on the moral force of the Emir in bringing the troops under control. He had called for the Emir to meet his flight at the airport, and, with Shuwa, they went into the rioting.

> They didn't stop shooting because they saw me and [ . . . ]Shuwa, no. As soon as they saw the face of the Emir, they ran away. They dropped their guns because of the respect they had for the Emir. . . . They could shoot me, because I was stopping them from what they wanted to do, [which was] looting. The citizens of Kano wanted to follow the soldiers into Igbo houses and loot their properties. . . . The soldiers were running back to the barracks not because of me, but because of the Emir. His turban was enough for them to run away.

All three men later addressed soldiers in the barracks.[49]

Stopping the soldiers, however, was not enough to end the killing. Some civilians had "gone wild" after the example of the mutinous troops.[50] Mobs of boys and young men continued attacks on Igbos. On 2 October, mobs searched Bompai and the former GRA for Igbos, entering the compounds of Nigerians and foreigners in the process.[51] Loyal troops and NPF worked to protect Igbos attempting flight, but fighting in and around Sabon Gari continued through Monday 3 October. While violent incidents continued for several days, patrols prevented further rioting as Igbos left Kano in droves. Most did so on overloaded trains, some of which were stoned as they left Kano or passed through other cities and towns before facing soldiers at the Benue River crossing at Makurdi. As late as 6 October, the *New Nigerian* reported that 1,456 left Kano and Zaria by train for Enugu.[52] Those more fortunate were evacuated by chartered aircraft.[53] With transportation both unsafe and overcrowded, many chose to remain in hiding before taking their chances; one Igbo informant reported hiding in the bush on the outskirts of Kano for several days before making her way to the train station and escaping south.[54] By the second week in October, however, the purge of the North was all but complete. The vast majority of the Igbos still in the North were either disguised, in hiding, or on the run. The large Igbo concentrations in cities like Jos, Zaria, and Kano, tens of thousands of people, had been dislodged.

There is an oft-repeated theory of the Kano mutiny that goes beyond the anti-Igbo sentiments that had become so pervasive in Northern Nigeria. At its core was the need of Northern troops, who constituted the overwhelming majority of the enlisted men in the garrison, to demonstrate to their comrades in other units that they too could rise up against Igbos. Unlike solders in other major units, the men of the Fifth Battalion had not participated in the January coup that brought Ironsi to power; more importantly, they had not helped to overthrow him or purge the Army of Igbos in July. Because its men had not watched their officers violate the chain of command in coup-related activities, the Fifth was the only major army unit outside of the East that had been neither relocated nor broken up.[55] On the other hand, the battalion had fired on Northern civilians during the anti-unification disturbances, and had been deployed on several occasions to protect Igbos. As a result, members of the battalion felt looked down on by other Northern soldiers who had staged actions against Igbo officers, men, or civilians.[56] Exacerbating matters was the fact that Lieutenant Colonel Ojukwu—by October an extremely unpopular figure in the North—had been the battalion's commander before being made governor of the East. According to this theory of the munity, being issued live ammunition for the Nguru operation presented an opportunity to take an unambiguous—and deadly—anti-Igbo stance. It appears likely that the statements by the Emir and the presence of NPF and army units in the streets before the mutiny had prevented any large-scale outbreak of violence by civilians. But once the mutiny happened, whatever pro-violence sentiment or planning the peace keepers had contained had an opportunity to spread.

The arrival of Governor Katsina in Kano is consistent with what appears to have been a good faith effort within his office to work to contain the violence and offer assistance to Igbos in distress. The office sent a series of telegrams to Provincial Secretaries urging them to use the Native Authority forces to help NPF and army units restore order. Perhaps more importantly, as early as 30 September it urged the secretaries to "ensure that you arrange repatriation of all southerners wishing to return home" in vehicles escorted by police and, in some cases, soldiers, who would see them to the border with the East. The Red Cross would receive them there.[57]

It is often overlooked that thousands of Igbos escaped with help from provincial authorities.[58] The regional government in Kaduna also used its own resources to protect Igbos; as it had in May and June, authorities there put shelter-seekers in ministerial housing in Kaduna, this time 800 Easterners awaiting transport home.[59] At the same time, even as Igbos left, Northern refugees from the East streamed toward home, many of them arriving in Kano by train or air. The governor's office issued orders that the new arrivals "not be allowed to spread exaggerated stories of their experiences in the East. Their activities, utterances, and wild allegations about incidents in the East are likely to stir up unrest in the community." Further, it authorized that "extremists may be isolated from the public for some time."[60] It is clear that the government's actions were not popular with many Northerners. Not surprisingly, it was its civilian representatives and not military personnel who bore the brunt of that sentiment. Even more so than during the May disturbances, civil servants who worked to protect Igbos or contain violence risked the wrath of other Northerners. Liman Ciroma, the Secretary to the Military Governor of the North, was told that his life was in danger for his role in working to stop the riots.[61]

Governor Katsina personally appealed to emirs and other traditional rulers to help prevent further outbreaks.[62] By that point, however, the ability of many traditional rulers to intervene had also been compromised. The Emir of Bauchi told an expatriate that for him to intervene on behalf of Igbos was to expose himself to danger.[63] Similarly, the Emir of Zaria and Waziri of Bornu were subjected to verbal abuse and had their cars struck for urging the cessation of rioting. Other traditional rulers were initially unwilling to oppose attacks on Igbos, and then found themselves unable to stop them after Katsina's appeal.[64] Like other people of means, however, those so inclined could, in many cases, use their access to material resources to help those in distress. An uncertain number of Igbos, by some accounts hundreds and certainly dozens, took shelter in the Emir of Kano's palace during the May and October disturbances.[65] In addition to the Emir, other residents of the palace provided sanctuary, sometimes getting Igbos in and out of the palace by dressing them in Hausa clothing. Such was reportedly the case with M.A. Agbamuche, a prominent attorney active in the Kano Igbo community; in October he was disguised with a turban and hidden in the palace for several days before being sent to Lagos.[66]

Like traditional rulers, the performance of Native Authority units also varied widely. The District Officer in Nguru, whose disappearance helped to create the circumstances for the mutiny, died apparently trying to protect Igbos there.[67] Similarly, elsewhere in Northern Kano Division, a local official intervened on behalf of Igbos in trouble.

> During trouble in Nguru, two Igbos, armed with Dane guns, fled on foot for Birninwa. Upon their arrival they were attacked and killed on 2 October. The same day another was chased and killed in Garun Gabas, where he had hidden in a school. Four others fled to Guri where the District Head (*Sarkin Bai*) offered sanctuary, though one died of injuries he received in Nguru. Police took the others to Kano.[68]

And, though many Igbos today express skepticism over the sincerity of its men during the crisis, the Nigeria Police Force, as much as any other branch of government, appears to have worked to protect Igbo civilian lives. Among its other activities were organizing evacuations by air of Igbos otherwise trapped. For example, during the first week in October, civilians—though some speculated they were soldiers in mufti—blocked the road between Maiduguri and Bauchi, to the southwest. With the most direct land route south effectively blocked, the NPF flew evacuees from Maiduguri out of the North.[69] On the other hand, the willingness of the NPF to stand up to transgressions by soldiers was limited. The available documentation reveals only one incident where NPF and mutinous soldiers clashed, on 2 October in Jos, when the NPF came to the aid of a group of Igbos as soldiers shot at them.[70]

Despite the interventions of authorities, killings continued as Igbos fled the North in large numbers for the third time in five months. On 5 October, for example, a group of soldiers in the Middle Belt town of Vom reportedly shot 30 wounded easterners.[71] Other soldiers continued their practice of stopping trains at the Makurdi and Lokoja bridges just north of the Eastern border. They had done this since July, in search of Igbo soldiers. It is unclear whether expanding their activities to include harassment of civilians happened with the approval of military authorities, though local officials as far away as Kano knew it was happening. In any case, as attacks on civilians had spread, trains provided easy targets for soldiers and civilian mobs, most of which appear to have operated with impunity. One of the last such incidents took place at Oturkpo on 7 October when a train bound for Enugu was attacked, apparently by civilians, while it overnighted there. Seven Igbos died.[72] Railway authorities in the East were aware of such violence, yet continued to rely on Igbo crews to operate trains, though they appealed to the military to guarantee the safety of crews as they passed through Makurdi and Oturkpo.[73]

In the wake of the killings in the North, Governor Ojukwu ordered non-Easterners to leave the East. He also directed Easterners outside the region to return to their home region for their safety. This reinforced a mass movement of people headed homeward, the majority to the East, but with each section of the country represented. While Ojukwu spoke in the language of regions and not ethnic labels, the Military Governor of the Mid-West was perhaps more candid when he advised Igbos—including the minority of Igbos indigenous to the Mid-West—who did not feel safe there to leave.[74] In Enugu, authorities struggled to deal with the newly arrived, many of whom were injured, some severely, and most of whom had no food and little money. By 8 October, the Eastern Region Rehabilitation Committee at Enugu registered 71,000 heads of households, and estimated another 10,000–15,000 awaited. This led them to estimate a total refugee population of between 405,000 and 430,000.[75] That number would grow as stragglers made their way south, many after emerging from hiding in the North. Counting the dead proved even more difficult than enumerating the living. In Kano there was no official casualty count, since authorities, pleading reasons of public health, buried the bodies without determining and recording causes of death, to say nothing of identifying them or their ethnic affiliation.[76] Estimates for the metropolis ranged between several hundred to more than 1,000. Ultimately, the regional death toll itself would become a political tool, as evidenced when Ojukwu placed it as high as 50,000.[77] Based on a tour of the North, the British High Commission conservatively estimated deaths at between 3,000 and 4,000, including 1,000 in Kano and 1,500 in Jos and Bukuru.[78] In any case, Igbo life had been rendered impossibly cheap. When Governor Katsina announced that thirty-one soldiers were to be tried for their part in the Kano mutiny, the District Officer in Hadejia noted that his statement "is worrying the minds of illiterate people. They wonder why should the soldiers be punished for merely killing Ibos."[79]

## THE OTHER SIDE: WARNINGS AND SHELTER

In sharp contrast to the sentiments voiced in Hadejia, it is important to keep in mind that most ordinary Northerners did not participate in rioting. Further still, some exposed themselves to personal danger to help Igbos. Elegalam, for example, recounted the story of Zephynir Anabirionye, who, taken for dead by his assailants, was smuggled away from a mass grave by a Northern friend who had followed the truck carrying Anabirionye and the bodies of other victims. Anabirionye's friend revived him and assisted him in leaving the region.[80] A more dramatic story transpired in Zaria, a core Hausa city north of Kaduna, where Yusuf Umar Dala, a Hausa trader from Kano, provided refuge for seven weeks to an Igbo business associate and fifteen other Igbos. Among them were four men, three women and nine children. After the worst of Zaria's rioting, Yusuf contacted the divisional police commandant, who advised him against moving the Igbos. He also gave Yusuf a telephone number to call if anyone threatened them. Yusuf fed and sheltered the group until a joint police-military escort carried them and other stranded Igbos to the East.[81]

Like Yusuf's Igbo associate, close ties with Hausas characterized other Igbos offered warnings or protection from Hausa neighbors during the riots. Speaking informally, a number of male *Kanawa* reached, independent of one another, similar conclusions about Igbos who got such help. Central to their descriptions of Igbos who would receive help was the habit of acting toward Northerners with respect or humanity (*mutunci*, from *mutum*, human being). In addition to avoiding the sort of condescension many Hausas associated with Igbos, practicing *mutunci* also included respecting Islamic dietary restrictions and the prohibition of alcohol when in the presence of observant Muslims, and being discreet about non-Islamic religious beliefs or practices.

Arguably, so doing placed these Igbo Christians symbolically close to—though not legally within—the Islamic category of *dhimmi*, or non-Muslims, usually Christians or Jews, who enjoy a protected status as tax-paying residents in a Muslim society. Speaking Hausa was also an important way of conveying *mutunci*. Hausa culture values learning the language, even without complete mastery, as a gesture of good will by outsiders. Speaking Hausa also allowed Igbos to speak to Hausas without using English, the language that had been such an important marker of Igbo privilege in Nigeria's colonial social order. Conversational Hausa also requires speakers to use Arabic loan words and phrases with religious denotation, the most common of which praise Allah or acknowledge his power. Speaking Hausa, therefore, causes speakers to refer to themselves and others within the context of an Islamic cosmology. These criteria apply in the cases of the three men, related earlier, who received warnings in advance of the disturbances. All three said that they were warned because they maintained significant social contacts with Hausas, and in that regard all three were exceptional: One directly supervised his Northern colleagues; the second conducted business with prominent local figures; and the third had been employed for years in local government; and all spoke Hausa fluently.

Another informant, in her late twenties in 1966, was able to save her own life and those of family members through her mastery of the Hausa language. The woman, who worked as a clerk, had grown up in Sabon Gari Kano and spoke Hausa fluently. While women and children were by no means safe during the October riots, adult men were almost certain to be targets. Knowing this, the family gambled with the limited hiding space available to them, reasoning that she and the children had a chance to escape harm if no men were present.

> We were hiding in our house; my husband and my father were hiding on the rooftop. The indigenes kicked open the door and asked for my husband. I told them he and my father had been killed. I had five children then. The smallest was on my back. The other four were scattered all over. [The men] asked me if I was born in Kano because I spoke the language without accent. I told them I was. They asked me to stay with them so that no one would harm me. They said I was one of them. It was when I was led out that I saw the corpses of the dead and the agony of the wounded.[82]

Her father and husband remained hidden on the roof of the family house. She was later able to rejoin them, and the family was able to make it to the airport from which they flew to the East. The family's assumptions about the role of sex in targeting victims appear to have been dubious. While most of the bodies observers reported there were those of adult males, Kano's Igbo population had been disproportionately male even under normal circumstances, and had grown even more so during the months of uncertainty since the May riots.[83] Other accounts make it clear that any inference that women or children were safe from attack is erroneous. They were not safe, though adult men appear to have been the preferred targets.

In cases where Igbos lived among Hausas, community members could choose to shelter their Igbo neighbors. There were several dozen Igbo employees of Nigerian Railways, many with families, who lived in government housing just inside the Kofar Nassarawa gate to Kano's old city, not far from the railway yards. Hausas living in Nassarawa ward hid a number of Igbos for between three and five days before turning them over to the police, who evacuated them.[84] Similarly, Hausa workers at the Challawa water works southwest of Kano escorted Igbo co-workers to a nearby police office; they were then escorted to Sabon Gari to arrange for transport south.[85]

Other Igbos benefited from different types of protection. There were almost certainly Igbo women who were members of Hausa households who, along with their children, were protected by the secrecy the practice of wife seclusion afforded. In all likelihood, as members of Hausa Muslim households, they faced no threat.[86] Similarly, though so few in number that they arguably represent the most exceptional of cases, the handful of Igbo men known to be Muslims were not threatened. One example is that of Alhaji Sani, an Igbo convert who, by 1966, had lived for twenty years in Dala ward of the old city and was married to a Hausa woman. He had, by that point, assimilated to the point of becoming Hausa, and had fathered children who identified as Hausa. He remained during 1966 and the war years, despite widespread knowledge of his Igbo origins.[87] Some non-Muslim Igbos also earned the benefit of the doubt. Shortly after the war began, police arrested "19 known Ibos" living in Kano, then released them. "This is because they are all known Ibos of long association with Kanawa who have localised through intermarriages etc. and have settled with no ill feelings with the natives."[88] Several Igbo employees of local contractor Sharif Bappa lived in the old city during the disturbances and war. During October and the months that followed, his Igbo foreman moved about town only in his company, though by the end of the war he was openly supervising crews of Hausa workers.[89] Other exceptions include a handful of Igbos who worked as drivers, technicians or household servants for wealthy Lebanese families in Fagge. These men, by limiting their movements, were able to remain during the disturbances without disguising their identities. An example is John, an Igbo accountant who resided in the home of his Lebanese employer and remained throughout the war years.[90] And in Sokoto, "Dekke," an Igbo convert born in the south, and hired as a driver for the Sultan of Sokoto in 1908, remained. By 1966 he had become a trusted member of Sultan Abubakar's household, and, not surprisingly, remained during the disturbances and afterward.[91]

## TARGETING VICTIMS

Identifying Igbos was an often tenuous step in the process of purging them. Appearance, dress, location, and speech provided clues that mobs used in determining whom to attack. Each of these measures, however, was inexact, and could work to the distinct disadvantage of non-Igbo southerners and Middle Belters. In other cases, Igbos exploited Northerners' assumptions to their advantage. For the majority of Igbos who did not have benefactors to protect them, the ability to make themselves invisible by looking and sounding Hausa—or at least to not appear or sound Igbo—was a tool for survival. Long-distance drivers in Kano reported that almost all of the bodies they had seen had been in western dress.[92] Not surprisingly, shedding one's shirt and trousers for a Hausa-style garment was a common tactic. One *Bakane* related the case of an Igbo acquaintance whom he saw move to safety inside a Hausa mob. The man spoke Hausa fluently and had donned Hausa dress, and was able to escape undetected. A second Igbo acquaintance was confronted by a mob of Hausas searching for Igbos near Sabon Gari. He responded to them, also in locally accented Hausa, "Me kuke nema?" ("What are you looking for?") and was left alone.[93] Most migrants spoke some Hausa, but often did so with identifiable accents. Across Hausaland, mobs sometimes confronted suspected Igbos and required them to pronounce certain Hausa words they believed difficult for native speakers of Igbo.[94]

Even after the violence ended and the Igbo community had been expelled, Igbos who found themselves in the North often relied on similar abilities and tactics. For example, one Igbo recalled an acquaintance who had been incarcerated in Kano during the disturbances and disguised himself as a Northerner after his release during the war.[95] And, according to a December report from Haɗejia,

> Easterners, mostly Igbos who fled to the neighbouring countries, are being dressed in Northern dresses and returning to the Division. A general [search] had been conducted at District Level and about 16 such

had been found and joined six resident in Haďejia Emirate [who] are being sent to the Nigeria Police in Kano. Already 19 of them have been sent and three [who] delayed to pack their property will very soon follow.[96]

Disguises extended to body modification. Very few Igbos had distinctive facial markings, and some gave themselves the *mali* mark, a small scar, as part of their disguises.[97] And, as late as March, 1967, ten Easterners surrendered to police in the Northern city of Minna, including two who had lived there for twenty years and given themselves facial markings associated with the Nupe ethnic group. One of them had walked to the border of the Republic of Benin, where he had been refused entry, and returned to Minna. [98]

During the riots it was not necessary to actually be Igbo to be a target for violence; simply being perceived as Igbo was enough. Further, under riot conditions, decisions were often hasty at best, sometimes instantaneous—and frequently wrong. Those who had the greatest difficulty distinguishing themselves from Igbos were non-Igbo Easterners, Mid-Westerners, and some Christian Middle Belters. Members of these groups tended to reside in the same areas of Northern cities as Igbos, and tended toward Western dress. In the words of one Northerner who witnessed the disturbances, "Even though the main targets were Igbos, anyone wearing western dress would be considered Igbo."[99] During rioting in Bauchi, a Ministry of Information sound truck drove through parts of the city broadcasting a message not to attack Yorubas and other "non-Ibos."[100] Embedded in that message is a none-too-subtle acquiescence to the killing of Igbos. At the same time, however, the message illuminates how the process of determining who was and was not Igbo was remarkably subjective and imprecise. In the face of such danger, many non-Igbos responded to the danger by banding together. Members of the southern Cameroonian community in Kano gathered in the house of Rafael Nyamasi on Emir Road. Hausa hawkers and beggars remained outside and protected them by telling potential marauders that those inside were not Igbos. The owner of the house, Nyamasi, had been an important NCNC figure in the North, and had delayed his return from a trip to Cameroon because he believed himself a likely target for political violence.[101] And in Haďejia, about 200 Mid-Westerners gathered for protection in the home of one Mr. Okena. Many were destitute after being robbed during the disturbances.[102]

As violence against departing Igbos abated, and transportation became safer, many other southerners and Middle Belt Christians also left the North.[103] Yet, in the absence of Igbos, the southerners and Middle Belters who remained played increasingly important roles in the maintenance of commercial and administrative infrastructures. When a group of Yorubas traveled from Gombe to Bauchi aboard a train carrying Igbos, a mob stopped the train, bound and ordered the Yorubas sent back to Gombe, and allowed the Igbos to continue on their way south.[104] In Kano, Yorubas had been among the safest migrant groups during the worst of the rioting. In large part this was because most of the Yorubas in Kano were Muslims from the portion of Yorubaland in the Middle Belt. These Muslim Yoruba men and women tended to wear clothing distinctive from but similar to Hausa styles, and many had distinctly Yoruba facial markings; and, if necessary, they could show that they were Muslims by reciting the *shahada* or demonstrating other Islamic knowledge.

Still, fear persisted. In Kano, like other Northern cities, rumors circulated that Mid-Westerners and Yorubas would also be attacked.[105] Authorities speculated that many such rumors were driven by would-be looters with designs on the property that those who fled would leave behind. Police and other local authorities offered reassurances.[106] A delegation of Westerners and Mid-Westerners petitioned the Emir for an audience to discuss their well-being a week after the October disturbances ended. They offered to remain in Kano if they were assured that their "lives and property" were safe. In exchange, they offered their "Technical, Clerical and Professional assistance wherever and whenever needed."[107]

The need, in fact, was substantial in cities across the region. Zukerman reported that 95 percent of the managers and maintenance workers in the region's mining industry were Igbos. Their departure forced a temporary shut-down. Industrial operations suffered the dual blow of staff loss and the failure of infrastructure. The Electricity Corporation lost half of its staff in the North, and communications suffered after Posts and Telegraphs lost four workers in five; in Jos and Kaduna, expatriate women who answered an advertisement in the *New Nigerian* staffed postal and telephone operations.[108] Hotel services were severely affected, as was over-the-road transport.[109] Branches of the African Continental Bank were closed, and other banks were open only an hour per day and relied heavily on expatriate staff.[110] Operations at Kano International Airport were curtailed, including a complete suspension of night flights. Perhaps the most significant disruption was to rail transport, as 6,000 employees abandoned their posts, and essential rolling stock was stranded in the East.[111] In Kano, almost 90 percent of drivers, all the guards assigned to trains, and two thirds of their crews were absent. They were joined by two-thirds of managers, station crews, and maintenance staff. Rail operations in Kaduna, Zaria, Minna, and Nguru also suffered serious disruptions.[112] Igbos assigned to the North ignored threats from the federal government to dismiss any civil servants who did not return to their posts by 15 October.[113] Other services suffered as well. In addition to rapid training of re-placement staff, the government brought in expatriate workers, many from India, to help restore rail service.[114] The absence of Igbo traders was significant as well. Though Sabon Gari Market reopened by 25 October, it was at greatly reduced levels of activity.[115]

## DUAL ETHNICITY: TWO EXAMPLES

Even after the disturbances, Igbos who remained in the North were subject to forced relocation to the East by the army or the NPF. As tensions between the East and the Federal Government increased be-tween October 1966 and the following May, authorities across the country began to treat any Igbos in their midst as potential saboteurs or spies. According to the November 1966 security report, "The gov-ernment will have to be vigilant on the activities of the Igbos (and they are not few) who now parade Kano presenting themselves as Mid-Westerners."[116] By January, 1967 "many Eastern Ibo elements now dis-guising themselves as Mid-Westerners" were being "traced and repatriated" to the East.[117] Two months later NPF operatives were aware that an Igbo, G.C. Nzeribe, had "disguised himself and avoided all his usual contact" when the Cairo-to-Lagos flight he was on unex-pectedly set down in Kano. He, along with other passengers, spent the night in the Central Hotel before departing the next day, appar-ently unaware he was under surveillance.[118]

After Ojukwu declared Eastern Nigeria to be the independent Re-public of Biafra in May, 1967, the Civil War began in earnest, and with it, the stakes for Igbos in the North increased. A month after the war began another Igbo, E.C. Imoh, a Nigerian Airways steward, was arrested at Kano's airport on suspicion of being a Biafran courier to Britain. He was released on orders from Lagos.[119] Citizens in Kano harbored fears of "widespread Igbo infiltration" across Nigeria's bor-der with Cameroon.[120] A letter to the editors of the *New Nigerian* gave voice to Northerners' concern that the federal government remain vigi-lant for sabotage by Igbos. When S.D. Peter of the Middle Belt town of Wamba wrote that "I want the Federal Government not to take things for granted. Igbos are Igbos, no matter where and what they may be," he was in large measure repackaging ideas that had circulated through official channels.[121]

Those who remained in the North knew the danger to which they were exposed, and most kept their identities secret. While disguising themselves during the war, some Igbos presented themselves as Northerners in acts of unabashed deception. On the other hand, those born of unions across ethnic lines had options that others did not. The Reverend Victor Musa and Mrs. Maria Montgomery (nee Ojeh) were able to select the parts of their heritage that worked in their interests, and to distance themselves from the Igbo affiliation that marked them as potential enemies of the state. For Mrs. Montgomery, that meant downplaying the Igbo affiliation that had been her primary ethnic identity before the war in favor of her mother's Tiv heritage. For Reverend Musa, the situation was more complicated, and involved weaving together elements of his father's Igbo and his mother's Hausa identities into the appearance of being a Northern Christian from one of the many small ethnic groups in which Hausa was widely spoken.

Mrs. Montgomery was born Maria Ojeh in Makurdi, the daughter of a Tiv mother and an Igbo father. She grew up in Jos and Kaduna speaking Igbo, Tiv, Hausa, and English, then relocated to Lagos. There, in 1964, she married Robert Montgomery, an African American who had gone to Nigeria in 1960 as a ground station technician with the United States space program and chosen to remain. Despite both having links to Kano, they spent the early months of the war in Lagos. When Biafran forces invaded Mid-Western Nigeria in August, 1967, others' knowledge of her Igbo roots led her to cross into neighboring Benin Republic, where she remained for several months. During her absence, her husband arranged for her to stay with Nigerian friends in a rural area near Kaduna where there was a substantial indigenous non-Hausa Christian population. There she avoided mention of her Igbo heritage and lived as a Tiv. Her husband relocated to Kano in February, 1968 and she joined him. In Kano, fluent in Tiv and Hausa, and carrying her husband's name, her ethnicity was not an issue and she remained throughout the war without incident.[122]

Reverend Musa's father was the Igbo captain of Kano's Fire Brigade who took for himself the Hausa-sounding name of Momo Sokoto. His mother was a Hausa woman, who gave birth to him in Kano in 1940. He grew up speaking Hausa as his first language, but also learned Igbo and English. Through a prominent maternal uncle, Malam Ango, Kano's first local-born pharmacist and a successful businessman, Reverend Musa came to know some of Kano's economic elite.

The crisis of 1966 pulled at the family, however. His father left Kano and spent the war years in Lagos; Reverend Musa's three sisters were inside Biafra. While he could communicate with his father, neither was able to get word to or from the three women. At the time, Reverend Musa worked with American and Canadian missionaries of the Sudan Interior Mission (later the Evangelical Community of West Africa), who "were very sympathetic to my dual identity and encouraged me to stay." Others he allowed to assume he was a Northern Christian from one of many smaller ethnic groups in the area. Unlike Maria Montgomery, who was able to comfortably adopt a Tiv identity without arousing any suspicions or creating any visible contradictions, the axiomatic association of Hausa identity with Islam—and the socially tenuous position of the few Hausa Christians in the area—made it impossible for Reverend Musa to, as it were, vanish into his Hausa heritage. His close association with the church, and the assumptions others made about his ethnicity nonetheless helped him to escape the stigma associated with Igboness even in non-Hausa areas; he recalled that during the war one way to embarrass someone in the market, for example, was to call him or her "Igbo."

A more serious consideration was the threat of arrest by local authorities who sought out known Igbos or people with Igbo-sounding names. Police and soldiers manned checkpoints along roads and railroads near Kano and Kaduna searching for "saboteurs." Reverend Musa was himself arrested in early 1968 after disclosing his ethnicity while detained for a traffic violation. Nigerian colleagues in the mission were able to assist in his release. By mid-1968, with the area's Igbo population long inside Biafra or in hiding, and the number of checkpoints diminished, he felt safe enough to guard his Igbo heritage less vigilantly. In 1969 he was assigned to pastoral duties in Kano, where he took advantage of his ability to fit into different environments and exploited the city's cosmopolitanism. Linguistically and socially fluent in both migrant and Hausa sections of Kano, Reverend Musa dressed to match his environment, and was able to go about his business in Kano without incident.[123]

There is embedded in many of the stories of 1966 a cautionary note against allowing the pull of simple binaries (in this case between Igbo and non-Igbo) to obscure the grey zones that occur along ethnic frontiers. In some cases, like those of Mrs. Montgomery or Reverend Musa, the origins of the ambiguities are fairly straight forward. In others, like that of Veronica Uzokwe, the woman who was spared because her potential assailants recognized in her a distant kinship based on her fluency in Hausa, the grey appears less stable. Mrs. Uzokwe was, of course, equally fluent in Igbo, and it is easy to imagine that fluency working to her detriment under only *slightly* different circumstances. This is a particularly powerful possibility when one recalls that many non-Igbo southerners met their deaths because they were mistakenly assumed to be Igbo; meanwhile, Mrs. Uzokwe, an Igbo woman, was, in a manner of speaking, escorted out of danger under a flag of ethnic ambiguity. Similarly, other Igbos, many of them practicioners of *mutunci* to their Hausa hosts, were led or directed into the relative safety of the grey zone. Lonsdale's concept of moral ethnicity may offer a window on this phenomenon.[124] He argues that ethnicity "instructs by moral exclusion; what is 'not done' is separated from what is 'done', what is done by 'others' is not done by 'us.'"[125] If, then, ethnicity attaches moral value to cultural practice, perhaps, in a climate in which Igbos were explicitly defined as the oppositional "other," elements of Hausa cultural practice provided a passport out of the condemned space of Igbo identity.

## CONCLUSION

The manipulation of ethnicity to engender violence in the service of political goals reached new heights during September and October of 1966. As during the May and June riots, patterns of organization and incitement are clear. Also, as during earlier disturbances, the responses of authorities varied enormously, and revealed some of the awkward fragmentation within and between different levels of government as traditional rulers, displaced civilian politicians and party operatives, civil servants, and military authorities sorted out their common and competing interests. In the process, the tapestry of Northern unity that the Ironsi government had made possible began to unravel. With no plausible outside threat to necessitate the setting aside of competing subregional and local agendas, many of the fissures that had characterized the Northern Region of the First Republic re-emerged. At the same time, with Igbo influence in the federal government and the military effectively at an end, Igbos in Northern Nigeria—indeed, outside of Igboland—were vulnerable to an unprecedented degree. Where local and regional authorities were unwilling or unable to protect them, they were left to their own devices, with little expectation of recourse. And where authorities did intervene on behalf of Igbos, it was generally not to protect their positions in the North or their right to remain there, but most often to escort them out of the region.

In the climate created by the manipulation of ethnicity during the Ironsi period, orchestrating the expulsion of Igbos from the North was not difficult; the floating of false rumors describing aggression or planned aggression against Northerners was a powerful tool in moving Northern citizens to violence, and the promise of loot was an inducement for others to join in. To be Igbo was to be subject to violence and dispossession; in many cases, survival itself depended on an Igbo's ability to escape being categorized as an Igbo, or, in rare cases, to somehow destabilize the assumptions that accompanied the label. Once the North's Igbos were dislodged, their property and economic niches fell under the control of local elites, in effect completing the purge.

At the same time that Igbos in the North took great care to conceal their presence, officials in Kaduna and Lagos saw to it that Igbos remained visible in other ways. As relations between Ojukwu's government in the East and the rest of Nigeria deteriorated, propagandists in the North set about generating inflammatory representations of Igbos. This was an early volley in a propaganda war that was to continue, in different phases, until the shooting war ended in 1970.

## NOTES

1. In fact, the label has been applied in retrospect. See Oha-Na-Eze Ndi Igbo, *Violations of Human and Civil Rights*, 11 (Section 3.3).

2. Andrew Bell-Fialkoff, *Ethnic Cleansing* (New York: St. Martin's Griffin, 1999), 1.

3. "Tour of Northern Nigeria," Report of the UK High Commission, 14 October 1966, 1, reproduced in USNA POL 23-8/2529/A-203, 20 October 1966.

4. USNA POL 23-9/2530, 3 October 1966; USNA POL 23-9/2530, 8 October 1966; FN 101: Interview with Alhaji Liman Ciroma, 4 July 1998, Kaduna.

5. See Muffett, *Let Truth Be Told*, 114. He argues that the impetus for secession came from enlisted soldiers, traditional rulers, and civil servants. See also Balogun, *The Tragic Years*, 48; Nwankwo and Ifejika, *Biafra: The Making of a Nation*, 156–7; and Kukah, *Religion, Politics and Power in Northern Nigeria*, 40.

6. The January coup cost the far North its highest-ranking officers. Of the four top Northern officers killed, three had been Kanuris from the far North, and Muslims; this left Hassan Katsina as the senior far Northern officer. See Muffett, *Let Truth Be Told*, 157.

7. Nnoli, *Ethnic Politics in Nigeria*, 244. During the First Republic, Native Authorities in predominantly Tiv areas had, at the behest of the regional government and the NPC, cracked down on UMBC supporters opposed to the NPC and who sought a separate Middle Belt state. The so-called "Tiv riots" represented a major political setback for the NPC. See also B.J. Tyoden, *The Middle Belt in Nigerian Politics* (Jos: ASA Publishers, 1991), 49–50.

8. John N. Paden, *Ahmadu Bello, Sardauna of Sokoto: Values and Leadership in Nigeria* (Zaria: Hudahuda Publishers, 1986), 697.

9. On August 31, Decree 59 of 1966 restored Nigeria's federal structure.

10. The "repatriation" was incomplete. In practice, Northern troops remained in the West and Lagos.

11. Nnoli, *Ethnicity and Development in Nigeria*, 136.

12. HCB R.227, 70, 18 September 1966.

13. HCB R.56, Vol. III, 552–3, Intelligence Report, 28 September 1966.

14. HCB R.62/324, n.p., Intelligence Report, 1 October 1966.

15. HCB R.227, 79, 23 September 1966.

16. HCR R.227, 73, 26 September 1966.

17. HCB R.62/324, 324, Intelligence Report, 1 October 1966.

18. HCB R.56, Vol. III, 554–4, Intelligence Report, 28 September 1966. This anachronistic reference to "The Republic of Biafra" remains mysterious.

19. HCB R.62/324, n.p., Intelligence Report, 1 October 1966.

20. USNA POL 23-9/2530, 28 September 1966.

21. USNA POL 23-9/2530, 30 September 1966.

22. FN-Anonymous.

23. FN-Anonymous.

24. FN-Anonymous.

25. HCB K/SEC/39, 230/Intelligence Report, September 1966. In an interesting bit of presage, the report also noted that: "The rumour is that the Eastern Military Governor has fixed a date to declare the East seceding from the rest of the country."

26. USNA POL 23-9/2530, 29 September 1966.

27. USNA POL 23-9/2530, 28 September 1966.

28. USNA POL 23-9/2530, 29 September 1966.

29. USNA POL 23-9/2530, 25 September 1966.

30. USNA POL 23-9/2530, 30 September 1966, 4 October 1966.

31. "Tour of Northern Nigeria," Report of the UK High Commission, 2, 14 October 1966, reproduced in USNA POL 23-8/2529/A-203, 20 October 1966.

32. *New Nigerian*, 30 September 1966.

33. USNA POL 23-9/2530, 9 October 1966.

34. FN 17A: Interview with Alhaji Aminu Sharif Bappa, 1 October 1994, Kano; FN 98: Interview with Prof. D. Murray Last, 5 November 1995, Orlando, Florida.

35. U.S. consular records, citing anonymous sources, reported that the Northern Ministry of Information ordered the *New Nigerian* to carry the story. USNA POL 23-9/2530, 9 October 1966.

36. USNA POL 23-9/2530, 30 September 1966; USNA POL 23-9/2530, 29 September 1966.

37. USNA POL 23-9/2530, 29 September 1966 and 5 October 1966.

38. USNA POL 23-9/2530, 30 September 1966.

39. HCB R.227, 83, 8 October 1966.

40. FN 101: Interview with Alhaji Liman Ciroma, 4 July 1998, Kaduna.

41. USNA POL 23-9/2530/A-190, 13 October 1966.

42. USNA POL 23-9/2530, 9 October 1966.

43. USNA POL 23-9/2530, 3 October 1966. The source was Secretary to the Military Governor Liman Ciroma.

44. FN 101: Interview with Alhaji Liman Ciroma, 4 July 1998, Kaduna.

45. USNA POL 23-9/2530, 2 October 1966.

46. HCB R.56, Vol. III: n.p., Intelligence Report, 31 October 1966.

47. USNA POL 23-9/2530, 2 October 1966 and 3 October 1966.

48. HCB R.56, Vol. III, n.p., Intelligence Report, 31 October 1966.

49. Katsina, quoted in Usman and Kwanashie, eds., *Inside Nigerian History 1950–1970*, 119.

50. Secretary to the Military Government Liman Ciroma, quoted in USNA POL 23-9/2530, 3 October 1966.

51. USNA POL 23-9/2530, 2 October 1966.

52. *New Nigerian*, 6 October 1966.

53. "800 Now Await Transport Home," *New Nigerian*, 3 October, 1966.

54. FN 71: Interview with Mrs. Uzoma Ojuku, 7 September 1994, Kano.

55. Tellingly, Governor Katsina told diplomats that, because of the mutiny, the battalion would have to be broken up. USNA POL 23-9/2530, 9 October 1966.

56. FN 101: Interview with Alhaji Liman Ciroma, 4 July 1998, Kaduna. See also USNA POL 23-9/2530, 3 October 1966. There was a very limited Igbo presence in the unit. According to one source, only a dentist remained among its officers in October, though it is possible he was a non-Igbo Easterner or Mid-Westerner.

57. HCB R.227, 75 (30 September 1966) and 80 (5 October 1966).

58. According to the *New Nigerian* of 20 October 1966, officials in Jos supervised the departure to the East of 4,093 by road, 950 by air, and 930 by train.

59. "800 Now Await Transport Home," *New Nigerian*, 3 October 1966.

60. HCB R.227, 84, n.d., probably 9–11 October 1966.

61. Liman Ciroma, quoted in Usman and Kwanashie, *Inside Nigerian History*, 94.

62. HCB R.227, 76, 7 October 1966.

63. USNA POL 23-8/2530/A-203, 2, 20 October 1966.

64. Secretary to the Military Governor Liman Ciroma, cited in USNA POL 23-9/2530, 26 October 1966.

65. FN 82: Interview with *Wambai* Alhaji Abbas Sanusi, 1 September 1994, Kano.

66. FN 38: Interview with Alhaji Abdulrahman Howeidy, 18 April 1994, Kano.

67. USNA POL 23-9/2530, 2, 7 October 1966.

68. HCB K/SEC/39, 232, Intelligence Report, September-October 1966.

69. USNA POL 23-9/2530, 3, 4 October 1966.

70. USNA POL 23-9/2530, 5 October 1966.

71. USNA POL 23-9/2530, 5 October 1966.

72. USNA POL 23-9/2530, 12 October 1966.

73. HCB 115/R.527, 33.

74. USNA POL 23-9/2530, 14 October 1966.

75. USNA POL 23-9/2530, 14 October 1966. Aluko estimated that more than 1.6 million people moved between regions during the 12 months ending April 1967. S.A. Aluko, "The Problem of the Displaced Persons," in *Christian Concern in the Nigerian Civil War*, Christian Council of Nigeria (Ibadan: Daystar Press, 1969), 22. Originally published in *West Africa*, 15 April 1967, 495. See also Wayne Nafziger, *The Economics of Political Instability: The Biafran War* (Boulder: Westview Press, 1983), 101.

76. HCB R.227, 83, 8 October 1966.

77. Soon after the disturbances, the Eastern Regional government put the figure at 10,000; in 1969 Ojukwu placed the number at 50,000. Chukwuemeka Ojukwu, "The Ahiara Declaration," speech delivered at Ahiara, 1 June 1969. See Kirk-Greene, *Conflict and Crisis in Nigeria*, Vol. II, 376.

78. "Tour of Northern Nigeria," Report of the UK High Commission (14 October 1966): 1, reproduced in USNA POL 23-8/2529/A-203, 20 October 66.

79. HCB K/SEC/39, 231-2, Intelligence Report, September-October 1966.

80. Elegalam, *Causes and Consequences of Igbo Migration to Northern Nigeria, 1900–1966*, 183.

81. The story has an interesting postscript. Sixteen months later, after the outbreak of war, Yusuf received a letter of thanks from one of the women, named Beatrice, who was by then an officer in Biafran forces. The letter was delivered by a Hausa trader captured along with five others near the front. She had ordered the men released. FN 21: Interview with Malam Yusuf Umar Dala, 20 July 1994, Kano.

82. FN 94: Interview with Mrs. Veronica Uzokwe, 26 August 1994. (Translation by Chidozie Umeh.)

83. USNA POL 23-8/2529, 9 June 1966.

84. FN 2: Interview with Alhaji Dauda Adamu, 8 September 1994, Kano. The police housed them briefly at Gandun Sarki before their evacuation.

85. FN 81: Interview with Alhaji "Likita" Nahiru Ringim, Alhaji Garba Tsoho, Alhaji Suleman Musa Garko, Alhaji Bala Isiyaku, 5 June 1994, Challawa.

86. There are unsubstantiated estimates of about 100 women and children remaining inside houses in the old city throughout the war. FN 26: Interview with Police Inspector Rilwanu Dutse (rtd.), 9 August 1994, Kano; FN 59A: Interview with the Reverend Victor Musa, 14 April 1994, Kano.

87. FN 21: Interview with Malam Yusuf Umar Dala, 20 July 1994, Kano. For a discussion of this phenomenon, see Douglas Anthony, "'Islam Does Not Belong to Them': Ethnic and Religious Identities Among Male Igbo Converts in Hausaland," *Africa* 70, 3 (2000).

88. HCB R.56, Vol. III, 614, Intelligence Report, July 1967.

89. FN 17B: Interview with Alhaji Aminu Sharif Bappa, 10 July 1998, Kano. See Anthony, "'Islam Does Not Belong to Them,'" 431-2.

90. FN 50: Interview with Mr. Abdul R. Khatoun, 10 September 1994, Kano.

91. FN 99: Interview with Prof. Jean Boyd, 6 November 1995, Orlando, Florida.

92. USNA POL 23-8/2529, 9 June 1966.

93. FN 3B: Interview with Alhaji Uba Adamu, 17 November 1993, Kano. There is precedent for this tactic; for example, Elegalam reports that some Igbos were able to escape violence during the 1945 Jos riot by lying about their ethnicity. Elegalam, *Causes and Consequences*, 98.

94. Such words included "gero," "tsamiya," "gyaɗa," "gwiwa," "ƙarfi," and "ƙarfe." The words themselves appear of no particular significance beyond their difficulty of pronunciation for native speakers of Igbo. Gero = millet; tsamiya = tamarind tree, its fruit, or a variety of cloth; gyaɗa = peanut; gwiwa = knee; ƙarfi = strength; ƙarfe = metal.

95. FN 70A: Interview with Chief Davis Ohaeri, 19 March 1994, Kano.

96. HCB K/SEC/39, 236-7, Intelligence Report, November-December 1966.

97. FN 38: Interview with Alhaji Abdulrahman Howeidy, 18 April 1994, Kano.

98. "Easterners Come Out of Hiding," *New Nigerian*, 11 March 1967.

99. FN 3B: Interview with Alhaji Uba Adamu, 17 November 1993, Kano.

100. USNA POL 23-9/2530, 1 October 1966.

101. FN 66: Interview with Mr. Mambo Nyamasi, 27 February 1994, Kano.

102. HCB R.227: 90, 20 October 1966.

103. FN 3B: Interview with Alhaji Uba Adamu, 17 November 1993, Kano.

104. USNA POL 23-92530, 12 October 1966.

105. HCB R.227: 86, 14 October 1966.

106. HCB R.56, Vol. III, n.p., Intelligence Report, 31 October 1966; USNA POL-23-9/2530, 26 October 1966. One such rumor identified 29 October as a date by which all Yorubas should vacate Kano. The rumor set in motion an evacuation of women and children.

107. HCB K/SEC/147, letter, B.A. Omeshebi, Chief Obia Omago, Olajide Badamasi, and H.E. Okena to Emir of Kano via Waje District Head, 10 October 1966.

During the war, relations between *Kanawa* and Yorubas were often tenuous, especially as the number of southern Yorubas, mostly Christians, increased not only in absolute terms, but also relative to the number of Muslim Northern Yorubas. In December 1966, police made arrests for anti-Yoruba rumor mongering. (HCB R.56, Vol III, 574, Intelligence Report, December 1966). Fears that Ojukwu was building a southern alliance with Yoruba leaders in the West during the early months of 1967 led authorities in Kano to fear the "possibility of an open . . . hostility to all Westerners and possibly, all Yorubas, even before the East is attacked." (HCB SEC 39, 7, Intelligence Report, April 1967). Then, in October 1967, the rapid influx of southern Yorubas led authorities to observe that in addition to filling white collar jobs,

they have also taken most of trade and hotel business and this is highly resented by the natives. There is now a highly charged atmosphere between the two groups that can explode at any moment. Feelings are high and the only thing that prevents any incident at the moment is the war to crush the rebellion[;] as soon as that is over and if by then nothing is done to restore the normal relationship by the authorities, there is bound to be an incident of a serious nature. (HCB R.56, Vol. III, 624, Intelligence Report, October 1967)

108. "Tour of Northern Nigeria," Report of the UK High Commission, 14 October 1966, 3, reproduced in USNA POL 23-8/2529/A-203, 20 October 1966. See also 23-9/2530, 6 October 1966.

109. See M.E. Zukerman, "Nigerian Crisis: Economic Impact on the North," *Journal of Modern African Studies* 8, 1 (1970). A plan to transfer 500 Westerners to the North, announced in early December, was eventually scrapped. *New Nigerian*, 6 December 1966.

110. USNA POL 23-9/2530, 7 October 1966 and 5 October 1966.

111. Zukerman, "Nigerian Crisis," 46.

112. Ministry of Economic Planning, unpublished survey (Kaduna: mimeograph, 1966), cited in Elegalam, *Causes and Consequences*, 91.

113. Nwankwo and Ifejika, *Biafra*, 179.

114. FN 49: Interview with Alhaji Shehu Usman Kazaure, 4 September 1994, Kano.

115. This change is discussed at greater length in chapter five.

116. HCB K/SEC/38, n.p., Security Report, November 1966.

117. HCB K/SEC/38, n.p., Security Report, January 1967.

118. HCB R.56 Vol. III, 590, Intelligence Report, March 1967.

119. HCB R.56 Vol. III, 605, Intelligence Report, June 1967.

120. HCB R.62 Vol. III, 350, Intelligence Report, August 1967.

121. "How Sincere are the Igbos in our Midst," letter to the editor, *New Nigerian*, 27 September 1967.

122. FN 55C. Interview with Mr. Robert Montgomery and Mrs. Maria Ojeh Montgomery, 22 June 1994, Kano.

123. FN 59A and FN 59B: Interviews with the Reverend Victor Musa, 14 April and 26 April 1994, Kano.

124. John Lonsdale, "The Moral Economy of Mau-Mau: Wealth, Poverty and Civic Virtue in Kikuyu Political Thought," in Bruce Berman and John Lonsdale, *Unhappy Valley: Conflict in Kenya and Africa, Book Two: Violence and Ethnicity* (Athens: Ohio University Press), 328.

125. Lonsdale, "The Moral Economy of Mau-Mau," 328.

# 4

# FROM "SAVAGES" TO "BROTHERS": OFFICIAL REPRESENTATIONS OF THE IGBO, 1966–1970

## INTRODUCTION

The circulation of unsettling ethnic orthodoxies continued after the departure of Igbos from the North, but the years that followed also demonstrated the versatility of ethnicity as a political tool. This versatility is most visible in representations of Igbos that official and quasi-official publications proffered, representations that went through a series of changes between 1966 and 1970.[1] During those years, the federal government worked to transform Northern propagandists' ethnic poison into medicine as part of its attempts to close some of the country's most gaping wounds. In pre-war and wartime publications and broadcasts, the characteristics that policy makers and propagandists assigned to Igbos remained remarkably stable, but the value that they attached to those characteristics underwent a nearly complete reversal. That Igbos were industrious and commercially adept, for example, was never questioned, but whether those characteristics were things other Nigerians should fear or welcome hinged directly on the political and economic context in which they operated, and that context was in flux. As public discourse on the place of the Igbo in Nigeria shifted its focus from Northern cities to the frontier between Nigeria and the Republic of Biafra, opinions from the North gave way to federal views. In the process, federal thinkers took elements of a discourse designed to incite and justify violence by amalgamating and

villifying Igbos and used them to challenge Igbos' faith in their leaders, and to begin rehabilitating the image of the group.

## MANAGING STEREOTYPES: NORTHERN AND FEDERAL AGENDAS

This manipulation of stereotypes to serve competing visions was
nothing new; as an observer wrote in 1961, "Sometimes the Ibo, like
the Jews, are called bloodcurdling grabbers; sometimes they are referred to as adventurous and hard-working . . . "[2] In the context of
open hostilities in which ideas surrounding ethnicity were important
sources of political and emotional capital, however, managing them
carefully was a necessity. The changes in representations of Igbos
corresponded directly to shifts in the stance Nigerian authorities assumed toward Igbos and their leadership in the Eastern Region (then,
after May 1967, the Republic of Biafra, and, as Biafra gradually fell
to Nigerian forces, the East Central State). In the months between the
exodus of October 1966 and the first shots of the Civil War the following July, the pamphlets that circulated in Kano and other Northern
cities were produced in Kaduna. Their representations of Igbos were
both sweeping and unabashedly hostile. The watershed in official pam-
phleteering came with the break up of the Northern Region in April
1968, when the four regions were divided into twelve states. From
that point on, the federal government became the dominant official
voice and the military governments of the new states followed its lead.
Federal propaganda was both less universalistic in its treatment of
Igbos and more conciliatory than the Northern pamphlets had been.
The speed with which representations of Igbos changed demonstrates
the ease with which political forces were able to appropriate, manipulate, and apply widely known and surprisingly uncontested stereotypes.
Once appropriated and packaged in official and semi-official publications, the stereotypes themselves became tools for mobilizing public
support within Nigeria for political change, for war, and ultimately
for post-war rapprochement.

The contrasts between the regional and federal propaganda are clearest
in their respective manipulation of stereotypes. The propaganda produced
in the North sought to justify the anti-Igbo violence that had taken place
in the North by mobilizing preexisting stereotypes to vilify a highly
essentialized "Igbo character." This Northern rhetoric branded Igbos as
arrogant, clannish, and materialistic. It also cast in universalistic and negative terms the high levels of formal education and business acumen it
ascribed to Igbos. Most importantly, it portrayed Igbos as unquestion-

ingly deferential to the banned Ibo State Union and NCNC, organizations the propaganda represented as having unswervingly advanced a monolithic Igbo cause. Thus characterized, Igbos and their institutions bore the blame for a host of Nigeria's political and social problems. Northern rhetoric contributed to the willingness of Northerners and other Nigerians to take up arms when the Eastern Region declared itself the independent Republic of Biafra in May 1967. Once the war began, however, the propaganda of the Gowon government used stereotypes as a wedge between Biafran leaders and citizens, both Igbo and non-Igbo. By 1968, federal rhetoric sought to disaggregate Igbos by focusing negative stereotypes on Biafra's leaders, especially Ojukwu, and encouraging ordinary Igbos to dissociate themselves from those leaders.[3] As the war progressed, large parts of Biafran territory fell into Nigerian hands and the number of Igbos openly advocating the federal position grew. With an Igbo appointed as the civilian administrator for "liberated" Igboland in Enugu, it no longer worked to treat the group monolithically. And, as the government began to anticipate an end to the fighting, federal rhetoric increasingly espoused brotherhood of those within Biafra with "other Nigerians." By the time that the collapse of Biafra appeared inevitable, the difference between "loyal" and "rebel" Igbos lost its meaning and all Igbos could once again be placed in the same basket. Stereotypes reappeared, and were again assigned in a universalistic manner, though this time it was the federal government applying them, and using them to extol rather than to assail. In a political climate focused more on reestablishing order than waging war, Igbos who had previously been branded as "clannish" and "greedy" became "self-reliant." New federal rhetoric touted Igbos' commercial drive and western education as national assets rather than threats to the economic and political well-being of other Nigerians. Most importantly, in the poverty and confusion that characterized so much of Igbo experience in the months and years after the war, pre-war perceptions of Igbos as being well-organized in order to dominate the country's government and economy lost their currency. And, under economic and political conditions that reinforced modest behavior among most Igbos, the pre-war "arrogance" protested by official rhetoric—and public demonstrations—had been transformed to a humility upon which other Nigerians looked with satisfaction.

## NORTHERN ANTI-IGBO PROPAGANDA

The line between official and quasi-official propaganda in the North is difficult to determine. In at least one case, government resources were used to produce a document under a collective pseudonym. Nonetheless, though inflammatory, the positions the document staked out were not remarkably different from later documents with official authorship. What is perhaps most striking about all of the Northern documents is that fact that they openly contradict the actions of so many civil servants who worked to minimize the loss of life in the North during the region's anti-Igbo disturbances. This tension is, no doubt, an indication of fissures within the apparatus of state in the North, and also reflects the degree to which the gulf between feelings and actions reached the level of the individual. The hard line that Northern propaganda took is also a reminder that, with the Igbo population largely out of the region, and with fingers in the East pointing North, assigning blame for the crises of 1966 was a major strategic undertaking. With the break up of Nigeria and war with the East looming, Northern leaders took steps to articulate and defend their positions to an audience of southern Nigerians and foreigners. At the same time, they manipulated anti-Igbo sentiment to begin preparing ordinary Northerners, should the worst come to pass, to fight a war.

The first such document does all of these things. Late in 1966, after the October disturbances, a group calling itself the Current Issues Society published *The Nigerian Situation: Facts and Background*.[4] The Society published the pamphlet through the Gaskiya Corporation, which was owned and operated by the regional government and which published, among other things, *The New Nigerian* and *Gaskiya Ta Fi Kwabo,* the North's main newspapers.[5] The military government was not openly involved in the pamphlet's production; rather, the Current Issues Society included members of the former civilian government and the regional civil service. In any case, the authors appropriated for the text an official-sounding tone, as they spoke for "the North."

> Large quantities of literature have been churned out in recent months on the situation in Nigeria. Northern Nigeria makes no apologies for adding this little booklet to the interesting collection.
>
> In its traditional way, the North has refrained from the precipitate action of rushing to print with trumped-up charges and unsupported facts. The North has waited until the troubled dust has settled down somewhat to present this calm and reasoned assessment of the whole situation.
>
> This little pamphlet is not a collection of charges and counter-allegations against the Ibos. It would be a waste of time and effort if it were so. It is in fact a dispassionate and forthright account of how the Igbos, through their devilish determination to dominate or break up Nigeria, plunged the country into the present crisis.[6]

Police recorded that readers in the North received the pamphlet enthusi-astically.[7] Most of the pamphlet was a litany of exaggerated anti-Igbo grievances, and its language was not subtle. It was openly ethnic in its focus on Igbos; throughout, its authors emphasized that they were not speaking of Easterners in general, but rather of Igbos in particular. This was consistent with a nascent strategy of undermining the Ojukwu government's influence among the non-Igbo minority in the East. The pamphlet appealed to non-Igbos who had suffered during the anti-Igbo disturbances. It told them that they had not been the intended targets of violence, and asserted that the riots had been the fruit of Igbo provoca-tions.[8] The authors took care to distinguish Igbos from other Easterners in language solicitous to the latter, and in so doing, dusted off the myth of large-scale attacks on Northerners in Igboland. "It must be pointed out that non-Igbos in the East deprecated the attack on Northerners and did all they could to save their lives and property," the authors wrote.[9]

The authors' second tact was to play on longstanding internal tensions in the East, which they accomplished by writing not of the Eastern Re-gion or its government, but rather the "Ibo East."[10] The clear implication was that the welfare of non-Igbos Easterners was separate from that of Igbos, in whose interests Ojukwu's government was acting. *The Nigerian Situation* built on that line of reasoning by emphasizing the ethnic chau-vinism of the Ibo State Union, and of Igbos in general. According to its authors,

> For their part, the Ibo lived like an island in the sea of others[,] not allowing themselves to be influenced by the cultures of those around them and lived a life directed by the caucus of the Ibo State Union. Their materialistic outlook beclouded their vision and motivated them into actions that are anathema to a cultured society. In the North they refused to identify themselves with members of the society in which they lived. A [study] carried out last year in the North showed that less than two percent of Ibos that had lived in the North for twenty years and over could tell how a Hausa marriage or Igala naming ceremony was conducted.[11]

Further,

> It might be asked, did Ibos ask for Northern participation in their busi-ness? The answer would be an unequivocal no. There never was any genuine attempt either in good faith or arising from guilty conscience to invite Northerners to join hands in their closed shop business. It was all Ibo business.

Although the North was their biggest market, there is no evidence
of participation or contribution to the progress of the North at [the]
local level.[12]

On the other hand, "Within the last few years, Ibos have imported a new
role into the orderly life of the North. They brought in the gun, robbery
with violence and thuggery to achieve political ends."[13]

At the same time that they treated Igbos monolithically, the authors
reinforced a bifurcated view by downplaying ethnic, religious, or political distinctions among Northerners. In the document, Northerners existed
primarily in contradistinction to Igbos, and the priorities of each group
appeared to be governed largely by its respective "nature." For the authors, three factors had determined "the role played by Ibos in Northern
Nigeria. These factors are the nature of the Northerner, the nature of the
Ibo and the historical developments in Nigeria[,] especially in the field
of Western Education."[14] These factors then combined in ways inimical
to Northern interests. During the period of decolonization and the First
Republic, Northerners

started to acquire sufficient qualifications to enable them [to] seek
employment in Government and other services; they obviously expected
the Ibo, who was already in the field, to receive them with pleasure as
fellow Nigerians. But the Northerners were wrong; the Ibo worker did
not want him in the service because he wanted his tribesmen alone to
monopolize the service perpetually. As a result, whenever a Northerner
applied for a job he would receive a letter of regret from the Ibo Chief
Clerk; but a few days later an Ibo man from the East, who might not
be better qualified than the Northerner, would be seen doing the same
job.[15]

This was because

The control of the public services is an essential cog in the wheel of
their plan to dominate the country and therefore all means including a
faked army coup must be employed to maintain their control of the
services.
    They put forward the bogey that they were regarded as second class
citizens and that the North wanted to dominate. In the meantime, they
continued to carry out their plan, master minded by the Ibo State Union
Caucus.[16]

The next year, after the Gowon government decreed the creation of
twelve states, but before the plan's implementation, the Northern govern-

ment published *The Creation of States*, in part to win over those elites vested in the regional system and resistant to the new administrative model. This time, the government took credit for the publication. While it contained few direct attacks on Igbos, central to its message was the articulation of a fundamentally "Northern Character," which its authors created in direct opposition to ideas about the Igbo already in circulation. For example,

> Like any people tutored by long experience and tempered by history, Northern Nigerians naturally would much rather stick to a system of life with which they are familiar than rush into the hasty acceptance of unfamiliar and untested innovations. For this they are branded as con- servative by their detractors, whereas the simple fact is that they are only cautious. Change for the mere sake of change has never been their philosophy nor anybody else's, but change which after full and careful consideration is found to be necessary and for the overall good, they have never been opposed to.[17]

Reflecting the dominance of Ahmadu Bello and the NPC in forging the idea of "the North," the "Northern Character" the pamphlet's au- thors described was, in large part if not in entirety, a reflection of what were conventionally viewed as far Northern Muslim values. Ac- cording to its authors, the "'Northerner' is not opposed to change as such; [but] he will not be bullied, threatened or harried; he likes to take his time to make up his own mind, but once he has made up his mind, he is absolutely reliable. He is used to constituted authority, but not to dictatorship and he is not afraid to say so."[18] Again conjur- ing stereotypes of the Igbo as contemptuous of Northerners, the au- thors wrote:

> Recent experience has exploded the myth that the "Northerner" is doc- ile, uncomplaining and undemonstrative. His reflective attitude has been mistaken for dumb docility, and although he is reserved and deliberate in his ways, and is not deeply concerned about trivialities, he does care, and profoundly too, about the issues that concern his fundamental rights and freedom. And any attempt to tamper with these unduly is enough to bring out the demonstrative side of the people of the "North." If the "North" resents any measure, the "North" can be relied upon to say so.[19]

Another pamphlet published by the government of the North, *Nige- ria: Realities of Our Times*, advanced a similar line of argumentation, but was more direct in its attacks on Igbos. It was published in Kaduna shortly after Biafra's secession, and unlike *The Nigerian Situation*, the North's Ministry of Information claimed authorship. By the time it was published, Enugu's propaganda mill had begun its own impassioned campaign to explain and justify secession, which it did by impugning the North for the slaughter of Igbos and other Easterners, to whom it appealed directly.[20] Taking up the challenge that Enugu's propaganda posed, the Northern authors of *Realities* identified their pamphlet as "a contribution by Northern Nigeria to the deluge of publications—true or false, well or ill-intentioned—covering the Nigerian crisis."[21] In presenting their version of the January 1966 coup and the Ironsi months, the authors of *Realities* used provocative language and harsh generalizations to vilify Igbos as a group. The characterizations of Igbos as domineering and uncivilized were familiar ones: "All the strife can be related to the intolerable behavior of Igbos who suddenly saw their long-awaited chance to grab and grab—their perpetual weakness."[22] More importantly, however, their very humanity came into question. The authors described the deaths of prominent Northerners in the January coup as

the sort of thing which could only be perpetrated by people who are, from first to last, savages. People who have no sense of decency, and who do not even know how to respect the dead. A dead Balewa lying peacefully and respectfully covered was no more alive than a dead Balewa reclining against a kolanut tree. A [Lieutenant Colonel Adogo Largema] dead and lying in Ikoyi Hotel was as unlikely to command the 4th Battalion as the dead Adogo dragged down five flights of stairs with his blood splattering the whole building. But the Igbos cannot be expected to know that.

Even in victory the Ibos were most mean. They allowed the Sardauna's body to lie exposed and [have] its photograph taken. They flew air force planes threatening people at his funeral. They denied officials in Kaduna vehicles to take his bereaved family back to Sokoto.[23]

The descriptions of the treatment of dead bodies appear keyed to be particularly repugnant to Islamic sensibilities. Sticking to the notion that Igbos operated as part of a monolithic whole, the pamphlet linked the behavior of Igbo soldiers with the Igbo political elite by asserting a broad Igbo conspiracy to dominate the country. Further, according to the pamphlet's largely unfounded account, after the coup, Igbo soldiers in Kaduna terrorized civilians, looted the property of government ministers, manhandled officials, and raped women, "while intoxicated Ibo civilians lined the streets and cheered them." Thereafter, "All over Nigeria the Igbos became unbearable—their traders, clerks, soldiers and even University students and lecturers, the last who were supposed to have the benefit of education—behaved in the same euphoric way."[24] This "congenital rudeness was unbearable, but they were too pleased with events to realise what fire they were playing with." Other sections of the pamphlet also took aim at Igbo intellectuals, who were "brandishing intellectualism" but not "thinking properly."[25]

*Realities* invoked the tensions surrounding the reversal of Northernization policies when it described a confrontation between an aggressive young Igbo job-seeker and a meek Northern bureaucrat. The seeker asked why his application for employment had been delayed.

> As no civilised man would do, he started to shout; the Permanent Secretary peeped out from an upstairs office to see what was happening, only to have the savage harangue at him that he should come down and show his certificate and explain how he got his job. This was just one incident out of a million such. Public Service application forms in Kaduna were exhausted by Ibo applicants, many of them from the University of Nsukka. The tone was "the Sardauna is dead; Northernisation Policy with him; Nigeria is one and the North is ours."[26]

That the confrontation was represented as having taken place in Kaduna, the Northern capital, served to make the young Igbo appear even more uncouth. And, the authors implied, the young man was not alone. "Every train brought loads and loads of Ibo job seekers who barged into government offices harassing young lady executives, throwing their certificates at everyone's face and demanding jobs."[27] Even setting aside questions of the veracity of its claims, nowhere in the document was there any attempt to differentiate between Igbos who had committed offensive acts and those who had not. "Most people in the South, especially Igbos, regard anyone from the North with absolute contempt. These feelings come out most clearly in a quarrel between two people. To Southerners, especially Igbos, the Northerner is incapable of achieving anything, especially in education."[28] The reference to the "young lady executives" is also significant. While there were no references whatsoever to Igbo women, all of the authors' references to non-Igbo women were as victims of aggression or violence by Igbo men. The wives of Ahmadu Bello and Brigadier Samuel Ademulegun are listed among the casualties of the

January coup, though not by name, and the "solicitous" wife of slain Colonel Yakubu Pam is described as having been betrayed by Igbo soldiers whom she knew personally.[29] Finally, the authors reserved their worst treatment for Ironsi. His plan to deploy military officers to each of Nigeria's provincial governments was, they argued, the final step in the master plan for national domination. According to the pamphlet, those officers would all be Igbos, and after the posting of "Ibo Military prefects" to each province of the North, "the Ibo conquest would be complete. For the remaining Northerners then it would be George Orwell's 1984!"[30]

The language Northern propaganda writers used was not new; in fact, it was well worn, rooted in generations of discourse. Beyond the political rhetoric of the First Republic, there were also older reservoirs of provocative generalizations to tap. One such source was the discourse surrounding the decision by voters in the southern half of British Cameroon to sever the region's administrative ties with Nigeria in 1961. Anti-Igbo sentiment had been critical in the campaign to join French Cameroun.[31] Southern Cameroonians who supported unification with French Cameroun presented as the alternative "Making yourselves and your children slaves of the Ibo now and forever and ever." They suggested that remaining affiliated with Nigeria "meant calling two million Igbos to the Cameroons."[32] And during the October 1966 crisis, the *New Nigerian* printed a number of letters to the editor critical of Igbos. One in particular, attributed to a non-Igbo Easterner, resonated with Northern discourses. Its author sought to distinguish non-Igbo Easterners from Igbos by describing the latter.

> These type of people migrate like the winter birds, looking for where to build their nests. Once upon a time, the East was transformed into their empire. Now all key posts in the government establishments, firms and industries, local and municipal councils, and schools are held by them to the detriment of the aborigines.
>
> These sects claim superiority over others, tribal origins notwithstanding. They dominate constituencies not theirs and use government machinery to suppress the people, acquiring land by force—all in the name of 'one Nigeria.'[33]

Similarly, many of the ideas about Igbos that Northern authors chose to exploit had colonial antecedents, reminiscent of what Malkki has called "a chilling traffic back and forth between the essentialist constructions of historians, anthropologists, and colonial administrators" as well as partisans. When this happens, "'Types' and 'traits' incautiously and sometimes fancifully ascribed by social scientists and bureaucrats have often taken on a terrible social reality as the reification and essentialization of cultural difference have been harnessed to deadly political vision."[34] In 1960, Margery Perham described calls by Igbos for national unity as a "very natural and very pregnant demand as they thrust their way all over Nigeria."[35] The description of Igbo job seekers in the *Nigerian Situation* and *Realities* echoed a well-circulated colonial report. In describing internal tensions in the East, the 1958 document reported that "It was suggested that it was the deliberate object of the Ibo majority in the Region to fill every post with Igbos."[36] And a widely read 1949 anthropological text was among the first of many to announce the "extreme aggressiveness" of the Igbo.[37] The images of Igbos as "savage" or "uncivilized" have colonial forebearers as well. In 1919, Lugard himself wrote that at the time of the British conquest, "The South was, for the most part, held in thrall by Fetish worship and the hideous ordeals of witchcraft, human sacrifice, and twin murder. The great Ibo race to the East of the Niger, numbering some 3 millions, and their cognate tribes had not developed beyond the stage of primitive savagery."[38] And two years later Basden described "savage customs."[39]

Despite the deep roots of such images, the demands of statecraft pushed federal writers in a sharply different direction than the one Northern writers had taken. The onset of open hostilities between Biafra and Nigeria in July 1967 signaled an end to Northern propaganda that vilified the Igbo and focused on the threat of Igbo domination.[40] Federal representations of Igbos would resonate with many Northern claims, but, on the whole, were more nuanced and less damning.

## FEDERAL PROPAGANDA, 1968–1969

By 1968, the Northern Region had ceased to exist and the federal government had become the primary distributor of official propaganda. Federal pamphlets circulated throughout Nigeria, among members of the international press and the diplomatic corps, and into Igbo hands through authorities in Enugu and Nigerian soldiers in the war zone. The literature produced in the North had helped to polarize Nigerians; in the far North and Middle Belt, men had flocked to local government offices to volunteer for military service. Now a goal of federal pamphleteers was to generate and exploit distrust between ordinary

Igbos and Biafra's secessionist leadership. A secondary goal was to begin to prepare Nigerians for Biafrans' return to the Nigerian fold.

A key step in accomplishing each was to shift the focus of hostility from ordinary Igbos to Ojukwu. In *Nigeria 12-State Structure: The Only Way Out*, some mention of a larger Igbo conspiracy to dominate the country remained, but the person of Ojukwu fully occupied center stage. No longer were Igbos the enemy; it was now "Ojukwu and his rebel gang."[41] Ojukwu appeared as petulant, obstinate, and fatally flawed by ambition. The authors described Ojukwu as having "preached defiance" to the legitimate authority of Gowon's government. They also attributed the failure of negotiations between Lagos and Enugu to "illegal actions and defiance of Federal Government authority" by Ojukwu.[42] The earlier preoccupation with Igbo aspirations for national domination was this time directed solely at him. Ojukwu was "spurred on in his ambition to rule an empire." Similarly, the authors emphasized his power and, by extension, his culpability, in this case in the context of abortive peace talks in Addis Ababa ("Mr. Ojukwu, the only person who can make decisions for the rebel regime . . . ").[43] Other Igbos, on the other hand, were welcome to rejoin Nigeria, with the federal government as the guarantor of their safety. In the March, 1968 radio broadcast on which the pamphlet text was based, Gowon reflected this staple of wartime rhetoric when he said that "Other Nigerians are ready to welcome back Igbos into their midst and to assure them of their personal safety. The government, for its part, is determined to do all in its power to ensure that no Ibo man is molested or intimidated anywhere in this country. We will direct our attention to the physical safety of every Nigerian no matter his state of origin."[44] In contrast, Ojukwu and other Biafran leaders were responsible for "the tragedy to which they have plunged the nation as a whole and in particular, the Ibos, whom they claim to serve."[45] Further emphasizing that not all Igbos were enemies of Nigeria, in another broadcast Gowon made a point of naming nineteen prominent Igbos—none of them military officers—whom his government would find acceptable as negotiators to end the war.[46]

The next step in the government's revision was to begin radically redrawing the portrait of Igbo economic, social, and political influence that had appeared in Northern propaganda. The pamphlet *Igbos in a United Nigeria*, also published in 1968, grew out of federal position papers presented in Addis Ababa. While it continued the rhetorical assault on Ojukwu, it took the important step of drawing a line between being Igbo and being an enemy of Nigeria. The war "has not been directed against the Igbos as a people but against an unpatriotic and rebellious clique," its authors claimed. The pamphlet's most ambitious shift was in taking Igbo involvement in public services, a lightning rod in pre-war discourse, and recasting it as an instrument for reintegrating Igbos into the fabric of Nigeria's national life. "The future of the Igbos as a people is clear. They will live with their compatriots again in the peace and prosperity which served Nigeria so well for over half a century—the peace and prosperity in which Igbos, themselves, thrived magnificently in leading positions in business, education, the professions and the public services."[47] The government also laid out its most detailed plan to date for the rehabilitation of war-affected areas and their populations. Key was the goodwill of Nigerians toward those in Biafra. The government would ensure that "nothing prevents the re-integration of the Ibo people into the Nigerian community in a wholesome manner, totally devoid of bitterness and rancour."[48] Another pamphlet, *Nigeria Answers Questions* categorically stated that "The Federal Military Government does not want a total victory or to humiliate the Ibos as a group," and promised the Igbo "the fullest scope to resume his trade and business."[49] And, as part of the effort to set a conciliatory tone toward ordinary Igbos, Gowon himself told an audience of students at Ahmadu Bello University that

> the ordinary Ibo man will have no guilty conscience after this war, because he was not responsible in any way for the one-sided coup of January 15 and its tragic aftermath. The ordinary Ibo man was not responsible for planning secession and its equally tragic aftermath. Secession and rebellion were planned and executed by the elite comprising the ex-politicians, university intellectuals, senior civil servants and, I regret to say, military officers.[50]

Gowon's explicit absolution of ordinary Igbos for the coup in particular stands in stark contrast to the blanket accusations made by Northern authors in 1966 and 1967.

Another 1968 publication took an even more critical stance on the events of 1966 when it revisited the "master plan" for national domination by Igbos that Northern propaganda alleged. Rather than reify the supposed plan as the Northern literature did, *The Collapse of a Rebellion and the Prospects of Lasting Peace* focused instead on fears among Northerners. According to the pamphlet, anti-Igbo violence had been the product of fear of "closely knit, single-minded organizations," suggesting the Ibo State Union and the NCNC. Also to blame was "the failure of the Ironsi regime to remove the impression that the one-sided coup of 15th January [was] part of the Ibo Master Plan to dominate the country."[51] In allowing that Ironsi's failure had been in not dispelling those beliefs, the government took a small step away from claiming that his actions had been part of a master plan in which all Igbos were implicated.

*Collapse of a Rebellion* also advanced the government's vision of Igbo reintegration. It pointed to the state governments' roles in preparing for "the re-integration of the Igbos into economic life in areas which they deserted as a result of the tragedies of 1966."[52] Another pamphlet, *Igbos in a United Nigeria*, also foregrounded the management of Igbo-owned property in the North.

> One fear which the Igbos may have about their future in the Nigerian Federation is the recovery of abandoned property. In their hurried return to the former Eastern Nigeria at Ojukwu's behest, many of them left behind real and landed property in other parts of the country.
>
> This fear has no basis, because the Federal and State Governments have made provisions for the maintenance and preservation of these properties until the return of their owners.[53]

Kano and Benue-Plateau States, the pamphlet assured readers, had set up caretaker committees. Through the actions of these committees with regard to abandoned properties, the government promised, "it will be a pleasant surprise to the owners that on their return substantial sums of money will be paid to them."[54] Abandoned property remained a major plank in the federal government's case that Igbos were welcome to return to the North, and officials carried that message to local audiences. As it became clear that the war was nearing its close, Malam Aminu Kano, former NEPU leader, took up the matter of Igbos and land. Malam Aminu, then a federal minister, addressed students at Abdullahi Bayero College in Kano in January 1969 on "the problem of reintegration of the Igbos." He told them that

> They left a large part of this country, and a lot of what they left has been taken over by the indigenes of the place. What are they to do? This is important since we are fighting them to stay in Nigeria. We are saying "You can't go away. You must remain Nigerian." When they come back, can you deny them the right to own plots or land? You can't do that.[55]

The Military Governor of Kano State, Police Commissioner Audu Bako made a similar point when he told the people of Kano that "my government will encourage all Nigerians to live wherever they want."[56] This was a direct reference to changes from the pre-war policies, inherited from the colonial period, that restricted land ownership. More important, it was a clear message that his government supported the return of Igbos to Kano once the war ended.

## FEDERAL MESSAGE WITH AN IGBO VOICE: UKPABI ASIKA

Perhaps the most important articulator of federal positions was the federal government's top civilian in Nigerian-held Igboland, Dr. Ukpabi Asika. The creation of states led to the separation of the Igbo-speaking areas of the former Eastern Region from non-Igbo speaking areas. Igbo-speaking areas were largely contained in the East Central State, while minority areas of the region became Rivers State and South East State. When Enugu fell to federal troops in September 1967, the Gowon government appointed Asika, an Igbo, as administrator of the East Central State (ECS). With the overwhelming majority of surviving Igbo officers fighting for Biafra, the appointment of an Igbo military governor to the ECS was hardly realistic, and the appointment of a non-Igbo military governor would have compounded the perception that federally held areas were occupied by a hostile force. The appointment of an Igbo would, in theory, undermine the persistent Biafran belief that the war was one of genocide, and the appointment of a civilian would suggest the reconciliation, rehabilitation, and reconstruction that would become the pillars of federal rhetoric. A lecturer in political science at the University of Ibadan, Asika had been born in Jos, had worked as a clerk for the Northern Regional government in Kano, and had remained on the federal side when war broke out. He is widely credited with coining the phrase "No Victor, No Vanquished," which became the unofficial slogan of federal wartime propaganda. It appears that little of what Asika said and wrote was directed at a Northern audience, though his words did circulate there. In part, he spoke to an international audience, but for the most part, his message was aimed at Igbos in federally held territory or inside Biafra, audiences with whom he had a modest popularity, at best.[57] In part, this was because he lacked public stature prior to the war, and in part because throughout the war most Igbos in Biafra persisted in believing that the federal government's goal was to continue the extermination of Igbos that they believed had begun in the North. Further, at least some Igbos had the perception that Asika had filled positions in Enugu and elsewhere in the state disproportionately with Igbos from his home town of Onitsha. Still, as the top

Nigerian official in Enugu, Asika controlled great resources in the midst of even greater need.

Asika's rhetoric echoed the points of contemporary federal propaganda, in particular the willingness of the North to welcome back Igbos, and the efforts made to protect abandoned property. In one of his early addresses, he told of his visits to sites of anti-Igbo violence. Just over a year after the Kano massacre, Asika described an official trip there.

> In Kano I was received by the Emir of Kano. And he said, among other things, that he was anxious, personally anxious, to have his friends, his brothers and his people who had lived for so many years in Kano, whose homes were in Kano, return to Kano, and that he was equally anxious that those former sons of Kano who had been living in the Eastern States, and who had been forced to leave the Eastern States during the period of the upheavals be free to return to their homes.[58]

And, less than two weeks later he told an audience

> In the Northern States I visited Kaduna, Kano, Zaria, Jos, Makurdi and Gboko. In these places, I was given a very warm welcome, a very spontaneous welcome. I wish, very, very much, my brothers, my sisters, that you had been there.[ . . . ] It is clear that this spontaneous welcome, this warmth of feeling . . . was not shown to me as . . . a private individual, as Asika; it was shown to me as an Ibo and as a representative of the Ibos in Nigeria.[59]

While he was willing to talk about Igbos in that collective sense, Asika also tugged at the threads of negative stereotypes. In a 1968 interview with *Drum* magazine, he went so far as to pick at the edifice of Igbo ethnicity in anthropological terms that were antithetical to the essentialisms of 1966 and 1967.[60]

> *Drum:* What do you consider—in the context of their being regarded as an ethnic unit—are the virtues and the faults of the Igbos?
>
> *Asika:* I think there are several misconceptions. The most basic is that Igbos are an ethnic unit. In terms of sociology, what is true of Igbos is that they form a language group made up of several tribal and ethnic groups who, as a result of the formation of the Nigerian political unit, have acquired an external definition as one social group. In order to talk meaningfully of characteristics of this externally defined group,

one would have to resolve the question of how significant external defi-
nitions are in giving group attributes.[61]

His artful, scholarly repackaging of Igbo ethnicity in the service of the
federal cause reached a peak when he wrote in 1968 that "In a sense,
one could say that the Ibo-speaking people of Nigeria were Nigerians
before they became Ibos."[62]

## CONCLUSION

Asika's message to Igbos that their place was secure in the new
Nigeria blended well with those emanating from the federal government: They need not be ashamed of their ethnic identity. On the con-
trary, the very affiliation which had so recently marked them for
violence—that many in Biafra argued marked them for genocide—
could now again be borne in safety if not necessarily with pride. They
were, first and foremost, Nigerians, and as Nigerians their ethnicity
marked them as particularly useful participants in the nation's future
prosperity. They would, presumably, return to "leading positions" in
the country's various (civilian) institutions, where they would dili-
gently and gratefully work for the national good. This startling re-
placement of Northern representations of Igbos as enemies of Nigeria
with federal visions of a peaceful reunion was an important factor in
setting the tone for the eventual return of an Igbo migrant population,
and represents an attempt by the federal government to make medicine from poison. Setting such a tone was not a step taken lightly, or
without contention. While it is difficult to assess the range of opinions within the military government on the treatment of Igbos, the
comments of a high-ranking Western State official speaking confiden-
tially with a British diplomat three months after the war suggest that
fissures existed. According to the official, a civilian, Gowon had endured criticism by Northern governors for "soft" post-war policies,
and for giving the ECS special treatment. Gowon, the official recounted, had said that perhaps the governors had a point, but that
publicly changing his policy could mean that Igbos "would never believe us again."[63]

Still, the public face of the federal government was conciliatory, and
for the most part the new state governments in the North followed the
federal government's lead. A concrete indication of the willingness of the
North to accept Igbos back is the wartime handling of abandoned property. As discussed in chapter five, the handling of such property in Kano

was also an important reflection of the new social and political realities the creation of Kano State brought about, though like the discourses surrounding Igbo ethnic identity during the war, the line between poison and medicine could sometimes be a thin one.

## NOTES

1. Popular representations, unfortunately, are more difficult to track, as many are by nature ephemeral. One exception to this pattern is a collection of Hausa-language poetry gathered in Kano during the war. Unfortunately, there is no comparable body of pre-war material, which makes a longitudinal analysis impossible. For a discussion of wartime poetry, see Graham Furniss, "Hausa Language Poetry on the Nigerian Civil War," *African Languages and Cultures* 4, 1 (1991). The poetry collection, based on a 1968 competition, is Abdu Yahya Bichi, ed., *Wakokin Yabon Soja* (Kano: Centre for the Study of Nigerian Languages, 1989). The question of Biafran propaganda's treatment of Northern Nigerians, which while related, offers little insight into the manipulation of Igbo representations, is the subject of a separate study. (Douglas Anthony, *forthcoming*.)

2. Eyo B.E. Ndem, *Ibos in Contemporary Nigerian Politics* (Onitsha: Etudo Limited, 1961), 16. Cited in Post and Vickers, *Structure and Conflict in Nigeria*, 29. Comparisons between Igbos and Jews have been common during the twentieth century, in ways both well-intentioned and malicious. In part, this is a reflection of what Oriji has called the "Jewish hypothesis of Igbo origin." See John N. Oriji, *Traditions of Igbo Origin: A Study of Pre-Colonial Population Movements in Africa* (New York: Peter Lang, 1990), 14. Comparisons with Jews go back as far as the slave narrative of Olaudah Equiano in the 18th century. Olaudah Equiano, *The Interesting Narrative of the Life of Olaudah Equiano*, in *The Classic Slave Narratives*, Henry Louis Gates, ed. (New York: Mentor Books, 1987), 22–23. See also Akwaelumo Ike, *The Origin of the Ibos* (Aba: Silent Prayer Home Press, 1951).

3. The focus on Ojukwu as "responsible for leading the Igbo people astray" surfaces in wartime Hausa-language poetry gathered in Kano in 1968. Furniss, "Hausa Language Poetry," 23.

4. Current Issues Society, *The Nigerian Situation: Facts and Background* (Kaduna: Gaskiya Corporation, 1966). The Current Issues society's membership included a number of past and contemporary civil servants, and was associated with the *Northern Echo* newspaper. Among its activities were public forums on political issues. A central figure was Malam Ibrahim Gamawa, a Northern civil servant who at one time worked for the government printer in Kaduna. Other members included Malam Ibrahim Abba Alhaji, in 1967 a Shell Oil Company employee, and Dr. Iya Abubakar, an ABU lecturer. The society's activities appear to have stopped by early 1967. My decision to assign plural authorship to this and other pamphlets published in the North is largely arbitrary. USNA POL 6/2371/A-55, 17 February 1967 and A-72, 20 June 1968.

5. Notably, the editor of the *New Nigerian*, Alhaji Adamu Ciroma, had been a long-time associate of Ahmadu Bello, and in many eyes, a protégé.

6. *Nigerian Situation*, 1.

7. HCB R.62, 331, Intelligence Report, November 1966.

8. This tactic would reemerge in mid-1967 in *Minorities, States and Nigerian Unity*, published by the "Old Calabar and Ogoja Communities [in] Lagos," but printed by the federal government printer. Among others, the pamphlet was dedicated to the "sons and daughters of Old Calabar and Ogoja provinces who fell during the disturbances of 1966 which they did not participate in planning." Its authors described non-Igbo areas of the East as "military occupation posts. Ibos in the East are armed and characteristically go about boasting of how they would destroy all the minorities." At the center, of course, was Ojukwu, whose "war is against the [minorities] of Eastern Nigeria" as part of a plan to perserve "Ibo domination, persecution, military occupation and colonization" of minority areas. This document is quoted in USNA POL 18/2371/A-017, 9 July 1967. It was apparently issued in a press run of 5,000 and was probably written before the outbreak of war, but distributed after.

9. *Nigerian Situation*, 9.

10. *Nigerian Situation*, 28.

11. *Nigerian Situation*, 18.

12. *Nigerian Situation*, 17.

13. *Nigerian Situation*, 18.

14. *Nigerian Situation*, 16.

15. *Nigerian Situation*, 19.

16. *Nigerian Situation*, 25.

17. Northern Nigeria, *The Creation of States* (Kaduna: Government Printing Office, 1967), 3.

18. *Creation of States*, 5.

19. *Creation of States*, 9.

20. For example, see: Ministry of Information, Eastern Nigeria, *The Problem of Nigerian Unity* (Enugu: Ministry of Information, 1967); Republic of Biafra, *The Case of Biafra* (Enugu: Ministry of Information, 1968); Biafra, *The Case for Independence* (London: Britain-Biafra Association, 1968).

21. Ministry of Information, Northern Group of Provinces, *Nigeria: The Realities of Our Time* (Kaduna: Government Printer, 1967), i. It is imperative to remember that the invective propaganda writers in the North used was, in the end, neither more nor less reductionist than that employed in Eastern propaganda vilifying Northerners. A similar study of contemporaneous images of Northern Nigerians in the rhetoric of Eastern Nigeria and later Biafra would find a virtual mirror image.

22. *Realities*, 4.

23. *Realities*, 2.

24. *Realities*, 2.

25. *Realities*, 4.

26. *Realities*, 4-5. The University of Nigeria-Nsukka is located in Igboland.

27. *Realities*, 4.

28. *Realities*, 19.

29. *Realities*, 6.

30. *Realities*, 7.

31. See Victor Bong Amaaze, "The 'Igbo Scare' in the British Cameroons, c. 1945-61," *Journal of African History* 31, 2 (1990). In 1960, Igbos from Nigeria made up a quarter of Southern Cameroon's federal civil servants, and constituted a third of the region's plantation work force. See also Ndiva Kofele-Kale, *Tribesmen and Patriots: Political Culture in a Poly-Ethnic African State* (Washington: University Press of America, 1981), 31.

32. Victor Levine, "'P' Day in the Cameroons, Part One," *West Africa*, 11 March 1961, 265.

33. C. Eke, "An Easterner Writes About Nigeria's Situation: Don't Blame All Easterners but Tribal Gods," *New Nigerian*, 10 October 1966. See also Post and Vickers, *Structure and Conflict in Nigeria*, 31.

34. Liisa H. Malkki, *Purity and Exile: Violence, Memory and National Cosmology Among Hutu Refugees in Tanzania* (Chicago: University of Chicago Press, 1995), 14.

35. Margery Perham, *Lugard, The Years of Authority 1898–1945* (London: Collins, 1960), 468. Both Perham and Jones, above, also described Igbos as "individualistic," a characterization that appears to have slipped out of favor with anti-Igbo propagandists as focus on the Ibo Union and the NCNC as manifestations of monolithic ethnic ambition grew.

36. Nigeria, *Report of the Commission appointed to enquire into the fears of Minorities and the means of allaying them* (London: HMSO, 1958), 39.

37. G.I. Jones, "Dual Organisation in Ibo Social Structures," *Africa* 19, 2 (1949), 150; see also Daryll Forde and G.I. Jones, *The Ibo and Ibibio-Speaking People of South-Eastern Nigeria* (London: Oxford University Press, 1950).

38. A.H.M. Kirk-Greene, *Lugard and the Amalgamation of Nigeria* (London: Frank Cass, 1968), 56.

39. G.T. Basden, *Among the Ibos of Nigeria* (1921, Frank Cass & Co., 1966 reprint), 37.

40. The images resurfaced before they vanished from official publications, however. After the invasion and brief occupation of the Mid-West by Biafran forces in August 1967, language very similar to what Northern propagandists had used appeared in the Mid-West government's tract *The Nigerian Crisis and the Midwest Decision* (Benin: n.p., 1968).

> The civil service, statutory corporations and state-sponsored companies were inundated overnight with hundreds of jobless Ibos from both sides of the Niger [i.e., from the East and Mid-West] who were appointed without any regard for established recruitment procedures and, in most cases, in the absence of vacancies. And when it became clear to the invading rebels that the reaction of the people, save the Ibos, who were, of course, part of the plot, was one of rebuff and open defiance, plans for the elimination of the cream of the non-Ibo communities were immediately laid. (4)

Further, "It had thus been quite clear for a long time that the Mid-west, almost from its inception, had been haunted by the nightmarish spectre of Ibo encirclement, subjugation and suppression." (7)

41. Federal Ministry of Information, *Nigeria 12-State Structure: The Only Way Out* (Lagos: Government Printing Office, 1968), 15. Mention of a larger Igbo con-

spiracy was limited to labeling the "incidents of January 15" as "a clumsily camou-
flaged attempt to secure Ibo domination of the Government of the country." (7) A
second publication containing largely the same text as *Nigeria 12-State Structure* is
Federal Ministry of Information, *The Collapse of a Rebellion and the Prospects of
Lasting Peace* (Lagos: Government Printing Office, 1968).

42. *Nigeria 12-State Structure*, 7.

43. *Nigeria 12-State Structure*, 17.

44. Broadcast (31 March 1968) quoted in *Nigeria 12-State Structure*, 21.

45. "Ending the Fighting," an address by General Yakubu Gowon, August 1968
(n.p.).

46. "Peace, Stability, and Harmony in Post-War Nigeria," an address by Gowon,
5 January 1968 (n.p.).

47. Federal Ministry of Information, *Igbos in a United Nigeria* (Lagos: Government Printing Office, 1968), 1.

48. *Igbos in a United Nigeria*, 1.

49. Federal Ministry of Information, *Nigeria Answers Questions* (Lagos: Government Printer, 1968), 9.

50. "National Reconciliation in Post-War Nigeria," address by Gowon at Ahmadu
Bello University, 30 November 1968 (Lagos: Federal Republic of Nigeria, 1968), 2–
3.

51. Federal Ministry of Information, *The Collapse of a Rebellion, and the Prospects of Lasting Peace* (Lagos: Government Printer, 1968), 3. *Nigeria Answers Questions* used similar language, though it prefaced it with mention that in 1966 "Ibo
traders and workers in the North taunted ordinary people in the majority ethnic group
in the area and boasted their full assumption of power." (4)

52. *The Collapse of a Rebellion*, 21.

53. *Igbos in a United Nigeria*, 2.

54. *Igbos in a United Nigeria*, 2–3.

55. Malam Aminu Kano, quoted in John Paden, *Religion and Political Culture in
Kano*, 356.

56. Broadcast (1 April 1968) by Audu Bako, quoted in Military Government Office, "Policy Statement Broadcast" (Kano: Information Division, Kano State, 1968),
4. The broadcast was also made in Hausa: "Gwamnantina za ta taimaki kowa zauna
inda ya ke so." (10)

57. Jerry Okoro wrote in the *Times* of London in 1971 that "The new Ibo
leader, Mr. Ukpabi Asika . . . is not very popular with the Igbos. But a small
group of more liberally minded Igbos argue that it was Mr. Asika's support for
the Federal Government that transformed the war from one against the Igbos as
a people to one against a 'clique of ambitious Igbos' led by Mr. Ojukwu." *Times*,
26 November 1970.

58. Ukpabi Asika, "We Shall Sorrow for our Dead but we shall not Weep," speech
28 November, 1967, in Asika, *No Victors, No Vanquished* (Apapa: East Central State
Information Service, 1968), 12.

59. Asika, "A New Maturity and Self Confidence," speech 9 December 1967, in
*No Victors, No Vanquished*, 18.

60. See M.M. Green, *Igbo Village Affairs* (London: Frank Cass, 1964), originally
published in 1947. The idea is most fully developed in Smock, *Ibo Politics*.

61. Asika, "No Reason to Fail," in *No Victor, No Vanquished*, 55. The interview was originally published in a slightly different version in the July 1968 edition of *Drum* magazine.

62. Asika, "An Afterward: Prospect and Retrospect," in *No Victors, No Vanquished*, 77.

63. USNA POL 15/2508, 3 March 1970. The source, a Secretary to a southwestern state government, said that Northern Governors argued that non-Igbo Easterners "had suffered more" because of Igbos than Igbos had suffered at the hands of the federal government.

Kofar Mata, one of several gates entering the "old city" as it appears today from Fagge ward. (Courtesy of Alan Frishman.)

Looking out from Kofar Mazugal. (Courtesy of Alan Frishman.)

Small stalls and hawkers line the streets outside of Kofar Mazugal. (Courtesy of Alan Frishman.)

143

Looking north along Hausa by Ibo Road, commonly known simply as Ibo Road, in Sabon Gari. Kano's Igbo population is concentrated in Sabon Gari. By the late 1990s rents in Sabon Gari were several times those of adjacent wards. (Courtesy of Alan Frishman.)

144

New buildings along the eastern edge of the Sabon-Gari market. Commercial and residential saturation in the area has led to the increasing popularity of multi-story shops (pictured here, on right) and dwellings. The arch in the background is a pedestrian overpass, and not a city gate. (Courtesy of Alan Frishman.)

A sign advertising computers and other electronic goods shares space with a food seller along Ibo Road. Across the street is one of Sabon Gari's many churches. (Courtesy of Alan Frishman.)

# 5

# "THEY WILL RETURN": THE CONTRADICTIONS OF ABANDONED PROPERTY

## INTRODUCTION

Between the expulsions of 1966 and the end of the war, the most concrete manifestation of Igbos' continued importance in Northern Nigeria was the property they left behind. Notwithstanding the near-total disappearance of trading stock and moveable personal property during the arson and looting that accompanied the disturbances, one of the most striking aspects of the ongoing relationship between Igbos and Northern Nigeria is the orderly handling of more substantial items of property, in particular buildings and capital goods. Local authorities, operating under federal guidelines, created elaborate mechanisms for handling such property in manners that preserved Igbo claims, but also allowed local citizens to exploit the property in the owners' absence. If federal propaganda represented a symbolic reversal of Northern discourses of expulsion, then the handling of property served much the same function in a less abstract manner. Like wartime and postwar propaganda, abandoned property represented an invitation to return to Northern Nigeria. Implicit in that invitation, however, was a set of conditions. By allowing Igbos to retain claim to residential and commercial property, Northern authorities sent a message that Igbos were welcome to return, provided that they did so in humility, and with the understanding that their presence in the North was at the indulgence of Northerners. The process of reclaiming property reinforced this message—and most Igbo property owners appear to have understood it clearly.

Recovering property, in this sense, simultaneously reinscribed the line between Igbos and Northerners even as it opened an important gateway into regaining some of the economic perquisites of citizenship. Not surprisingly, property owners who had survived the war, and the heirs of those who had not, responded variously to the challenges and opportunities that reclamation presented them. In so doing, cases arose where the process of reclaiming property highlighted the boundaries between Igbos and *Kanawa*, as local officials grappled with elements of Igbo "traditional" law, and a variety of formal and informal intermediaries stepped in to bridge both legitimate and illicit points of slippage between communities.

## THE CONTRADICTIONS OF ABANDONED PROPERTY

The first Igbos to return to Kano arrived before the cessation of hostilities between Nigeria and Biafra, and joined the handful who had remained behind. When the war ended in January, 1970, the trickle of migrants from Igboland increased. One of the things that drew them back was the property they had left behind in 1966, and the promises the government had made that it would be restored to them. In Kano and other Northern cities, Igbos and Hausas alike point to the handling of abandoned property as a central ingredient in the successful reconciliation that occurred between the groups. While the return of abandoned property has become emblematic of the North's willingness to accept Igbos back, and to ease their reentry, it also reveals many of the contradictions of the same period. On the one hand, official policies protected the enormous wealth that property-owning Igbos left behind, and demonstrated the expectation that the owners or their heirs would return to claim it. And when Igbos did return, recovery of property was a central ingredient in the economic recovery of survivors, even for those who did not reestablish residency in the North. Symbolically, its return was an important gesture of reconciliation between individuals and communities. On the other hand, the exploitation of Igbo property during and after the war did much to benefit local people, and the reclamation of property became, for many Igbos, a trying exercise in tenacity and humility, a reminder that while they could return to the North, most of them were politically impotent, and that, in many ways, they were at the mercy of local authorities. That many owners experienced long delays in having their property restored to them only reinforced that point.

The saga of abandoned property began when Igbos left the North in 1966 and military authorities charged local governments with the task of looking after their property. Once the war began, this relationship was formalized with the creation of Abandoned Property Committees to oversee the sale or storage of movable assets, and to manage the renting of houses and commercial property to caretakers. These caretakers included local citizens, but also arms of government and, especially in large cities like Kano, Nigerians from other areas. The return of property in the North was a centerpiece in the government's reconciliation program. A front-page story in the *New Nigerian* on the anniversary of the war's end was typical in including abandoned property in what had become standard, if overly optimistic, praise for the government's success in managing a return to peace.

> Reintegration is being affected all over the country. Citizens of the East Central State are now fully resettled in all parts of the federation and enjoying their full citizenship—freedom of movement, association and choices.
> Their abandoned houses and stalls are being returned to them with accumulated rent proceeds; their enterprises resuscitated with the help of other Nigerians and state government; thousands have been reabsorbed in their former places of employment.[1]

In practice, however, even in places where it generally went well, the return of property from caretakers was often tainted by delays, and few owners recovered the rents that the government promised them. Still, these failures are secondary to the fact that most property itself was handed back—which was not the case in many of the minority areas of the former East.

The experience of property owners in Kano was quite varied, however, and some property owners were able to recover their property with a minimum of difficulty. Frequently these were individuals with personal or commercial links to people with influence within the new state government. Other owners were directly victimized by corruption within the bureaucracy that dealt with abandoned property, while still others—many penniless—were pressured to sell their property to local people, in some cases with the apparent complicity of some within the caretaking bureaucracy. In addition, some properties large and small were handled outside the official system, usually by Kano citizens on behalf of Igbo business associates or friends. The significance of the general absence of open enmity with regard to the handling of abandoned property in Kano is clearest when contrasted with such southern cities as Port Harcourt, Calabar, and to a lesser extent Lagos. The resistance to returning property in the south and the relative willingness to return it in the North reflects the different political and economic significance of the Igbo populations in those locations. This is particularly true when one considers the degree to which Igbo businesses were viewed as a potential threat in, for example, Port Harcourt, as opposed to Kano where they were accepted as welcome assets to the local economy. For this reason, Kano, as the first city of the North, became a symbol of the relative ease with which Igbos reclaimed their property in the region, and, in turn, became a national symbol of successful reconciliation and reintegration.

## EARLY CARETAKING EFFORTS

Many fleeing Igbos were able to take substantial amounts of property with them when they left, including personal or commercial vehicles. In particular, the fortunate minority who were warned in advance of the October riots were able to arrange for the safe removal of valuable commercial and personal belongings to the south, to sell off property, or to arrange for its indefinite safekeeping in Kano. In his study on Kano blacksmiths, Jaggar describes such an incident between a Kano blacksmith, Alhaji Audu, and his Igbo hardware suppliers. "[I]n 1966 a number of these Igbos, sensing that trouble was imminent, came to Alhaji Audu and asked him if he would be prepared to buy them out since they had all decided to leave Kano for their homeland."[2] Alhaji Audu bought trading stock and took over market stalls, all at prices well below market value at the time.

Despite many such hasty sales, the moveable property that Igbos left behind was substantial. In Kano, property classified as "perishable," defined by the government as items such as furniture or personal effects that were easily stolen, were auctioned by the Local Authority, with the intention that proceeds be retained for the owners. The yard at the Ministry of Works within the old city, as well as Local Authority facilities in the Government Reserved Area were used as storage facilities for other moveable properties. Over the course of the war, however, the property that was stored disappeared, and no Igbos recalled any owners receiving remuneration. Some moveable property, such as tools, trading stock, and in at least one case, a printing press, ended up in the hands of non-Igbo apprentices, business associates, or friends who remained. Much of this property was stored or remained in use before eventually being returned; alternately, it was sold and the proceeds invested or saved. And in some cases, particularly in rural areas, district heads kept animals, including horses, donkeys, or cows owned by Igbos.[3] However, as one Igbo, a community leader before the war, explained, few Igbos who returned to Kano expected to recover their moveable property. In his words, "You don't expect to get your motor bike back when you left it during a riot."[4]

Government records suggest that during the seven-month period between the flight of the Igbo population and the outbreak of war, civil servants and Nigeria Police made efforts at assisting refugees in Igboland with a variety of concerns. On the last day of 1966, I.A. Nkwocha wrote from Owerri to the Ministry of Finance in Kaduna seeking the £35 pension payment that his former employer, the Zaria Native Authority, had failed to forward to Owerri. "Would you imagine the difficulty in which I am now placed with a family of ten with no means of livelihood and after returning from the North without a brass farthing and or property[?] I was a trader in Kano and my market stall with merchandise were burnt and my property looted. I was managing until the September incident befell me and I narrowly escaped death."[5] Then, in February, 1967, Raphael Nnadozie wrote from Onitsha to the Provincial Secretary in Kano to seek help in locating the Northern owners of two properties in the Fegge section of Onitsha. Like many Eastern cities, Onitsha was overcrowded and housing was in short supply. Nnadozie apparently wished to occupy or use the buildings. By March 15, the Waje District Office in Kano had located the landlords; one was reportedly living in Cameroon, though the Waje office succeeded in passing a message to the other.[6]

Officials also took steps to help Igbos recover their moveable property, and in some cases to locate family members. These efforts are evidence that even as some elements within the Northern establishment worked against Igbo interests, in other cases the institutional apparatus continued to function as intended. Each of the four cases below was routed from the Military Governor's office in Kaduna to the appropriate local authorities in late 1966 or 1967.

• An Igbo blacksmith who had fled Jos in 1966 wrote the following April to the office of Military Governor in Kaduna asking for the "repatriation" of his work tools from Jos to the East. The tools, which represented a substantial accumulation of capital, were in the custody of a non-Igbo apprentice. The letter passed through police headquarters in Kaduna before police in Jos investigated his claim and located the tools in June. However, when communication with the East was banned with the outbreak of war, they were unable to take further action.[7]

• An Igbo railroad worker's attempt to track down household property in Wushishi suffered a similar failure after a mishandled letter wound up in Bauchi rather than Minna. The railroad worker, A.C. Obodo, was following up a letter from the station master, E.O. Oyekunle. The station master had written Obodo in Enugu to inform him that he had stored Obodo's property in the railway yard in Wushishi and was awaiting his instructions. Obodo, in turn, wanted the government's assistance in getting the station master to send his belongings by train to Ibadan, where he would retrieve them. By the time the letter was rerouted, however, the first shots of the war had been fired.[8]

- In April, 1967, a photographer from Umuobom, Orlu Division, sought the government's help in retrieving not only his equipment but also in locating his wife and three children, whom he "handed over" to a "local chief" in Takum, Benue Province. Like many Igbo refugees, he found it difficult upon his return to secure either employment or land for farming. "I am a Photo Grapher. I am now an applicant [for government assistance] in my home Ubuobom, I want to start local farming such as cassava [but] my bloodly related brothers do not want me to use any of our father's land [and] even want me to leave the village. [ . . . ] I am not a useless man in the Town."[9] By June the Makurdi Provincial office located his wife and children in good health, but advised authorities in Kaduna that "in view of the present condition in the country it is not deemed advisable that he either comes in person even if he had transport money, or that consideration should be given to his wish that his family join him."[10] The Kaduna office retired the letter because contact with Eastern Nigeria had been broken.

- A fourth incident concerned a separated family. An Igbo who had operated a filling station in Maiduguri wrote to Kaduna in December, 1966 seeking help in locating his son and wife, a nurse from Bornu. In February, 1967 investigators in Maiduguri reported both living there, "fit as a fiddle," though apparently the wife had no intention of rejoining her husband.[11]

Even more significant than moveable properties in both symbolic and economic terms were the landed properties Igbos owned. Most were houses, but also included hotels, town union halls, and, in Kano, a school. In Kano the houses themselves were most frequently "one and two-storey block built compound residences used very largely as rooming houses." Internal spaces within the compounds were frequently put to use for income-generating activities such as mechanical work and carpentry.[12] Other commercial activities in the primarily residential areas that lay outside the market included the provision of accommodation, food and drink. Researchers tallied 2,074 houses in

Sabon Gari-Kano in 1966; the founding chair of Kano's Abandoned Property Committee conservatively estimated Igbos owned 80 percent of the structures in Sabon Gari; if true, the number of Igbo-owned houses in Sabon Gari-Kano would have been at least 1,650.[13] Of those, the government took over 1,502.[14] This number, of course, does not include houses in outlying towns, such as Hadejia and Dutse, and villages where Igbo traders, produce buyers, and skilled workers worked and in many cases lived. Nor does it take into account rural and semi-rural locations like the Challawa waterworks.[15] In Jos, the home of the former Northern Region's second-largest Igbo community, officials counted 1,446 abandoned houses.[16] In Kaduna, the estimate was over 1,000.[17]

Initially there was some confusion about how abandoned houses were to be handled. For example, as late as January, 1967, the Kano Local Authority deflected a request from a non-Hausa employee of a bottling company for permission to occupy an abandoned flat in a damaged house owned by an Igbo woman who had fled. The Authority responded that "we have no legal right to authorize anyone to enter into other people's property."[18] The following month, however, the Military Governor in Kaduna delegated such authority to local governments, ostensibly out of concern that the unattended property presented a threat to public health.[19] Not all early caretaking arrangements went smoothly. For example, in May, 1967, the Waje District Head in Kano issued a "certificate to be Care-Taker" to J.P.D. Ogbise for one of two houses on adjacent plots. Ogbise had identified himself as an "Ijaw from Rivers" in the East, a Kano resident for sixteen years, and the owner of a registered construction business. In response to his initial query, Ogbise was instructed to apply in writing to the owner for permission to caretake. The Igbo owner, D.O. Okechukwu, apparently writing from Igboland, gave written permission in which he specified that he authorized only Ogbise to use the two houses. In September, however, a new District Head refused to grant a certificate for the second house, on which Ogbise claimed to have spent £90 on repairs and unpaid plot dues. According to Ogbise, the District Head also threatened to rescind the certificate his predecessor had granted.[20] How the dispute was resolved, unfortunately, is unclear. The incident suggests that southerners had particularly limited leverage as caretakers in the early days. The Waje office began formally interviewing caretaker applicants in April, 1967.[21] Most were Hausa, though letters from 1967 identify two caretaker applicants as Ijaw and Yoruba, respectively; other early caretakers were Lebanese and Chinese.[22] In some cases, non-Hausa caretakers who faced or expected difficulty in gaining access to abandoned property enlisted the help of *Kanawa* in facilitating their arrangements.

It was with the April 1968 inauguration of Nigeria's twelve states that the procedures governing abandoned property took the shape that they were to maintain throughout the war and into the period of post-war reintegration.[23] The federal government did not specify how abandoned property was to be handled, only that it was to be held for its owners. With the abolition of the regions, the particulars landed in local hands. In August the Kano Native Authority handed over responsibility for abandoned buildings to the head of the Local Authority, who was at that time chairman of the Rehabilitation Committee.[24] This marked a deviation from previous patterns since the regular jurisdiction of the Local Authority was limited to the GRA, and most of the property in question was located in Sabon Gari, since 1941 under the jurisdiction of the Native Authority. The task befell the Local Authority because it was better equipped to deal with the property in terms of personnel and storage space.[25]

## KANO STATE AND THE ABANDONED PROPERTY COMMITTEE

The first task of Kano's Abandoned Property Committee (APC) was to locate capital with which to physically restore Sabon Gari and, eventually, to return its buildings to paid occupancy.[26] Without tenants, plot dues, an important source of revenue for government coffers, would go unpaid. The area had been heavily damaged during the 1966 riots; a survey conducted in November, 1966, found that 45 percent of the houses in Sabon Gari were damaged, and another 30 percent were undamaged but vacant.[27] The capital the APC sought was to come from private caretakers.[28] The APC's plan was to charge caretakers low rents so that they would invest their own money in restoring the property; in exchange caretakers got the right to use or sublet the property until the owners returned. The basic plan was simple: Caretakers would pay rent on the property, not to the absent landlord, but rather to the Local Authority, who would then hold the money on account for the landlord. The gain for caretakers was potentially substantial. They could sublet to residential or commercial tenants, who would then deal only with the caretakers, or the caretakers themselves could use the property as they pleased, provided that they agreed not to remove any contents or fixtures. The APC sought out individuals established in the community with radio and television announcements.

After being interviewed, successful candidates registered with the Local Authority. Private caretakers put properties to a variety of uses, mostly as rental property. With Sabon Gari's population down, however, about half of abandoned property remained uninhabited through all or most of the war. And since almost all of the houses were designed for multiple households, even those with caretakers and tenants were not necessarily at full occupancy. This was particularly true of houses that had been badly damaged or that were less attractively located.[29]

Large blocks of contiguous accommodation made abandoned property attractive to government agencies that needed to provide accomodation to employees or clients in a hurry. An early example of this occurred shortly after Kano's Igbos departed. At the same time, the Hausa communities in Onitsha and other parts of the southeast returned North. Just as Igbo refugees occupied whatever accommodation they could find in the East, so some Northern refugees from the East moved into abandoned property in Sabon Gari without authorization, a practice which the Ministry of Social Welfare tried to control. Most "Northern refugees," as they were called, traveled through Kano, some directly from their host communities in the south, others via Lagos. While many were bound for Kano, others went on to other parts of the North. Social welfare officers at different levels of government cooperated to repatriate these travelers to their respective home areas.[30] Early in 1967 the government established a fund for Northern refugees that was sustained largely by private donations from businesses and individuals. They also rallied local businesses to hire "refugee" heads of households.[31] As part of the rehabilitation effort, the Local Authority housed many refugees in abandoned houses in Sabon Gari.[32]

Later, as caretaking arrangements became more formal, other agencies took advantage of the opportunities for inexpensive or even free accommodation that Sabon Gari presented. During 1968–1969 the Kano State Pilgrims Welfare Board, with cooperation from the Local Authority, took over large portions of Weatherhead and Burma Roads in Sabon Gari to provide temporary lodging for pilgrims flying from Kano to Saudi Arabia on *hajj*.[33] (Ironically, it was on these same roads, and particularly Weatherhead, that much of Sabon Gari's pre-war commercial sex trade had been centered, which was a major reason many of the hotels there had failed to attract private caretakers.[34]) In addition to the pilgrims themselves, the Board housed friends and relatives who accompanied the pilgrims as far as Kano, and who would often await their return. Besides occupying empty houses, the Board erected temporary shelters on the street. At times the official count of those temporarily lodged went as high as 5,000. As a state government agency, the Board paid no rent to use abandoned houses, but did pay for repairs to power and water lines. Further, according to a former Local Authority head, some funds generated by abandoned properties went not to owners, but toward the construction of a permanent camp for pilgrims. The Board made occasional use of unclaimed property in the area until 1973.[35]

Nigeria Airways, the Immigration and Customs services, the police and the military also made use of abandoned buildings as short-term housing. And, during the last year of Nigeria's civil war, Ghana's "Aliens' Compliance Order" resulted in the expulsion of 200,000 foreign nationals, most of them Nigerian citizens. While Yoruba from southwestern Nigeria represented the largest group of Nigerians, a number were from the Kano area. The Kano State Ministry of Internal Affairs used abandoned houses as temporary shelter for them for up to four weeks at a time.[36] One advantage to the Local Authority of such institutional caretakers was that the transactions were between government agencies, which simplified bookkeeping.[37] Even after the majority of property had been returned to owners, the National Youth Service Corps in 1973 used and later purchased from the state two houses on Gold Coast Road that remained unclaimed.[38]

## SABON GARI, 1967–1970

Commercial and residential patterns in Sabon Gari provide a snapshot of the ways in which non-Igbo Nigerians established footholds in the area during the war years. Even after the initial departure of Igbos between late May and early October, 1966, the population of Sabon Gari continued to decrease. Statistics from the Waje office indicate an almost 95 percent drop in Sabon Gari's population between 1965 and 1968. Between 1965–1966 and 1966–1967 the official figure dipped from 41,956 to 15,997. The following year, 1967–1968, the number again dropped drastically to 2,196 before the activity of Hausa and Yoruba traders in the Sabon Gari Market began to pick up in 1968.[39] At the same time, the number of income tax payers in Waje, most of them salaried workers, picked up. The number nearly doubled between 1967 (704) and 1969 (1,317).[40]

During the war the ethnic makeup of Sabon Gari's residential population was, like the market, predominantly Hausa and Yoruba. In addition to traders, many of the Yoruba were among the hundreds of skilled workers from the West, Mid-West, and Middle Belt who had found accommodation with caretaker landlords, or squatted in buildings left vacant by the Igbos whose jobs they had assumed.[41] As Paden pointed out, while most of the Yoruba living in Kano before the war had been Hausa-speaking, the bulk of those who came during the war were not.[42] During the Civil War the Waje office took the important step of reallocating Sabon Gari Market stalls that Igbos had held, most to local traders from Kasuwar Kurmi, the main market in the old city. Sabon Gari market had displaced Kurmi as the city's—and the region's—most active market by 1965.[43] Now the war provided an opportunity for locals to establish themselves there without competition from Igbo traders. They moved in, and by mid-1967 the market was back to full occupancy, its ethnic makeup changed profoundly.[44] One consequence of Hausa penetration of the Sabon Gari Market was the growth of the Hausa population in Sabon Gari from a tiny percentage to a wartime plurality.[45] An unofficial estimate by the Native Authority put the number of Hausa living in Sabon Gari at the end of the war at 5,000, most of them traders and their families.[46]

While most wholesale and retail trade was limited to the market, other commercially attractive properties lay in the largely residential area north of the market. These were mostly hotels, restaurants, and drinking spots, but also included union halls, which could be rented out as meeting spaces or for social gatherings. Locations near the market in particular were commercially attractive. Then, in 1968, Kano and other northern state governments made plans to appropriate abandoned schools, hotels, union halls and commercial buildings as government property.[47] The plan—which, if executed, would have grossly contradicted the spirit of reconciliation being so carefully cultivated—was eventually curtailed, but only after the federal government announced its disapproval of any plans to confiscate property.[48] In the end the northern states took over only schools, including the Ibo Union Grammar School.[49] Though exempted from appropriation by the state, hotels presented a special difficulty for the APC. Their central role in the sale and consumption of beer and other alcoholic beverages made them unattractive to many Muslims who were potential caretakers. The additional association of some hotels with the sex trade compounded the problem.[50] Nonetheless, after the initial depopulation of Sabon Gari, both the alcohol and sex industries regained some of their profitability, attributable both to the influx of new residents to the area, and the presence of soldiers on leave from the front, as well as those treated at Kano's orthopedic hospital.[51] While *Kanawa* shunned public association with most hotels, many consider it an open secret that some local Muslims profited from such properties by working with southern partners who were the public owners and operators.

## RECLAMATION

For many Igbo owners the experience of reclaiming landed property did not live up to its promise. Little if any of the moveable property in government care found its way back to its owners. While buildings, as a general rule, were returned, most owners were not able to reclaim them quickly or easily, and very few received any of the rents collected on their behalf. What made the deepest imprint on Igbo migrants, however, was the simple fact that they were able to reclaim their houses at all. When contrasted to the enormous difficulties faced by Igbo landowners in the south, Northern cities were a welcome relief. Patricia Ogbogu, the daughter of Igbo traders, had spent much of her childhood in Kano. Her undergraduate thesis on Igbo reintegration in Kano was based on interviews with Igbo traders and workers in Kano in 1973, and is the only contemporary research that records Igbos' thoughts on the matter. Her findings sum up the ambivalence many Igbos later expressed.

> Though quite a lot of Ibo property owners I met in Kano have got their houses released to them, generally they all expressed dissatisfaction at the way and manner the houses were released to them. Many of them came back to Kano a few months after the end of the war and did not get back their houses until a few months ago. Even where the owners of the properties have the completed documents needed, they had to go through an indigen to speak on their behalf before they get their house.[52]

Even after it became clear that there would be no rents for most, property still represented a number of options. Some owners intended to sell what they owned to purchase necessities, or to capitalize business ventures. Others were fleeing an acute housing shortage in the war-affected area, and, finding the security climate in Kano acceptable, intended to set up residence. Still others tried to beat the system by filing dubious claims.

The procedure for reclaiming property was, in theory, simple. Owners would report to the Local Authority office with whatever documentation they could produce. Most important was the "certificate of occupancy" originally issued owners by the Native Authority; most granted usufructuary rights for a period of ninety-nine years contingent on small annual plot fees. These documents were among the most valued possessions of most owners, who went to great lengths to protect them. Stories circulate about certificates carefully buried or otherwise elaborately hidden during the war. Most property owners were able to produce certificates for the property they claimed. The second part of the identification process was to confirm the identity of the person making the claim. Where Igbos could provide official documentation, this was a simple matter. If the claimant was personally known to someone in the Local Authority or Native Authority offices, claims might also proceed. In most cases, however, individuals did not have official identification or personal contacts in the offices. In these cases, most found a local person to vouch for them. A scenario described many times had the returning Igbo seek out a local Hausa citizen—frequently a former customer, business associate, or in rare cases a neighbor—to accompany him or her to the Local Authority office to confirm his or her identity. One enlisted the help of former Hausa classmates from the Ibo Union Grammar School.[53] Pre-war tenants—some of whom had acted as caretakers—could also identify owners. Sometimes it took three or four people to establish a chain of first-hand acquaintances between the Igbo and officials. This was, however, the most important step in the process since if the identity of an owner could be established, but ownership could not be confirmed, it was policy to allow the claimant to occupy the property in question if all or part of it was vacant.[54] In other cases, Igbos who had not yet begun to process claims or were temporarily unable to prove their claims lived as squatters, sometimes in their own property. Those who reclaimed property frequently took in those who did not have their own accommodation; new arrivals were also able to rent sleeping space, sometimes from owners, sometimes from caretakers, or squat. The high degree of transience in Sabon Gari made squatting difficult to control, especially during 1970 and 1971.

Owners with political or commercial connections had an easier time than others. The importance of personal contacts is clear in the case of the International Hotel and its owners, the Northern Traders Corporation, headed by Felix E. Okonkwo. Okonkwo had been the first president of Kano's Ibo Union, head of the local NCNC chapter, and a one-time special member of the Northern House of Assembly in Kaduna. He had also been a member of the Waje district council. The

Northern Traders Corporation, of which he was president, was a group of Igbo traders organized in 1955. By 1966 the corporation had about forty shareholders, most of whom resided in Kano. It specialized in textile trading and commercial transport along the Onitsha-Kano axis, and also operated the International Hotel, Sabon Gari's largest and one of Kano's most prestigious. Okonkwo made a short visit to Kano in 1969, then returned to stay in 1971. It was then that he tried to take control of the hotel, which had been operated during the war by a Lebanese caretaker. As a former NCNC officer, Okonkwo had worked closely with NEPU leaders, including Tanko Yakasai, by 1969 the state's Secretary for Information. Okonkwo was also a longtime acquaintance of Governor Ahmed Bako.[55] When he encountered difficulty within the Local Authority in regaining control of the profitable hotel, he went directly to its head, a former NEPU member who, with support from the Governor, released the hotel to him immediately.[56]

The greatest difficulties occurred in cases where the owner named on the certificate of occupancy did not return, and a second party initiated a claim. Paden, for example, noted in 1973 that there had been three times as many claims filed as there were abandoned houses in Sabon Gari. Almost certainly many of those claims were dishonest attempts to take advantage of the confusion that surrounded property.[57] On the other hand, in many cases the APC had to deal with multiple claims to properties whose owners had been killed during the 1966 disturbances or the war. In other cases owners were either unable to travel or simply refused to return to the North after the experiences of 1966, and empowered relatives or other agents to act on their behalves. While both sets of records that the APC generated have been lost, hidden, or destroyed since Paden examined them, the state published second-person claims. They reveal that all the petitioners declared some form of kinship with the deceased owner. The largest group of second-party claimants were widows, followed by children, about half of whom were specified as "eldest son." "Widow and son" combinations and brothers constituted most of the rest. In only one case did parents claim their children's property.[58] Of the seventy-five cases preserved, all but two of the deceased listed were men. To what extent this is a reflection on women's ownership of property is unclear; more reliably it is a reminder that men made up the majority of casualties in 1966, which, based on second-person claims, was a far more lethal period for property owners than the war itself.[59] Conventional wisdom also holds that more men than women died during the war.

## Igbo Inheritance in Hausaland

The Kano APC had little expertise with the laws governing inheritance in Igbo society. A former APC chairman recalled a number of disputes surrounding the rights of daughters to inherit property belonging to their parents, cases that he forwarded to local rulers in Igboland to adjudicate. In another instance, the practice of wife inheritance created difficulties in a case where civil and traditional law already appeared at odds. The senior wife of a deceased property owner was unable to travel, and the junior wife made a claim to the husband's property. She was accompanied by two of her dead husband's brothers. The senior brother also wished to claim the dead man's property, a claim he based on Igbo law. In addition to claiming the man's property, the senior brother further wished to marry the junior widow by right of inheritance; the widow, however, preferred to go to the man's junior brother. The APC chair recalled determining that his understanding of Igbo law led him to believe that the senior brother would have inherited both the widow and his brother's property. The widow's claim to his property, however, was based on civil law. If the senior brother's claim to the wife was successful, the APC's solution to the question of who inherited the dead man's property would have been to turn it over to the couple and let them resolve ownership between themselves. However, in the eyes of the APC, the widow's wish to be inherited by the junior brother gave added weight to her claim to her late husband's property. Lacking the expertise to make a decision, the APC turned over all authority in the case to the East Central State for its courts to decide. The senior brother prevailed, and inherited both the widow and his brother's Kano property.[60]

An extreme example of the difficulties relatives could face in claiming property is the case of the Inuwa Hotel, a popular drinking spot.[61] The owner, Mrs. Inuwa, was widely known to be childless. She left during the 1966 disturbances and died during the war. After the war a young woman with documents identifying her as Mrs. Inuwa's daughter claimed the hotel. The Local Authority head, who had known Mrs. Inuwa personally, rejected her claim based on Mrs. Inuwa's childlessness. The woman returned a week later with two of Mrs. Inuwa's brothers, who verified her story, explaining that she was Mrs. Inuwa's daughter through a female-female marriage.[62] Unfamiliar with the institution of female marriage, the Local Authority again refused the woman's claim. She then appealed to the Kano State government, and a month after the daughter's initial claim, the Kano State attorney issued a letter informing the Local Authority of the practice and instructing him to release the property to the daughter.[63]

## The Economics of Reclamation

Once identity was confirmed and ownership was established, the task of settling financial matters remained. For most owners, this was perhaps the most contentious stage of the process. Paden reported that more than £100,000 in rents were collected.[64] However, only one Igbo informant knew for certain of an owner receiving rent money. That echoes Ogbogu's 1973 findings. She wrote that "virtually none of them received any money and many of them feared to put forward the claims. There was a feeling that they would be maltreated if they try to talk about money."[65] Some abandoned property remained under the day-to-day supervision of caretakers for months or even years after its owners returned to Kano to reclaim it. Frequently this was the result of the inability of owners to meet their financial obligations to the APC. Returning owners were required to pay overdue land dues, usually a modest £1 10/— per annum, to the local government before their property would be released. It was the decisions that the caretakers made, however, that often wound up costing owners money, and forced some to sell. Caretakers enjoyed a great deal of latitude in making improvements to property, and recouped their outlay from rents that they paid the APC.[66] In cases where caretakers made repairs or improvements that cost more than the APC collected in rents, the owners were required to repay caretakers for those expenses.[67] These demands on the limited resources of most returnees contributed to the frequency with which cash-strapped Igbo landlords sold their properties to caretakers or other buyers, in most cases *Kanawa*.

An example of this process came in the case of a house on Burma Road. The owner had fled before completing construction of the building. The caretaker, in this case a Mid-Westerner, took advantage of its incompleteness to turn the front of the building into a beer parlor and restaurant. The Igbo owner, upon her return was reportedly initially pleased with the improvements. In order to benefit from her property, however, one of three things had to happen, in each case to the benefit of the caretaker. She could have paid the government for expenses the caretaker incurred on the property; the government would then have reimbursed the caretaker. The second option was to not reclaim the building until the caretaker paid to the government an amount in rents equal to the cost of improvements. The government would then have, in essence, given the caretaker back his money in lieu of rents payable to the owners. Her final option was to sell the house, either to the caretaker or another buyer. Following the sale, she would reimburse the caretaker. The APC, however, as formal custodian of the property, had the right to set the selling price. In the end, the owner waited until accumulated rents were enough to pay off the caretaker, which took about a year. She then reclaimed the house and sold it to the caretaker at a price the two negotiated without interference from the APC.[68]

Another example is the case of Raphael Nyamasi. Nyamasi, the Cameroonian who had been NCNC secretary for the far north from 1960–1962, had strong political and social links to the Igbo community. He returned to Kano in 1970. In addition to a house, he owned a hotel that was under the care of a Midwestern woman who claimed to have spent £300 on repairs and improvements. Administrative delays and difficulty in raising the money to cover repairs and land dues prevented him from regaining formal control of the hotel until 1972, and from completely divesting the caretaker until 1976.[69]

Some owners did not demonstrate the Nyamasi's level of patience. In fact, one of the APC's biggest problems was returning owners, eager to reoccupy their property, asking tenants to vacate on short notice, sometimes before taking formal possession. The tenants, who had agreements not with owners, but rather with the caretakers, often refused. Collectively owned properties with income-generating potential such as town union halls were also particularly vulnerable to long delays. Following a series of delays, the Amucha Patriotic Union sold its hall to a local man in 1975. Selling the hall, union members said, was the only way to recoup any of its value from its caretaker, owing to delays within the APC. The price of £4,500 was much less than the £20,000 they argued was the market value of the sixteen-room structure built on a double plot. The twenty union members who had been in Kano before the war reinvested the money in Aba, Igboland's commercial second city. Later, under the new name of the Amucha Youth Association, they began work on a new building in Sabon Gari.

There were also informal caretaking arrangements that grew out of pre-war business relationships. While some such arrangements never came to the attention of authorities, others did. In addition to written documentation, oral testimony by local people was key in supporting undocumented claims by Igbos. This is clear in the case of a Hausa palm oil trader in the Riman Dada section of Kano who had an Igbo apprentice, Andrew, living with him. A second Igbo, a trading partner, had given the Hausa trader ownership of a house in Sabon Gari in lieu of an unpaid debt. The trader, a devout Muslim, was reluctant to own a house in Sabon Gari, because of the ward's association with sex work and alcohol, and he offered to sell it to Andrew. Andrew agreed, and the two made an oral contract with one witness, a Hausa neighbor. Andrew would pay £1,100, in installments, and then take possession of the house. When Andrew fled Kano, he had paid £350. The Hausa trader died during the war, and left instructions to his heirs that the house in Sabon Gari not be included in his estate; rather the family was to give Andrew the opportunity to resume payments if he returned to Kano. If Andrew did not return, the trader instructed, the family was to turn the property over to the government. Andrew did return, and he and the traders' children agreed on new payment terms. They then approached the Local Authority for permission for Andrew to take possession of the house. The Local Authority rejected the claim based on the absence of written proof of Andrew's ownership. When the witness to the oral contract testified on Andrew's behalf, the Local Authority released the property to the children who turned it over to Andrew.[70]

Finally, some property remained under the control of caretakers simply because it was unclaimed. For example, an Igbo informant described his father's house in Kiyawa, a village approximately 150 kilometers from Kano, near Dutse. As of 1994, the house had been abandoned since 1966. After the owner's death, possession of the certificate of occupancy passed on to his oldest son, the half-brother of the informant. The new owner, however, had not claimed the property in 1994, and the house remained in the care of the state government. The informant, who lived in Kano and physically maintained the structure, was unwilling to press any claim to the house because of the oldest son's customary right to the property of the father.[71]

## CORRUPTION

Bribery was an important component in the return of abandoned property, though accounts differ on how pervasive it was. Some details of its operation, however, are clear. A number of Igbos interviewed reported reclaiming their property without offering bribes or being asked to pay them. Others reported being forced to pay in order to avoid delays in the return of their property. Payment of a bribe to someone within the APC bureaucracy could ease minor problems with owners' paperwork, guarantee prompt processing of their claims, or expedite transitional arrangements with the caretaker. On the other hand, two Hausa informants suggested that in many cases returning

Igbos offered bribes unnecessarily to people in the Local Authority and Waje offices to expedite their claims; in the words of one, "The Igbos believed that nothing would go without anything." Similarly, they said, upon the closing of claims, some Igbos offered "gratuities."[72] Still, some within the Local Authority and Waje offices consciously slowed the return of property, apparently to take advantage of cash-strapped and politically impotent migrants. When this happened, it appears to have been done in cooperation with caretakers who sought to extend their access to rents and commercial profits, or to frustrate owners into selling their property. Several informants reported being approached by "underground negotiators" claiming connections to the APC. These underground negotiators, in each case presenting themselves as *Kanawa*, promised to expedite the release of property if the owners would promise, in turn, to sell the property to clients of the negotiator.[73] As discussed in the following chapters, the sell-off of land in Sabon Gari by some Igbo owners during the 1970s is part of a larger pattern of changing investment tendencies among Igbos living outside of Igboland. During the 1980s, much of the land Igbos sold off the previous decade would find its way back into Igbo hands.

## KANO AS A POINT OF CONTRAST

Despite incidents of corruption, two things are striking about the abandoned property story in Kano, and to varying degrees, other parts of the North. First, while bribery was a problem, it was not pervasive, and did not derail the process of handing over property. The second point is the general absence of public controversy over the return of abandoned property. This was very different than the experience of Igbo property owners in non-Igbo areas of the old Eastern Region, areas that had been inside the borders of Biafra early in the war. Conventional wisdom holds that once federal troops occupied these areas, locals seized Igbo property "with the connivance of the federal government," and "divided it among themselves."[74] Igbos in Kano frequently described their experiences in contrast to those places, where much—often most—of Igbo property was not returned. This is clearest in the case of Port Harcourt, the major center of Igbo property ownership outside of Igboland in pre-war Eastern Nigeria, and after 1968 the capital of Rivers State. The ECS-controlled *Renaissance* noted that "It is an irony that it is the Northern States which the secessionist authorities declared collectively as the arch enemy of the Ibos that have demonstrated better understanding in their approach to the problem . . . "[75] While the federal government encouraged the return of Igbos to the North, Gowon was reluctant to push for their return to Rivers State. In May of 1970, he noted that hostility to Igbos in the state "had not gone unnoticed," but justified it by explaining that non-Igbos had suffered at the hands of Biafrans.[76] A letter from a Rivers citizen was less circumspect: "It would be too audacious for certain perpetrators of certain brutal atrocities on the Rivers people and their property to hurry back to Port Harcourt at this time; it would be taking the Rivers people and their Government . . . for granted. This would add to the complex refugee problems of the young State; there would also be a great security risk for these people themselves."[77] Private companies were responsive to such sentiments. Oil company executives and others in the private sector reported pressure from locals to avoid rehiring former Igbo employees. There were also allegations of unpublicized attacks on Igbos attempting to enter the city.[78]

Igbo property remained at the center of events, however. In early 1971 the East Central State government claimed that its citizens owned £56 million worth of property that sat unused in Rivers State, including undeveloped land and 5,600 buildings. Later that year an ECS official estimated that the rents collected monthly on Igbo-owned property in Rivers State was £500,000.[79] Early the next year, the Rivers government promulgated a decree that severely curtailed the power of nominal owners to control their property. The decree prohibited the eviction of anyone who had occupied a property for more than two years without explicit permission from the state's Abandoned Property Authority.[80] The two-year window appears designed to help consolidate the gains of wartime occupants. U.S diplomats quoted a high-ranking Rivers State official who, in discussing the edict, told them that Igbos could not be allowed to reassume control of their property, "or why have we fought the war?"[81] Similarly, the fomer Secretary to the Kano State government and a former APC chairman recall a top Rivers State official expressing shock that Kano state was returning Igbo property.[82]

In May 1973 ECS administrator Ukpabi Asika launched another volley when he laid the blame for the problem in Rivers at the feet of "vested interests . . . anxious to expropriate and to continue to enjoy their illegal booty from the efforts of others, some of whom even now live in Port Harcourt but who have no access to their legitimate property."[83] And, in July of that year, *West Africa* reported that the Rivers State government had "acquired 1,000 items of 'abandoned' property" in the state, and had canceled leases on an additional 856 plots of land in Port Harcourt, most of which Igbos had held.[84] In September, the state government announced it had completed arrangements to pay compensation to owners whose property it had acquired.[85] Similar struggles had taken place on a diminished scale in Calabar, capital of South East State, where the state government also announced plans to acquire "unclaimed" property.[86] By October, 1973, the South East State government claimed to have released only 130 houses, and to have "acquired" another 250 from their owners.[87] Igbo owners pressed their cases, but to little avail. The problem persisted, and in 1976 the Nigerian government intervened in both states. The next year, however, a top administrator in Port Harcourt barred citizens of Imo and Anambra States (successor states to East-Central)—in other words, Igbos—from buying abandoned houses in the city.[88] The expropriation of Igbo property in Port Harcourt, Calabar, and other parts of the southeast remains an open sore. It is common for Igbos to refer to such property as "captured" rather than abandoned.

Several factors contributed to the difference in attitudes toward abandoned property between Kano and the southeastern cities. The first factor at work was the Igbo population's more important commercial role in Kano and other northern cities than in non-Igbo areas in the south. As the following chapter details, returning Igbos brought with them many of the same skills and access to trading networks that had characterized their presence before the war. Those skills and connections were at far less of a premium in the southeast. More importantly, after the war Igbos appear to have been both less feared and less resented in the North than they had been in the southeast. The Igbo presence in Kano, though substantial, had never approached in either number or proportion that of Port Harcourt, which lay on the southern frontier of Igboland. The 1958 report of the Willinks Commission on the status of Nigeria's minority groups within the regions concluded that "Port Harcourt is an Ibo town; it is growing rapidly and the indigenous branch of the Igbos who were originally inhabitants are already out-numbered by Igbos from the hinterland."[89] Within the former Eastern Region, where Igbos had been the numerical majority, those who exerted the greatest control over political and economic life had been Igbos, even in non-Igbo parts of the region. According to the report, "In the whole of this non-Ibo area there is present in varying degrees some fear of being over-run, commercially and politically, by the Igbos . . . "[90] Land ownership, in particular, was at issue.

There is no doubt that on the Ibo plateau there is insufficient land for the people; the Ibos are thrusting outwards into the surrounding areas and where possible they do acquire land and use it either for cultivation or for building. Where land is held communally, as is usually the case, they cannot acquire freehold; what is probably most usual is that they obtain possession as a favour or for some trifling consideration and then are hard to evict. This is a matter that will require legislation sooner or later and it will be delicate to handle . . . [91]

Indeed, in a response to the commission's report, the Ibo State Union articulated fears that should non-Igbo areas of the Eastern Region be separated from the Eastern Region, "The Igbos would be disenfranchised and their properties seized."[92] The creation of states separated Igbo and non-Igbo areas; further, it did so during wartime, when resource-strapped Biafra was experiencing internal crises, and the federal government was using ethnic differences there to maximize divisions. According to *West Africa*,

> The trouble is not merely that it is widely believed by Rivers people that in the former Eastern Region Igbos used their political power to further their economic domination in non-Ibo areas—though now that the Rivers people are firmly in control of their own state they could surely prevent such domination emerging again. The real problem is that however exaggerated the stories may be, Rivers people are full of resentment at what they believe to have been cruel rebel treatment meted out to them—sometimes by their own people who supported the rebellion.[93]

On the other hand, the Igbo presence in Kano during the war had been minimal, and the war itself had been fought far away. So, while resentments in the southeast had grown, in the North, they had cooled.[94]

## CONCLUSION

There is no clear end point to the abandoned property saga. There was a marked drop-off in property claims in Kano after 1973. The APC ceased to exist officially in 1975, when the state umbrella organization under which it then operated, the Ministry of Internal Affairs' Rehabilitation and Reconstruction Committee, disbanded.[95] Data gathered in 1973 from the Local Authority reported that 1,002 of the 1,502 houses taken over by the APC had been returned.[96] No more recent official information on the remaining 500 has become available. A few cases lingered, however. In the case of the Orlu Division Union hall, it took time, money, and political connections to recover the hall. Caretakers retained control of the Orlu Division Union hall until 1983, when the Union took advantage of political rivalry within Kano State and appealed to civilian Governor Abubakar Rimi to release the property.[97] A locally owned insurance and development company had taken over the building, one of the largest union halls in Sabon Gari, and put it to use as a gambling club and beer parlor. When the union reclaimed the building in 1983, it paid N12,000 for the improvements to the property. Promises for payment of rents were never made good.[98]

Still, despite the difficulties, the recovery of abandoned property was an essential component in rebuilding Igbo lives. The ability of property owners to assist other migrants with lodging, employment, or capital amplified its importance to the wider Igbo community in Kano, and even into Igboland. That property owners in the North encountered, in general, substantially better treatment than their counterparts in areas like Port Harcourt was an important indicator that they were welcome to return to Kano and other parts of the region. On the other hand, that there were delays to be endured, bribes to pay, and pressure to sell their property at low prices reinforced the gulf between communities, a gulf where ethnicity and state citizenship overlapped to reinscribe old divisions. The delays, bribes, and pressures to sell were also reminders that Igbos who remained in Kano did so on terms set by the local populace. Under the circumstances of post-war poverty and dislocation, these terms were acceptable to the migrants who remained in Kano. That the state and care-taker landlords were able to benefit from their homes, rental properties, and places of business was part of the price Igbo owners paid for having lost the war, and for being politically marginal aliens in a state not their own. The following chapter explores the ways in which these migrants reestablished themselves economically beyond the question of abandoned property, and the ways in which they negotiated their status as defeated, but economically necessary Nigerians.

## NOTES

1. *New Nigerian* 16 January 1971.

2. See Philip Jaggar, *The Blacksmiths of Kano City: A Study in Tradition, Innovation and Entrepreneurship* (Cologne: Köppe Verlag, 1994), 90–92.

3. FN 3A: Interview with Alhaji Uba Adamu, 13 November 1993, Kano.

4. FN-Anonymous.

5. NAK ASI/17.115, 212, letter, I.A. Nkwocha to Minister of Finance (Kaduna), 31 December, 1966.

6. HCB 562 CER/3/Vol. III, 544, letter, Raphael Nnadozie to Provincial Secretary (Kano), February 1967.

7. NAK ASI/17.115, 227, 240, letter, Mr. E. Onyika to Military Governor of Northern Nigeria, 10 April 1967.

8. NAK ASI/17.115, 230, letter, A.C. Obodo to Minna Native Authority, 12 April 1967.

9. NAK ASI/17.115, 235, letter from Paulinus Mbachu to Provincial Secretary (Makurdi), 13 April 1967.

10. NAK ASI/17.115, 242, letter, Provincial Secretary (Makurdi) to Secretary to the Military Governor (Kaduna), n.d.

11. NAK ASI/17.115, 214, letter, Vincent N. Ummerah to Secretary to the Military Governor (Kaduna), 7 December 1966. Ummerah was from Awgu Division in Igboland.

12. B.A.W. Trevallion, *Metropolitan Kano: Report on the Twenty Year Development Plan, 1963–1983* (Oxford: Pergamon Press 1963), 47–48.

13. The figure of 2,074 originates in KSPO LAN/50, cited in Alan Frishman, *The Spatial Growth and Residential Location Pattern of Kano, Nigeria* (Ph.D. dissertation, Northwestern University, 1977), 192. The estimate of Igbo land ownership comes from FN 3A: Interview with Alhaji Uba Adamu, 13 November 1993, Kano. Other estimates by individuals with similar access to first-hand information ran higher, usually 90 percent.

14. This is according to the records of the Abandoned Property Commission, as cited in Ogbogu, "Ibo Integration in Kano After the War," 45. The records themselves are no longer available, and Ogbobu's thesis is one of the few links to the records that remain.

15. *Nigeria Population Census: Northern Region, Vol. II* (Lagos: Government Printer, 1963), cited in *Kano State Statistical Yearbook, 1972* (Kano: Military Governor's Office, 1972), 21. The census counted a total of 11,474 Igbos in Kano Province, including 2,489 outside of cities and towns. The data from the politically charged 1963 census recorded only a fraction of the normal Igbo population, since most Nigerians returned home to be counted in their home regions.

16. *West Africa*, June 13 1970, 658.

17. S.E. Mosugu, *Abandoned Property Edicts in the Northern States* (Zaria: Nigeria Institute of Administration, Ahmadu Bello University, 1972), 35–36.

18. HCB 562 CER/3, Vol. III, n.p., letter, from S.B. Olaye to Kano Local Authority, 24 January 1967.

19. HCB 562 CER/3, Vol. III, n.p., letter, Office of the Secretary to the Military Governor to all Provincial Secretaries (Northern Nigeria), 18 February 1967.

20. HCB 817/LAN/28, Vol. III, 687, letter, J.P.D. Ogbise to Waje District Head, 19 September 1967.

21. HCB 562 CER/3, Vol. III, n.p., memo concerning query from M.A. Akinsanni, 8 April 1967.

22. HCB 562 CER/3, Vol. III, letters. In a letter to the District Officer, Kano, dated 3 April 1967, M.A. Akinsanni writes "I am Yoruba by birth." HCB 817/LAN/28, Vol. III; FN 53: Interview with Alhaji Sharu Audu Mili, 22 September 1994, Kano; FN 84: Interview with Malam Sunusi, 17 September 1994, Kano.

23. For a discussion of the state creation exercise in Kano, and its ramifications for the local economic, political, and religious life, see Paden, *Religion and Political Culture*, chapter nine.

24. HCB 218/R.974, 47, letter, *Madakin* Kano to Acting Secretary to the Governor, 27 August 1967.

25. FN 16: Interview with Alhaji Sani Bala, 8 August 1994, Kano.

26. The committee's first chair was Alhaji Sani Bala, head of the Local Authority (*Kantoma*), and a former Kano representative in the Northern House of Assembly during the First Republic. The APC's membership consisted of representatives of the Native Authority, the state Ministry of Health, and the Police, Army, and Air Force.

27. KSPO LAN/50 cited in Frishman, *Spatial Growth*, 192.

28. FN 3A: Interview with Alhaji Uba Adamu, 13 November 1993, Kano; FN 16: Interview with Alhaji Sani Bala, 8 August 1994, Kano; FN 96A: Interview with Alhaji Tanko Yakasai, 3 January 1994, Kano.

29. FN 70A: Interview with Chief Davis Ohaeri, 19 March 1994, Kano.

30. HCB 760/IMM 45, 8-11, letters Alhaji A. Galadi, et al., to Refugees Union, Kano Branch (routed to Native Authority Social Welfare Officer), 20 July 1967.

31. HCB 760/IMM 45, 12-14.

32. FN 96A: Interview with Alhaji Tanko Yakasai, 3 January 1994, Kano.

33. FN 3A: Interview with Alhaji Uba Adamu, 13 November 1993, Kano; FN 16: Interview with Alhaji Sani Bala, 8 August 1994, Kano.

34. FN 26: Interview with Police Inspector Rilwanu Dutse (rtd.), 9 August 1994, Kano.

35. FN 3A: Interview with Alhaji Uba Adamu, 13 November 1993, Kano.

36. FN 16: Interview with Alhaji Sani Bala, 8 August 1994, Kano. For more on the 1969 order, see J.S. Eades, *Strangers and Traders: Yoruba Migrants, Markets and the State in Northern Ghana* (Trenton: Africa World Press, 1994).

37. FN 3C: Interview with Alhaji Uba Adamu, 1 December 1993, Kano.

38. FN 16: Interview with Alhaji Sani Bala, 8 August 1994, Kano; FN 87: Interview with the Very Reverend Samuel Uche, 1 June 1994, Kano.

39. Population statistics from the Waje Office cited in Frishman, *Spatial Growth*, 193.

40. For perspective, the number quintupled between 1969 and 1973, when 6,700 workers paid tax. Lubeck, *Islam and Urban Labor in Northern Nigeria*, 323.

41. FN 3B: Interview with Alhaji Uba Adamu, 17 November 1993, Kano; FN 50: Interview with Mr. Abdul R. Khatoun, 10 September 1994, Kano; FN 69: Interview with Father John O'Brien, 11 March 1994, Kano; FN 96A: Interview with Alhaji Tanko Yakasai, 3 January 1994, Kano.

42. Paden, *Religion and Political Culture*, 357.

43. Paden, *Ahmadu Bello, Sardauna of Sokoto*, 587. According to Trevallion, there were 4,150 stalls in Kurmi in 1965, versus 6,800 in Sabon Gari. See Trevallion, *Metropolitan Kano*.

44. Bako, *A Socio-Economic History of Sabon Gari Kano*, 268.

45. In 1955 less than .5 percent of Sabon Gari residents identified as Hausa or Fulani. "Tribal Population Statistics," cited in Paden, *Religion and Political Culture*, 315.

46. Ogbogu, "Ibo Integration," 57.

47. FN 3A: Interview with Alhaji Uba Adamu, 13 November 1993, Kano.

48. FN 38: Interview with Alhaji Abdulrahman Howeidy, 18 April 1994, Kano.

49. FN 3A: Interview with Alhaji Uba Adamu, 13 November 1993, Kano.

50. A former APC chair remarked, "No Hausa man would run a hotel. We would call them to be caretakers of hotels and they would run away." FN 3A: Interview with Alhaji Uba Adamu, 13 November 1993, Kano.

51. FN 66: Interview with Mr. Mambo Nyamasi, 27 February 1994, Kano.

52. Ogbogu, "Ibo Integration," 45.

53. FN 4: Interview with Chief D.O. Adinuso, 1 July 1994, Kano.

54. FN 96A: Interview with Alhaji Tanko Yakasai, 3 January 1994, Kano.

55. FN 3C: Interview with Alhaji Uba Adamu, 1 December 1993, Kano; FN 27A: Interview with Chief J.B. Egbe, 27 December 1993, Kano; FN 32A: Interview with Mr. J.C. Emodi, 6 May 1993, Kano; FN 66: Interview with Mr. Mambo Nyamasi, 27 February 1994, Kano; FN 76: Interview with Mr. Robert Onuora, 31 March 1994, Kano; FN 79B: Interview with Chief Michael Onyeador, 30 September 1994, Kano.

56. FN 3A: Interview with Alhaji Uba Adamu, 13 November 1993, Kano.

57. Paden, *Religion and Political Culture*, 356.

58. Available editions of the *Kano State Gazette* document 75 second-party claims. *Kano State Gazette*, (Kano: Ministry of Information, 1970–75). Of the claims, wives filed 28, children 23 (12 of whom were identified as "eldest son"). In nine cases "widow and son" combinations made claims.

59. Of the 75 second-person claims, 27 owners were killed in 1966, all but one in October; three died 1967, eight in 1968, and five in 1969; seven died in 1970, after the formal cessation of hostilities. Publication of the *Gazette* was sometimes irregular, and its numbering inconsistent. It is likely that the surveyed sample represents about three-quarters of published cases. The question of violent crime in postwar Igboland is discussed in chapter six.

60. FN 100: Interview with Alhaji Lawal Tudun Wada, 10 June 1998, Kano.

61. Many so-called "hotels" were actually bars with very limited, if any, overnight accommodation.

62. The institution whereby women in some Igbo groups could marry wives and benefit from their productive and reproductive activities is described in great depth in Ifi Amadiume, *Male Daughters, Female Husbands: Gender and Sex in an African Society* (London: Zed Books Limited, 1987). As Amadiume has described the practice in Idemili, a woman of economic means might marry a wife to free herself from domestic or conjugal responsibilities. Female-female marriages could also be invoked in cases where there was no son to carry on a patrilineage; in these cases the eldest daughter could assume the status of a "male daughter" and marry wives whose children from other men would belong to and perpetuate the patrilineage. Unfortunately, based on available sources it is unclear from where Mrs. Inuwa originated, and which, if either, situation described by Amadiume applied to her case.

63. FN 3A: Interview with Alhaji Uba Adamu, 13 November 1993, Kano.

64. Paden, *Religion and Political Culture*, 356.

65. Ogbogu, "Ibo Integration," 45.

66. The rent caretakers paid to the APC was usually £2 10/– per month for a multi-tenant dwelling. With full occupancy, a caretaker could gross ten to twenty times that amount from tenants.

67. FN 3A and FN 3C: Interviews with Alhaji Uba Adamu, 13 November and 1 December 1993, Kano; FN 16: Interview with Alhaji Sani Bala, 8 August 1994, Kano.

68. FN 3C: Interview with Alhaji Uba Adamu, 1 December 1993, Kano.

69. FN 66: Interview with Mr. Mambo Nyamasi, 27 February 1994, Kano.

70. FN 3A: Interview with Alhaji Uba Adamu, 13 November 1993, Kano.

71. FN 42: Interview with Mr. Emanuel Irozuru, 8 September 1994, Kano.

72. FN-Anonymous.

73. FN-Anonymous.

74. See, for example, Nnoli, *Ethnicity and Development in Nigeria*, 143. Assigning "Igbo identity" in this context presents difficulties. Nnoli noted, "The Igbo indigenous who remained found it advantageous to deny their Igbo origin and claimed, instead, a non-Igbo Ikwerre identity."

75. "Abandoned Property," *Renaissance*, 17 January 1971.

76. *West Africa*, 9 May 1970, 537.

77. *West Africa*, 30 May 1970, 590. The author is W.H. Kio Lawson, an officer in the Rivers State Students Union of Great Britain and Ireland.

78. USNA POL 15/2508, 7 April 1970.

79. *West Africa,* 6 February 1971, 178; Sam Ikoku, ECS Commissioner for Economic Development and Reconstruction, quoted in *West Africa*, 17 October 1971, 1097.

80. Decree 21 of 1971 was in fact published in the Rivers State *Official Gazette* of February 1972. Excerpted in USNA POL 15/2505/A-88, 1, 25 March 1972.

81. F.S. Abraskasa was the Rivers State Permanent Secretary in Lagos, quoted in USNA POL 15/2505/A-88, 2, 25 March 1972.

82. FN 3D: Interview with Alhaji Uba Adamu, 18 April 1994, Kano; and FN 38: Interview with Alhaji Abdulrahman Howeidy, 18 April 1994, Kano.

83. *West Africa*, 14 May 1973, 650.

84. *West Africa*, 23 July 1973, 1015.

85. *West Africa*, 24 September 1973, 1362.

86. *West Africa*, 11 February 1972, 169.

87. *West Africa*, 15 October 1973, 1471.

88. Nafziger, *The Economics of Political Instability*, 178.

89. *Report of the Commission*, 51.

90. *Report of the Commission*, 37.

91. *Report of the Commission*, 42.

92. Ibo State Union, *Memorandum to the Willinks Commission* (Port Harcourt: NPP Press, 1958), 24.

93. *West Africa*, 25 April 1970, 463. In his work on reconstruction in Igboland, Harneit-Sievers has made a similar argument. Axel Harneit-Sievers, "'No Victors, No Vanquished'? Reconstruction and Reintegration after the Nigerian Civil War" (unpublished paper, 1994), 15.

94. This is not to say that the North was without incident. In a number of Northern cities, tenants lodged complaints against landlords who reclaimed property and then raised rents or evicted them. More seriously, at a handing over ceremony in

Kafanchan, the Zaria Provincial Secretary condemned the "uncooperative attitude" of returning Igbos, whom he alleged had presented false documentation. This followed a protracted and public dispute in which Igbos in Jema'a alleged delays of up to five months in return of property. Such public disputes, however, were unusual in the North. USNA POL 18/2516/A-59, 3, 6 August 1971.

95. FN 38: Interview with Alhaji Abdulrahman Howeidy, 18 April 1994, Kano.

96. Ogbogu, "Ibo Reintegration," 45. Ogbogu gathered her information directly from the Local Authority.

97. FN 70B: Interview with Chief Davis Ohaeri, 18 June 1994, Kano.

98. FN 15: Interview with Mr. K.J. Asika, 12 February 1994, Kano; FN 70A: Interview with Chief Davis Ohaeri, 19 March 1994, Kano; FN 90B: Interview with Mr. Humphrey S.C. Umeh, 25 January 1994. See also chapter seven. One informant, an Igbo businessman who served as a ward chairman in the short-lived Social Democratic Party during the early 1990s, reported that some properties remained under state control as late as 1994. During 1988 and 1989, before the creation of parties, he represented an area that included Noman's Land, parts of Gwagwarwa and Brigade, and the northern half of Sabon Gari on Kano's municipal council. He reported that in that capacity he became aware of up to fifty cases of unresolved abandoned property dating to the Civil War era. While there is no way to confirm this number, neither is there any way to determine the total number of abandoned properties under the supervision of the government at any subsequent time. Both copies of the abandoned property registry, one with the Kano Waje office and the other with the Ministry of Social Welfare, have been reported lost, and official estimates were not forthcoming. Whether the registries were lost as the result of multiple moves and changes in administration, or for the convenience of those caretakers reaping the benefits of the large margin between their cost and their intake is impossible to say. Both explanations are equally plausible. It is reasonable to believe that in an area representing approximately half of Sabon Gari there would be fifty houses still under caretakership, particularly when one also considers that some property of deceased landlords was unclaimed in 1994 and remained, formally, under government supervision. During the early 1990s, caretakers paid a fixed amount of N30 per month in rent to the Kano State Ministry of Social Welfare, to be held in account for the owners. Actual rents paid to the caretaker by tenants, however, were as high as N400 per month, and subject to increase. FN 13: Interview with Chief C.O. Anyaka, 5 July 1994, Kano; FN 70A: Interview with Chief Davis Ohaeri, 19 March 1994, Kano.

# 6

# "I NEED TO GET TO KANO": POST-WAR IGBO MIGRATION

## INTRODUCTION

For most Igbos at the end of the war, a decision to venture into the North was not an easy one. Questions of safety loomed large. Inescapable were recollections of 1966, when simply to be Igbo was to be targeted. Those who had not been in the North themselves had encountered refugees, or heard stories the refugees brought with them. Could the federal government's promises be believed? Were Northerners indeed prepared to accept back those they had expelled? Further, open hostility toward Igbos in other parts of the former Eastern Region gave these questions an added currency. Despite changes in its tone during the war, the discourse of ethnicity had persisted. Igbos, in the eyes of other Nigerians, were perhaps siblings under the national flag, but they were still Igbos, and it seemed improbable that the venom directed against them could be so easily set aside. Accounts of the months and years following the war by both Igbos and *Kanawa* reflect an acute awareness of belonging to different communities, and of building or reestablishing relationships across a fundamental divide.

As before the war, Igbo ethnicity remained politically charged in ways that other ethnic identities were not. While some Igbos had remained loyal to Nigeria during the war, the association of Igbos with Biafra had been very strong. Federal propaganda had largely succeeded in distancing non-Igbo Easterners from Biafra in the eyes of most Nigerians, leaving Igbos to bear the stigma of secession alone. Further, new modes of political discourse that emphasized the states and state citizenship did little to mute the visibility of Igbo ethnicity since the overwhelming majority of Igbos were now citizens of the new East Central State. Igbo ethnicity and ECS citizenship were virtually interchangable to a degree not true for any other ethnic group, since Hausas and Yorubas each constituted majorities in more than one state, and the country's minority groups shared states with one another and the large groups.[1] In this climate, Igbos had little choice but to accept that they were easily identified in ethnic terms. In rebuilding their lives in the North, most Igbos embraced that assumption.

### "NO VICTOR, NO VANQUISHED"

Despite the government's stated policy of "No Victor, No Vanquished," and rhetoric espousing the "brotherhood" of all Nigerians, the war had devastated the lives of most former Biafrans. Official documents and broadcasts spoke often of the "three R's" of reconciliation, rehabilitation, and reconstruction. Of these, reconciliation is not only the most compelling, but also the most difficult to define or recognize. Rehabilitation can, to a large degree, be measured in terms of wealth, income, or property ownership, and by using conventional gauges of social status and stability within households and communities. Reconstruction lends itself to even more concrete measures, since we can, with relative ease, track the reversal of material devastation. Reconciliation, however, happens largely beyond the reach of historical inquiry; it is subjective, conditional, and ongoing. Among its currencies are forgiveness, and, more elusively, trust. It is certainly not a process to be taken for granted in post-Civil War Nigeria. Yet, to the extent that reconciliation occurred, it was closely linked to rehabilitation and reconstruction.

Slogans proclaiming "No Vanquished" notwithstanding, there was no doubting that Igbos had indeed lost the war. Probably of equal importance, they had lost the pre-war conflicts as well. And while federal rhetoric had created a framework to seal over some of the fissures created by the war, it had done little to address the pre-war period. There had been no apologies for the killings in the North, no attempts to identify and expose those behind them. The people who had conceived of, organized, and perpetrated the purge were, at least in official terms, forgotten. The anger, bitterness, and fear that many victims of the violence of 1966 felt prevented them from returning North; their stories remain to date largely untold. It is in some ways remarkable, then, that many other Igbos chose to return, or to emigrate for the first time.

It is equally striking that the broad consensus among Kano's Igbos is that, despite their many misgivings about going North, there was very little hostility to their return. Most use the expression "warm reception" in describing their experiences. Individuals recall not only friendly reunions with Hausa friends and associates, but describe an atmosphere of general receptivity to their return.[2] In economic terms, besides the lure of abandoned property, there were jobs for technicians and skilled laborers, bookkeepers and teachers, nurses and mechanics. In the face of destitution, the promise of collecting even small debts made a trip North tempting. Material assistance and help in re-establishing economic connections was available from Kano citizens to many professionals and, more importantly, traders. And, from the early 1970s, a small but symbolically important number of jobs in the new Kano State's public services went to Igbos, many of whom were actively recruited, and most of whom were first-time migrants.

Economic and social conditions in Igboland, including a devastating set of decisions by the federal government that wiped out the bank accounts of former Biafrans who held them, pushed people to emigrate. On the other hand, Kano's booming economy and the promise of the rents from abandoned property pulled at those willing and able to look past the physical and emotional trauma of 1966. The humility that individual Igbos displayed after the war appears to have eased their reentry into Kano society as much as their now sought-after commercial connections and professional skills. Those who could speak Hausa used it in public rather than English; those who did not know Hausa learned it; and few spoke Igbo publicly. Displays of ethnic chauvinism by Igbos disappeared. As a result, migrants, so recently defeated in war, were able to negotiate for themselves places in a political and economic climate fundamentally changed by state creation and the first ripples of Nigeria's oil boom. The overall climate was one in which Igbos in Kano, as elsewhere, regained their economic footing through a combination of aid in cash and kind from friends, associates, and even strangers, but most importantly through individual and collective self-help.

It is important to recognize that the Igbos' return to the North differed sharply from their departure. The violence of 1966 had the effect of driving away most of the North's Igbo population in waves, first in late May and early June, then in late September and early October. In contrast, the returnees and new migrants arrived in a trickle, a trickle that, in fact, had begun before the cessation of hostilities in January 1970. Those who came in the first two years after the war appear to have been mostly returning migrants, many of whom owned property, though a small cadre of first-time Igbo public servants that arrived in 1970 was an important exception. Early post-war migrants were overwhelmingly male, though from late 1970 on, there was a small but unprecedented number of Igbo women living on their own in Kano. There, as in other Northern cities, they filled jobs in retail, at telephone exchanges, and in offices. A substantial number of the first Igbos to arrive did not remain in Kano as residents; rather they reclaimed what property they could, then either sold it or rented it out to cash-paying tenants and returned south. By 1973, however, the rate at which abandoned property was reclaimed fell off substantially.[3] Igbos who migrated to Kano after 1971 included reluctant returnees and first-time migrants, many of whom went only after hearing from others that the situation in Kano was stable and secure. At the same time the number of Igbos who spent time in Kano without residing there grew as well. Trucks bearing East Central State license plates were a regular sight by 1971, as their drivers brought manufactured goods, women's clothing, and textiles from southern ports, and purchased and transported loads of Northern groundnuts and rice to markets in the south.[4]

There are few reliable estimates of the numbers of returnees, in part because of the high level of transience that characterized the first several years. An early returner estimated there were 500 Igbos in Kano by April, 1970,[5] which, allowing for gradual growth, is consistent with the 800 Kano's military governor estimated in August of that year.[6] Paden reported that by March, sixty or so Igbos were reopening bank accounts in Kano each week.[7] Numbers continued to increase throughout the 1970s, with 1972 and 1973 the consensus peak years, and the Igbo population probably reached pre-war levels by the end of the decade. Other parts of the North followed similar patterns. In Jos, the Catholic bishop estimated 3,000 had returned by mid-1971, many to jobs in Posts and Telegraphs, and as laborers, mechanics, and tradesmen in the Ministry of Works. In Kaduna, Igbo women and men were visible in white collar jobs and as skilled laborers.[8]

While the gradual nature of the Igbos' return contributed to the welcome they received by minimizing any potential threat they might have represented, equally important was the fact that most returned in poverty—in many cases literal destitution. Their poverty was particularly acute relative to the pre-war affluence many Igbos enjoyed or appeared to enjoy. Economic and political realities contributed to a willingness to welcome the Igbos back as well. The national economy had expanded substantially during the war, and continued to do so afterward, particularly after petroleum exports increased markedly in 1973. Kano's economy was also expanding, boosted by the city's elevation to the capital of Nigeria's most populous state. Many of the occupational and economic gaps the Igbo exodus had created had been filled, in many cases by Yorubas from the west or the Middle Belt.[9] Non-Igbos had been less successful filling the void left by Igbo traders, and many of the goods and services they had traded in Kano's markets had been either largely absent since 1966, or available only at inflated prices.

And, quite significantly, the reality of an administratively separate Kano State government from 1968 contributed to an increased sense of control over their political and economic destiny among Kano people; this in turn fed an environment in which Igbo migrants could be more easily seen as contributors to local development than before the war. Unlike 1966 in particular, it was implausible to see them as part of a conspiracy to usurp local agency. Much of this change, of course, derived from the increasingly local focus that state creation had brought to questions of governance. Even Igbos in the federal services, however, had experienced severe setbacks because of the war. Though a substantial number of Igbos were "reabsorbed" into their federal jobs after the war, they had lost at least three years of seniority to their colleagues; others had not survived, did not return to government work, or were reluctant to accept postings in the North. Further, a federal decree allowed for the compulsory retirement or dismissal for former Biafran officials, though it was used selectively.[10] Before the war, federal positions had been an Igbo bastion in Kano and other Northern cities. After 1966, non-Igbos, most of them southerners and Middle-Belters, filled nearly all the federal public service positions from which Igbos had been driven. As a result, the number of Igbo federal employees who returned to Kano was substantially smaller than the pre-war number, and, across the country, the corps they joined had far fewer Igbos in it, including the politically sensitive middle and senior levels.

## POST-WAR ECONOMIC AND LIVING CONDITIONS: THE EAST

Economic conditions in post-war Igboland were generally harsh.[11] At the close of hostilities in January 1970, food shortages were the most immediate problem, and persisted in some areas for several months. Igboland had been one of Africa's most densely populated subregions before the war, even before the return of refugees, and remained so afterward, despite wartime deaths in the hundreds of thousands or more.[12] Reconstruction within the East Central State hinged initially on food assistance for the period between planting and harvest, and on individuals regaining access to Nigeria's cash economy.[13] While large stocks of food were brought in by non-governmental relief agencies, damaged infrastructure and economic stagnation slowed its penetration away from distribution centers. Currency shortages meant that many areas relied on elaborate systems of barter. In April, the *Times* of London reported that "Food is cheaper in the East Central State than in any other part of the country. The only trouble is that there is no money with which to buy it."[14] This was, in large part, because in January 1968, in a move to financially cripple the Biafran government, Nigeria unveiled a new currency, and invalidated the old one. In response, Biafra issued its own currency.

During the war, limited quantities of the new Nigerian money filtered into Biafra where it intermingled with Biafran and the old Nigerian currency still in circulation, including coins, which had not been affected by the currency change. Spending by Nigerian soldiers along the shifting Nigeria-Biafra border accounted for a small portion. Another source was money Biafrans took from dead or captured Nigerian troops, though a number of former Biafran soldiers said that Nigerian attacks occurred most frequently in the days preceding pay day. This, they alleged, was a ploy to allow corrupt officers to appropriate the pay of soldiers who did not survive the assaults.[15] For the Biafrans, it meant that the amounts of money they recovered were usually small. In addition to captured specie, illicit commerce—the so-called "attack trade"—conducted mainly by Biafran women with Nigerian traders in the mangroves and creeks of the Niger Delta had the side effect of importing small quantities of Nigerian money into Biafra.[16] Nonetheless, when the war ended, Nigerian currency was in very short supply in Igboland. In January, *West Africa* reported that 90 percent of the refugees in Owerri had only Biafran money, though Nigerian currency was the preferred medium of exchange in the city. Rural areas took longer to accept the change. In nearby Orlu, Biafran money remained in use, and traders appeared suspicious of the new Nigerian currency. As a result, even Nigerian soldiers and police in the area reportedly used Biafran currency.[17] Biafran money—though officially worthless—remained the main medium of exchange in some areas for weeks or even months, though it devalued constantly as town and village economies restored direct links with major centers and the increasingly sought-after Nigerian money pushed it out of circulation.

In post-war Igboland, acquiring Nigerian currency was a top priority for most. Most informants reported selling some form of personal property to Nigerian soldiers soon after the end of the war. Items ranged from jewelry and clothing to chickens and goats to a Morris automobile purchased before the war for £650 and sold afterward in Onitsha for £350.[18] Consignment sales went on also, with Igbo agents traveling from village to village connecting sellers and buyers. Others tapped into soldiers' wealth by carrying water, washing and ironing, or selling high-turnover goods like food, palm wine, or firewood to them, frequently for minimal profit, but often with perquisites such as occasional access to transportation or the intangible benefit of protection. While relations between soldiers and Igbos were generally good, given the circumstances, there were important exceptions. Shortly after the war, there were reports of soldiers looting—"authorized theft" in popular parlance.[19] More disturbing was the continuation of the wartime practice whereby soldiers abducted Igbo women, though in other cases women initiated relationships. According to Emezue, not only did some of these unions become formal marriages, but in many cases the soldier paid bridewealth to the woman's family after the war.[20]

Other important injections of Nigerian money into the economy of the war-affected areas in the months following the war included the salaries of the soldiers stationed there, which totaled more than £2 million per month in 1971, salaries paid to employees of the federal and East Central State governments, and foreign remittances.[21] In rural areas, by late 1970, the marketing of palm kernels picked up temporarily.[22] All of these helped the state's economy to recover. It did so, however, without the benefit of much of the savings some Biafrans had either preserved or, in some cases, accumulated during the war.

## THE FINANCIAL COST OF DEFEAT: FROM THE CURRENCY CHANGE TO THE INDIGENIZATION DECREE

The financial disaster that began with the currency change came to full fruition with the redemption of bank accounts in 1970. The redemption was, for former Biafrans, a concrete reminder that they had lost the war. Soon after the war, the federal government announced plans to register old Nigerian currency and bank accounts in either old Nigerian or Biafran currencies. It would redeem them in new Nigerian funds. In anticipation of the pending exchange, former Biafrans deposited £16 million in Biafran funds and £2.5 million in old Nigerian notes with the Nigerian Central Bank through local banks. In May, however, the government changed the terms of the plan. Under the new scheme, each account registered with the Central Bank for exchange, as well as any other account that had been active during the war, was redeemed at a flat rate of £20, regardless of the amount it held. The cost to the federal government was, reportedly, £4 million.[23] At the time, the government justified the change in policy as necessary to foil currency speculators. That claim met with great skepticism in Igboland, where most viewed the redemption as both opportunistic and punitive.

The financial impact of the flat redemption on Igbos as a group is difficult to overstate. Achebe wrote that it "had the immediate result of pauperizing the Igbo middle class."[24] Among Igbos it was—and is— widely viewed as punishment for having waged and lost the war.[25] Not everyone was adversely affected, however. A few who apparently anticipated the change in policy—or perhaps had prior knowledge of it—were able to divide their assets among multiple accounts, thereby minimizing their losses, or even making gains. And for many who had held devalued Biafran notes, the effect was minimal; according to one Igbo: "To some it came as a relief, because if you had the Biafran money, say £200 Biafran, or five shillings of Nigerian money, that five shillings would buy you more."[26] In most cases, however, the redemption represented a major setback. And those who had been able to take either the old Nigerian or Biafran currency out of the country were simply out of luck. As Harneit-Sievers has pointed out, with the government disbursing £4 million, a maximum of 200,000 people out of an affected population of several million received anything at all; and, with some holding multiple accounts, the number of actual recipients was much smaller.[27] A trader based in Kano before the war reported losing £6,000 in Nigerian currency deposited outside Biafra, and more than £420,000 Biafran, some of it pre-war assets, the rest accumulated during the war. Out of anger he refused to collect the £20 on any of his accounts.[28] Others reported that redeeming accounts frequently entailed long waits and other frustrations—including cash shortages and corruption within the banks—that prevented them from redeeming their accounts. They speculate that their money wound up in the accounts of bank officers or government employees.[29]

The ramifications of the exchange were amplified after the Gowon government promulgated the Nigerian Enterprises Promotion Decree in 1972, widely known as the Indigenization Decree. During the Civil War Nigerian leaders had become acutely aware of the degree to which foreigners controlled the country's economy. Almost all of Nigeria's large-scale industry, and most of its medium-scale enterprises, were in foreign hands, most European. The decree established two lists of enterprises that would be restricted to Nigerian capitalists, or to Nigerian capitalists in partnership with foreign interests. This represented a potential windfall for Nigerian investors as foreign companies scrambled to find Nigerian partners. The thirty-three types of business so reserved included several types of manufacturing, construction, the brewing of beer, vehicle distribution and service, ownership of department stores and supermarkets, and shipping. Similar opportunities existed for Nigerians with access to capital as foreign interests were required to withdraw entirely from another twenty-two types of less capital-intensive industries that included advertising, distilleries, bakeries, cinemas, newspaper publishing, over-the-road haulage, and the operation of buses and taxis. While a few Igbos had regained their feet by the time the decree went into effect in 1974, far fewer had enough capital to compete with those who had not suffered the same setbacks, or who had even profited from the war. Even as the decree went into effect there were concerns that it was "creating opportunity for a handful of Nigerians to enrich themselves at the expense of the masses."[30] That "handful" consisted of Nigerians who were not only wealthy, but included very few Igbos. The post-war liquidity crisis and political marginalization all but excluded Igbo entrepreneurs from the indigenization process. According to Nnoli, Igbo leaders believed "the timing of the exercise was ethnically deliberate. Its objective was to put the Igbo at an obvious disadvantage in this new process of sharing the national cake."[31]

## THE PULL OF THE NORTH

In addition to financial difficulties, administrative conditions in Igboland also contributed to emigration, especially for public employees. The populace of the new East Central State, despite the ravages of the war, was, in formal terms, among the best-educated of any Nigerian state. The hiring practices of the new states, all of which gave preference to their own citizens, severely limited the state's ability to export teachers and civil servants. As a result, the ECS contained more civil servants and teachers than it could employ. The state responded by retiring most civil servants beyond age fifty, which left some breadwinners unemployed, and put pressure on other family members.[32] Further, those salaried employees who retained their jobs were subject to special levies on their earnings to subsidize reconstruction. For example, Humphrey Umeh, at the time a secondary school teacher, reported that as late as 1974 half of his monthly salary went to the "survival levy." He himself was tempted North the following year by advertisements for teachers in Northern institutions of higher learning that appeared in the *Daily Times* and *Renaissance* newspapers. These advertisements were supplemented by active recruiting in the ECS, including small caravans of Toyota Corollas and Volkswagen Rios that recruiters from the North drove past schools while public address systems advertised the availability of jobs. A clear subtext of the caravans' message was the availability of cars to successful candidates. "That motivated very many people then to know that their way to opulence in their professions lay in the North. They went North."[33] Umeh was hired by Ahmadu Bello University (ABU) to teach at their Advanced Teachers College in Kano, and received a car loan soon after his arrival, something he could not have expected in East Central State.

Another factor that contributed to the decision of many Igbos to head north was the demand for humility that former Biafrans, and especially former soldiers, felt at the hands of Nigerian soldiers and federal and ECS bureaucrats. Humility was also an important consideration in the North, though it manifested itself quite differently. For Northerners, the matter of humility tended to rest on the contrast between perceptions of arrogance among pre-war Igbos and the humility demonstrated by former Biafrans. For many of those former Biafrans, however, going to Kano or other points North was an escape from constant reminders of their defeat at the hands of soldiers and government officials, reminders that continued through the mid-1970s. For Chief W.O. Anunobi, a police officer who was reabsorbed by the Nigeria Police after the war, the matter of postings reinforced humility among former Biafrans. "After the war, nobody was standing with feet firm. Whatever we did, we were doing it with fear. Whatever we did, right or wrong, we did it saying 'yes, sir.' This meant, for the law-abiding, not contesting postings."[34]

And Umeh, a former officer in the Biafran Army, described the situation in occupied Igboland thus: "Humility—you were humiliated. It was demanded from you at every turn. And if you didn't meet it that way, you made mistakes. Here [in Kano] I had fuller freedoms. My humanity, my dignity, were all taken care of."[35] As a government employee in East Central State, he had been routinely confronted with an aggressive and frequently offensive bureaucracy.

> At every turn you were made to feel grateful for having employment at all. It wasn't official policy that was articulated openly, no. But again and again, everywhere at all, you were reminded of your defeated status by agents of government, especially those who had the opportunity of staying on with the government in Enugu—those who managed to get themselves involved in government in Enugu while we were on the other side going away from them fighting the Nigerian soldiers. Also [by] people who, by virtue of their position, you seemed to be obligated to for something or another—accommodation, your pay, leave allowance, *et cetera*, even employment as such. They didn't behave very nicely to us people. They made you feel as if you weren't entitled to what you were asking for, but that if they felt like it, they might grant it to you by their own kindness.[36]

His dealings with bureaucracies in Kano were much simpler. "I had never seen this lack of red tape. It was incredible."[37]

Most young men in Biafra had fought against Nigeria; subsequently, the presence of thousands of Nigerian soldiers throughout the East Central State presented a frequent challenge, especially for former Biafran fighters—or men Nigerian soldiers presumed were former Biafran fighters. "If a soldier looked at your carriage, he could tell if you'd had any training in how to manage your body and movement. It didn't matter how you shuffled along, it would be known you were disguising things. You didn't make a journey that you didn't have very much to make. The conversations at these road checkpoints could lead to anything."[38]

Language was one way that Nigerian soldiers, most of whom were from the Middle Belt or the far North, asserted their authority. Failure to greet, or at the very least, to be able to respond to these soldiers in Hausa, or sometimes Tiv or Yoruba, was, as often as not, to invite harassment. Adopting the proper disposition was also necessary.[39]

> We managed, inevitably, to develop a degree of humility that was quite alien to our natures. The Igbo man is not very humble, usually . . . not at all, really. We managed to ingratiate ourselves with these people. Sometimes before you even approached the checkpoint you were brandishing a cigarette or something like that, or saying "*sannu, sannu, sannu,* One Nigeria, One Nigeria," you know, to put everybody in a good frame of mind for your passage.[40]

Umeh's descriptions resonate with those of other former Biafrans, some of whose encounters with Nigerian soldiers happened as late as the mid-1970s.

## A NORTHERN LIFESTYLE

While Umeh was a first-time migrant to the North, a large proportion of the earliest arrivals were Igbo men who had grown up in the Northern Region, or spent years living there. Among these men, many said that their experiences left them better able to function in the North than in the south. It is a widely accepted truth in Nigeria that there are fundamental differences between urban life in the North and in the south. Without exception, *Kanawa* and Igbos agreed that life in the far North—even in Kano, Nigeria's second city—was slower-paced, and generally less stressful than in southern cities. They pointed to the "hustle and bustle" of Lagos and Onitsha, places many migrants said they were avoiding by living in Kano. The most frequently cited factor was crime. Incidents of armed robbery had long been higher in the south than the far North even before the war. While they went up across the country after the war, they did so precipitously in the south. Chief Anunobi served in the Nigeria Police Force in the south both before and after the war, then was transferred to Kano in 1973. In his words, "You cannot compare Nigeria before and after the war. Before the war Nigeria was very sleepy."[41] Economic hardship swelled the ranks of criminals, and they were much better armed than before. Anunobi attributed the post-war increase to the widespread availability of weapons, especially those from the Biafran side. Further, the war had facilitated the development of channels for smuggling guns and ammunition into the country. In addition, many young men who found themselves jobless after the war had military or paramilitary experience in Biafra. *West Africa* concurred. In 1970 the magazine described entire villages being attacked by robbers, some of whom had access to army uniforms and equipment, and raised the spectre of complicity by members of the military and police. The role of former Biafran forces was central as well.

> Many of the criminals are probably ex-soldiers, plus a few deserters. The rebel army was disbanded virtually overnight, leaving thousands of men trained for violence with no livelihood (in an area where it was not safe to travel at night even in pre-war days). It is only too clear why the Federal Army cannot be reduced except by a carefully-phased

demobilisation programme. And the hungry men with no money have access to a vast amount of arms and ammunition; caches have been found by police in raids throughout what used to be Biafra.[42]

While crime statistics are unavailable, a Hausa police inspector confirmed the popular belief that post-war Kano also experienced a moderate increase in what had been the extremely low rate of armed robbery, though it was nothing like what obtained in the south.[43] For Igbos who were choosing between life in the south and returning to Kano, however, such changes were immaterial in the face of the differences. A Kano-born Igbo who left the south in the late 1970s to return to Kano was struck by the differences. "There's lots of night life here; you find people at all hours moving around with ease. It's not like the south. You might have money, but you can't enjoy it there. By eight o'clock you've locked yourself in."[44] Concerns about inter-communal violence persisted, but for some were outweighed by the day-to-day risk from crime in the south. The comments of a Kano-born engineer are indicative of many others. "When tension here comes, it comes in volcanoes. It comes in waves and make headlines. People like me who like taking life easy prefer the North—with due consideration to the eruptions. Three days in three years makes a very low risk compared to the everyday risk in a place like Benin [City] or Lagos." He pointed out that, having grown up in the North, he had grown "tuned to this pattern of life."[45] The idea of being better "tuned" to life there than in the south was common. For some, the war years marked the longest time they had spent away from the far North. When confronted by relatives in Igboland who feared for their safety, the engineer and others made the usual counter arguments about reclaiming property. They also argued that their skills were more in demand there than in the south, where several informants described professional, white collar, and technical fields as "saturated." And, having grown up in the North, many had missed the chance to nurture the patronage networks that were so important in finding and retaining work in the south. In the words of one, "in the south, you need someone to help you out." In the North, he had contacts, and his skills and credentials were highly sought after.[46] Other Igbos developed similar feelings. Even a majority of those who came for the first time after the war said they felt more comfortable living in Kano or other far Northern cities than in the south, and would have a difficult time re-establishing themselves in the south's tighter labor, residential, and entrepreneurial markets.

## KANO: THE PUBLIC SECTOR

The contrast between economic and social conditions in Kano and those in post-war Igboland was stark. The military, though present, played a much less visible role in Kano life than in Igboland, the new state government enjoyed a great deal of popularity, and the city's economy was healthy and expanding. It is difficult to make comparisons of economic activity in Kano between the pre- and post-war periods, because administrative divisions and accounting systems changed with the creation of states. It is clear, however, that Sabon Gari Kano played an important role in the state's economy. Internally generated revenues in Kano State increased modestly between 1968–1969 (£4,998,754) and 1969–1970 (£5,058,446). However, in 1970–1971, they leapt to £6,996,400, in large part because of a resurgent Sabon Gari market. There were modest increases over the next two years, then another dramatic leap between 1972–1973 (£7,299,548) and 1973–1974 (£8,565,975) as the national economy began to reflect the oil boom.[47]

In Kano State, an official attitude of conciliation had been evident even before the war ended. In his first official policy statement as Military Governor of Kano State, Police Commissioner Audu Bako echoed the timbre of federal rhetoric when he expressed his "earnest hope that Ojukwu's rebellion would soon be crushed, so that my country men from the East-Central State could come back to live happily in our midst."[48] That the abandoned properties of Igbos who had fled had been preserved for them was taken by many returning Igbos as evidence that Bako had spoken in good faith. In a secret January 1970 security report, the District Officer in nearby Kazaure wrote that "the Ibos who have been subdued" by the war "will feel quite reluctant and will think it unsafe to mingle freely with their fellow Nigerians, especially when they are confined to work" in their home areas. He concluded that people in Kazaure, a site of violence in 1966, felt that the federal government should assist displaced Igbos in returning to their former working places. In addition he passed along a suggestion that "to avert and alleviate any fear that may be harboured by Igbos, the Government should introduce the system of inter-state transfer of senior civil servants from extreme North to work in the three eastern states and vice versa."[49]

No such system emerged, but the realities of staffing the public services of the new northern states had a similar effect. The Kano State government, like the other state governments, followed hiring policies that strongly favored its own citizens. Other Nigerians were, in theory, hired only in cases where qualified *Kanawa* were unavailable. This maximized opportunities for the cadre of young, western-educated Kano citizens, members of which had spearheaded the anti-unification demonstrations of May 1966. By 1970 the state had largely absorbed the pool of qualified *Kanawa*, and the mechanisms of state government offered great promise that the pattern would continue. The Northernization policies of the late colonial period and First Republic had been explicit in their preference for expatriate workers over southern Nigerians in cases where qualified Northern candidates were not available. In 1971, however, the Kano State Public Service Commission stated a fundamental reversal of that aspect of hiring policy. "The Commission's Policy has always been to fill existing vacancies with qualified Nigerians whenever these are available and only recruits and appoints expatriate officers where qualified Nigerians have not been available."[50]

During the first two years of Kano State's life, the number of state government employees nearly doubled between 1968 (2,260) and 1970 (4,040). During that time, the percentage who were from out of state remained fairly constant at just under 30 percent. By 1974 the number of state employees reached 8,696, of whom about a quarter were out-of-state Nigerians, though their absolute number (2,147) was substantial.[51] Igbo public service employees made up a small but important portion of post-war migrants to Kano State, and their symbolic value was particularly significant in rebuilding some measure of trust between communities. This is especially true in view of the vilification of Igbo public service employees that happened in the North prior to and during the war. In July 1970 Governor Bako and the chairman of the state's Public Service Commission visited Enugu, where Bako made public statements emphasizing that all Nigerians were free to live and work in Kano. More importantly, the two men made plans for state recruiters to make a follow-up visit. Accordingly, in November, a delegation from Kano State including the permanent commissioner of the Public Service Commission and members of four state ministries undertook a week-long recruiting mission in the East Central State. They interviewed seventy applicants and made thirty-one offers, including nine to teachers, three to nurses, and three to accountants.[52] Nineteen of the candidates accepted postings.

One of them was D.O. Nnadi, who, by the 1990s had become Deputy Accountant General of Kano State. He began a contract appointment with the state after hearing a radio announcement in late

1970. Encouraged by a friend he was visiting in Enugu, he went to the ECS civil service office where representatives from Kano were interviewing. Though he had been an officer in the Biafran army, the recruiters did not ask about his service. He recalled that at the time most Igbos were afraid to go North, but he accepted the position in Kano over one he had been offered in Lagos, intending to remain for the three-year term of his contract, and then return to the ECS. He lived in government housing in the GRA, one of the few Igbos who resided outside of Sabon Gari at the time. Because of this, and the fact that most of his co-workers were from Kano, his social network included Hausa colleagues. Three times he accepted invitations to homes in the old city before becoming discouraged by the social and religious obstacles to interacting with the families of his hosts. After that, his socializing with Hausa friends centered on public spaces in Sabon Gari and other parts of Waje. When his three-year contract expired, the state offered him a permanent position, which he accepted, in part because he had been promoted more quickly than he the would have been at home. Even as he advanced professionally, however, he exercised caution. Nnadi married in 1970, but, like many migrants, did not bring his family to Kano until he was financially stable and confident of their safety. In his case, they arrived in 1975, the same year that his town union established a Kano chapter. Almost all of its members were traders, but that changed in the late 1970s when the Nigeria Police ended its practice of stationing most of its members in their home states. In the eyes of other union members "those of us who came in 1970 and 71 were looked upon as crazy."[53]

When interviewed in 1994, Nnadi was the last Igbo in his cohort still working for the state; the numbers, he said, fell off as Kano became better able to meet its manpower needs with its own citizens. Unlike Nnadi, most of the other Igbos did not receive permanent appointments, and moved on to positions elsewhere or went into business for themselves. Based on hiring records and employee registers, Kano State public services employed at least thirty-six Igbos in its professional and administrative grades during 1970 and 1971. At least twenty-three new hires followed in 1972. Of those fifty-nine hired in the first three years following the war, at least twenty-seven remained in the employ of Kano State in 1976, which then had at least seventy-five Igbo professional and administrative employees on a staff of about 2,200, in addition to a handful of National Youth Service Corps workers.[54] While the percentage of Igbo employees in the Kano State public service of 1976 was probably slightly lower than in the pre-war Northern Regional service in Kano, it was significant. The absolute number of public service jobs at all levels in Kano, as elsewhere in Nigeria, increased remarkably between 1967 and the mid-1970s. During the war, Kano had drawn heavily on other states and on expatriates in meeting its rapidly expanding manpower needs. Data from 1970–1971 suggests that largely Yoruba Kwara State was by far the single largest supplier of out-of-state workers.[55]

As the comments of Nnadi's fellow town union members suggest, the role of fear among Igbos in accepting postings in Kano and other Northern cities is important to acknowledge. Like other Igbos, civil servants who had been in Kano before the war were often reluctant to come back.[56] Fear of postings in the North and loss of seniority contributed to a general drift away from public service jobs and toward independent means of support in the years after the war. While there are no numbers available, several informants expressed the belief that most of the Igbos posted to federal positions in Kano—in public utilities, the post office, or working for the railroad or Nigerian Airways— had worked there before the war. First-timers, they say, did not begin to arrive in meaningful numbers until the mid-1970s. Nonetheless, since most federal and state public service jobs offered housing or housing allowances, salaries that were competitive with the formal private sector, and the possibility of salary advances, the temporary security of such posts made them attractive to many unemployed or underemployed professionals.

## KANO: THE PRIVATE SECTOR

While the activities of government did much to set a tone for the reentry of Igbos into Kano society, it was traders who made up the largest and most visible block of those participating in the city and state's economy. There is a startling orthodoxy to beliefs expressed in Kano about the business practices of various ethnic groups. They are expressed in comparable terms by Hausas, Igbos, and members of other groups, with little exception, and are virtually indistinguishable from nationally prevailing ethnic stereotypes. The orthodox view of Igbo traders is that they prefer to make profits through high volume rather than high mark-up, and share a willingness to travel far and wide in search of goods to market. The words of a successful Igbo businessman based in Kano are indicative.

> To trade properly you need connections. The work is going to scout and look for the item—enduring the hassle. The Igbo man is on the move. That's the difference. Even a big [i.e., successful] Igbo man will

go ahead and do the looking that an equally rich [non-Igbo] trader might consider beneath his dignity. A lot of these Igbos don't send their boys [apprentices] to go and buy their goods. They go themselves. If an Igbo trader doesn't have what a customer needs he says "Give me two or four days." That night he's on the night bus to Onitsha and early the next morning he's in the market. That night he's on the luxury bus back to Kano, and the next day the goods are ready. That's the Igbo man.[57]

This widely shared perception had a powerful influence on the willingness of Kano citizens to welcome back Igbo traders and to offer them financial assistance. There were many cases like that of a trader, well-established before the war, and among the first Igbos to return to Kano, who got credit assistance from a Hausa former business associate. The trader, who arrived in March 1970, recalled that his business associate, though unable to lend money from his own pocket, used his personal connections to arrange a bank loan that allowed the trader to set up a market stall and purchase stock.[58]

Other forms of credit were available as well. Some who had established themselves before the war as dealers or distributors for larger companies—sellers of medical supplies, hardware, or machine parts, for example—were able, with the help of those companies, to take goods on credit. Most often this type of connection appears to have been arranged from the south; the dealers in Kano were frequently younger relations or former apprentices of established dealers based in Onitsha, Aba, or Lagos. Banking also figured prominently in the recovery process, and the African Continental Bank (ACB) was the institution of choice for most Igbos. Before the war, most Igbos in Kano with bank accounts had them with the ACB, which had been closely associated with Nnamdi Azikiwe and the Eastern Region government. The Kano branch of the bank began to solicit business from Igbo customers very soon after the war. Its efforts included canvassing traders in the Sabon Gari market, adjacent to the bank. Bank agents offered the possibilities of overdrafts and loans as inducements to traders and were liberal in offering them to pre-war customers. And, as the Igbo population of Kano increased in the months and years that followed, ACB managers worked through previously reliable customers to get access to less-established business people, and maintained a liberal overdraft policy.[59]

Informal credit played an important role for most returning traders. Hausa traders eager for supplies of yam, palm oil, and other food stuffs in short supply during the war were able to lend capital to Igbo traders, frequently but not always in relatively small amounts. Even with such assistance, however, the circumstances of most returnees required them to take decisive steps to set themselves on solid financial ground, steps which quite frequently entailed moving between southern and northern markets, organizing capital, and transporting small quantities of goods, usually by public transportation. Though he was not primarily a trader by profession, the example of Felix Agwuenu is instructive. Literally penniless at the end of the war, Agwuenu was able to take advantage of his Hausa language ability and pre-war experience in the North to take the first steps toward economic recovery.

## THE CASE OF FELIX AGWUENU

Felix Agwuenu was born of Igbo parents in 1942 in the Middle Belt city of Minna, where his father was a stone mason for the Ministry of Works. Agwuenu grew up there speaking Igbo, Hausa, and English. In 1960 he left for southern Zaria Province where he taught in a village primary school, then at a nearby Catholic school. In 1964 he accepted a teaching position at a branch of the St. Thomas school in Challawa, near Kano, then moved to the main campus of St. Thomas in Sabon Gari in late 1964. He left the North on scheduled home leave on 9 August 1966, less than two weeks after the July counter-coup. Aboard the train on which he traveled were a group of widows of officers killed during the July coup. The women were angry when soldiers at Makurdi "ransacked" their property.

> As it turned out, that train was the last safe train to move to the East. They [soldiers of Northern origin] made us get down at the Makurdi bridge; they got all the young men, looking for soldiers. They asked us if we were going there to make an army. I told them I was a student from St. Thomas—I didn't tell them I was teaching. I told them "You have your army, why shouldn't they make their own?" They looked at me and told me I had a very hard head.

The soldiers allowed the men to reboard the train, which arrived in Enugu without further incident. On the eve of his planned return to Kano, he received a letter from the parish priest in Kano dated a week after his departure instructing him not to return because of the decaying security situation. "The letter said to forget the news that everything was quiet." He spent the pre-war months at St. Charles College in Onitsha before enlisting.

The end of the war found him in the family home of Ifite Ukpo.
"Some federal troops were in my place. I moved around and met some
people; because I spoke Hausa it was easy." In February 1970, he
struck up a conversation with a federal soldier who was impressed
with Agwuenu's command of Hausa and wondered where he had
learned it. Another soldier, a non-Hausa Northerner, was from the village where Agwuenu had taught. As it turned out, he was also engaged to marry the daughter of one of Agwuenu's former colleagues
in southern Zaria. "I said 'You're planning to marry Lucy?' He said
yes, he was. I told him to wait, and ran to get a photograph I had of
the man and the girl." Seeing his economic options and personal connections severely limited in the East, Agwuenu accepted the soldiers'
invitation to join them on home leave in Kaduna. This he did over the
objections of family members who feared for his safety, but with the
blessing of the family patriarch, Agwuenu's uncle. "'Why would you
go back there?' they said. I told them I was born and bred in the
North and understood it better there than here. The longest time I had
ever spent at home was during the war." On 24 February, penniless,
but in the company of soldiers, Agwuenu was able to travel to Kaduna
by rail without paying. There he lodged with them in private homes,
and searched for former classmates. A Northern friend who had heard
Agwuenu was in Kaduna sought him out.

> He took me to a hotel to buy me a bottle of beer. I don't drink
> beer. I told him rather than buy me that bottle of beer, give me that
> four shillings and six pence and let me have something in this
> pocket. He was surprised. I told him, "Look, I'm from the war area
> and I don't have anything." He gave me five shillings and bought
> me a bottle of Sprite.

Agwuenu waited four days before deciding to catch a Kano-bound train,
which he also boarded without paying. Confronted by a ticket collector,
he explained his situation.

> I told her "I am from the war area and I need to get to Kano." They
> put me in the staff coach and told me that I would be handed over to
> the police at the next stop. There was one Hausa man in there, with a
> drink and smoking. He asked me why did I want to make things diffi-
> cult for myself. I told him where I was from and how much money I
> had. I said "I'm not prepared to part with five pence of this money.
> When we got to Kano I went down. No police.

He found non-Igbo friends in Sabon Gari in Kano, including a Fulani woman with whom he had corresponded for as long as possible before the war broke out. She had believed him dead. Another friend offered him accommodation and gave him £10. The next day he spent £6 on forty packs of cigarettes of different brands—a scarce commodity in the war-affected area. After two days and one night in Kano, he paid for a ticket back to Kaduna. There he rejoined the soldiers and several days later they set off for Enugu together, and again Agwuenu avoided paying the fare. The train was delayed at Kafanchan, and he got off with a soldier to look for friends. They missed the train, on which he had left the cigarettes. The soldier sent a message to comrades in Enugu to pick up Agwuenu's bag when the train arrived; when he and the soldier reached Enugu, Agwuenu was reunited with his property.

Upon returning home, Agwuenu quickly sold the cigarettes, mostly to soldiers, and often on credit. He quickly doubled his money. Since Nigerian currency was still in short supply in Igboland in March 1970, £12 represented a substantial stake. He invested some of his capital in palm wine produced by local tappers and sold it to soldiers. His Hausa language skills guaranteed his social mobility among Northern soldiers, who shared their food and drink with him, and gave him small tips in return for extending them credit. With his need to buy food for himself minimized, his steadily growing income from trading was enough to feed and shelter his family, and to prepare for a second trip North. In April he returned to his job in Kano, where he estimated the Igbo population to be fewer than 500, including many who "came to check things out." The Catholic church, which operated the school, did not offer either money or accommodation to returners, but Agwuenu collected four months salary from 1966. During his next visit home in August he carried cloth wrappers from Kano to sell. He remained employed at the school in Kano until 1979 when he went into business for himself.[60]

## STRATEGIES FOR REHABILITATION

Agwuenu's actions in the months following the war mirror several patterns common among Igbo migrants in the months following the war. While travel from most parts of Igboland to Kano cost less than £1 at the time, that sum represented a hardship for most, and a temporary impossibility for others. Some sold belongings or were given small sums of money for transportation. Others, like Agwuenu, took advantage of the movement of soldiers. Several described opportunities for rides from garrisons in Igboland to Kaduna on military transport. Similarly, Agwuenu's manipulation of public transportation resonates with other accounts. For example, one Igbo trader wounded in action fighting for Biafra was issued a government letter in 1970 entitling him to free transport to Kano to undergo treatment at Kano City Hospital. According to a relative, for more than a year he was able to reuse the letter to move back and forth between Kano and the southeast, where he purchased clothing to sell in Kano. Once railway employees detected his deception, he was sometimes able to pay them small bribes to look the other way.[61]

Agwuenu's acquisition of his initial working capital is also typical; many of the Igbo men returning during 1970 and 1971 received cash gifts from non-Igbo friends and associates, usually Northerners, but also southerners.[62] Traders, in particular, seem likely to have been given cash, though a former Nigeria Airways employee recalls colleagues receiving cash gifts from Hausa co-workers, in addition to help in locating accommodation.[63] It is also noteworthy that Agwuenu, a teacher by training, relied on trading to generate cash flow immediately after the war. Substituting or augmenting one's regular profession with trading was a common strategy. Chief Davis Ohaeri, trained as a surveyor and craftsman, returned to Kano in 1971 after spending a year farming. He arrived with only enough money to feed himself for a week. Aware of the stereotype of Igbos as hard-working and loyal employees, he advertised his ethnicity and found work as a day laborer on a construction site within hours. Within a week he challenged erroneous measurements made by an Italian engineer, and was promoted to foreman. While he waited for his new job to pay, however, he supported himself by selling used clothing supplied to him by a relative in the south.

Igbos with scarce skills or powerful connections found help particularly forthcoming. Chief Agu Ezetah had both. Ezetah, later the founding president (*Onu Nekwuru Igbo*) of the post-war Kano Igbo Community Association in 1983, had help from Malam Aminu Kano when he arrived in Kano in 1971. Malam Aminu, the former leader of the NEPU political party was, in 1970, Federal Communications Commissioner. The two had met in 1970 while Ezetah was a law student in Lagos, but had known each other previously through their political activities. Ezetah had spent fifteen years in Kano as a trader between 1948 and 1963 before entering the University of Nigeria with sponsorship from the Orlu Divisional Union. While he had lived in Kano he had been an assistant chair of the Kano branch of the NCNC and general secretary of the Orlu divisional union. Upon Ezetah's return to Kano, the former NEPU leader provided him with rent-free legal chambers, and gave him a letter of introduction to use in soliciting clients. In addition, other former NEPU members, including Alhaji Tanko Yakasai, at that time Kano State's Secretary for Information, gave him modest gifts of money.[64] Another example is that of Chief O.T. Nnadi, who in 1994 became the first "traditional ruler" of Kano's Igbos (*Eze Ndi Igbo*). Nnadi arrived in Kano for the first time in March 1970. Also an attorney, he stayed with family friends upon his arrival. A friend in the East had paid for his transportation. He met a Yoruba lawyer he had known from study overseas, who gave him accommodation and took him into his law practice.

Government contracts were one area where public and private interests overlapped. One pattern, though difficult to detail, clearly grew out of the state's new administrative independence and its shortfall of western-trained technicians and craftspeople. Kano's rise to state capital status fueled a proliferation of development projects, nearly all of them reserved for contractors indigenous to the state. Though generally unable to secure government contracts on their own, subcontractors from other states were in many cases able to perform the work in its entirety by paying a kickback—usually ten percent off the top—to the local firm or individual holding the contract, and who might or might not have been a *bona fide* contractor.[65] Supply contracts frequently operated similarly, with out-of-state subcontractors with commercial links to markets in Lagos and Onitsha providing bulk goods ranging from building materials to office and school supplies to local contractors who, in turn, sold them to the state. Again, the pre-war reputation of the Igbo as reliable, skilled traders and workers contributed to the willingness of local contractors to enter into arrangements with them.

### Small Business and Rehabilitation

A sample of data available from a 1973 small business survey offers important insights into the financial realities Igbo entrepreneurs faced, and illustrates how those with marketable skills were able to set up shop with very little capital.[66] The survey excluded traders in favor of service providers and producers of goods.[67] As early as 1969 there were clues to the marketability of technical skills. Of the three Igbo-owned businesses established in 1969 on which data exists, one was a bar established in Sabon Gari by a twenty-four-year-old woman from the Mid-West with a £70 investment. Of the remaining two, however, one was an automobile repair shop, and the other a motorcycle workshop, each established by men in their mid-twenties. The motorcycle mechanic described his initial capital as a £20 investment in basic tools, most apparently purchased after starting the business. The auto mechanic, on the other hand, reported a £60 investment in new tools in 1969, which he funded from savings. Both established themselves where they could take advantage of traffic from the old city: The motorcycle mechanic worked outdoors at the northern edge of Fagge, and the auto mechanic in a small shelter near the motor park outside the Kofar Mata gate. Before the war Igbo mechanics had been a highly visible presence. The relative shortage of mechanics in Kano during the war years, combined with the fact that a skilled mechanic could perform many basic repairs with a few simple and inexpensive tools, made automobile and motorcycle repair relatively low-risk enterprises. In fact, of the 77 Igbo businesses visited during the survey, mechanical workshops made up the largest cluster. Nine (12 percent) were automobile or motorcycle repair workshops, and another six (8 percent) specialized in bicycle repair. Significantly, where only 45 percent of the enumerated businesses were established in 1969 and 1970, eight of the nine automobile and motorcycle workshops were in operation by the end of 1970, suggesting that these services were very much in demand. Most of the other significant clusters reflected a similar emphasis on technical skills. They included operations specializing in welding or iron work (8 percent), watch repair services (8 percent), carpentry workshops (6 percent), shoe manufacture and repair (6 percent), and electronic repair (5 percent).[68]

Most of the small business owners capitalized themselves. Only twelve (15 percent) reported using borrowed money for all or most of their start-up capital. The remainder indicated that their enterprises had been capitalized from savings. Interestingly, of the six businesses with clear pre-war roots in Kano, five were able to draw on borrowed capital, suggesting that returning migrants were able to organize financial support from pre-war associates. The amounts ranged from a £3 loan to a bicycle mechanic and a gift to a carpenter covering part of his £10 start-up capital, to an £8,000 loan for a bakery reestablished in 1972. Another six of the seventy-seven businesses were able to begin operation with equipment purchased in 1966 or before (though not necessarily in Kano), suggesting that the equipment had either been left behind and subsequently recovered, or had been brought to Kano after the war.

The sixty-nine responses to questions on initial capitalization demonstrate that the amount of start-up money migrants were able to invest in their businesses varied widely.

| Initial Capital | All Enterprises Established 1969–73 | Early Enterprises Established 1969–70 |
|---|---|---|
| Less than £10 | 9 (13%) | 3 (10%) |
| £10-19 | 14 (20%) | 3 (10%) |
| £20-49 | 14 (20%) | 6 (20%) |
| £50-99 | 13 (19%) | 7 (23%) |
| £100-249 | 13 (19%) | 9 (30%) |
| £250-499 | 4 ( 6%) | 2 (7%) |
| £500 or more | 2 ( 3%) | 0 |
| | 69 (100%) | 30 (100%) |

Those fortunate or industrious migrants who were able to bring capital out of Biafra or to raise it in the weeks and months following the war invested it quickly. While those businesses capitalized at the lowest level (£10 and below) were spread out over the three years following the war, twelve of the nineteen businesses capitalized with more than £100 opened in 1970. Of the twelve, only one operator reported borrowing capital; another used equipment owned before the war, and the others drew on savings.

The local government's reallocation of market stalls to *Kanawa* had implications for cash-strapped Igbos as well, who found that they could no longer rent stalls directly from the Waje authorities. Instead, they had in many cases to sublet them from the *Kanawa* tenants. This had the effect of pushing up the rents Igbo traders paid. Where monthly rent on stalls was between five and 10 shillings before the war, by 1973 most Igbo tenants paid between £3 and £10 monthly for stalls averaging nine square yards, and some paid as much as £15 for larger stalls. By contrast, working space in areas of Sabon Gari outside the market was much less expensive. For many skilled workers, such as painters, carpenters, and watch repairers, and traders in specialized products such as automotive parts or electronic goods, this increase in overhead pushed them out of the market itself. A sign painter, for example, paid £3 monthly rent for 36 square yards of shed space on Yoruba Road, several hundred yards from the market, and a pomade maker reported paying £1 per month for the same amount of indoor space on Onitsha Road, perhaps a twenty-minute walk from the market. This disparity in costs, in turn, contributed to the commercialization of areas of Sabon Gari outside the market. Nonetheless, for many traders—in particular sellers of high-turnover goods such as food, clothing, and small manufactured goods—the advantages of the market outweighed the added expense.[69]

### Apprenticeship and Rehabilitation

The strength of the apprenticeship system also contributed to the Igbo population's ability to rehabilitate itself. Apprenticeship meshed well with the social realities of the post-war period to the extent that it provided a formal apparatus that simultaneously addressed educational and economic needs. Apprenticeship did so by defining conditions under which those with means took into their households or commercial enterprises younger relatives or people from their home areas who had been orphaned or otherwise displaced by the war. This, in turn, reinforced the salience of ties from home. Like the union system which did the same, the post-war apprenticeship seems to have fundamentally changed little from its pre-war incarnation.

The practice of drawing apprentices from one's home community is probably the greatest force behind the strong association of certain parts of Igboland with certain types of trade. In the well-known case of automobile parts, traders from the Nnewi area of Igboland have established a virtual national monopoly. In other areas, while monopolies or near-monopolies have not necessarily resulted, areas of local specialization emerged as established traders and artisans protected access to supply networks and skills. In the post-war period, for example, Orlu traders have been closely associated with stationery and pharmaceuticals; Okigbwa has proliferated textile traders, and Ifitedunu has become known for its carpenters. When the teacher Felix Agwuenu joined the Ifite Ukpo Progressive Union in 1972, he was the only of its eight members who was not a carpenter.

The terms of apprenticeships have varied according to the type of work, and, more significantly, according to sex. Apprenticeships follow the rather rigid gendering of work; not surprisingly, male apprentices learn from men, and females from women. Before the war and during the 1970s, most apprentices began immediately after leaving primary school, though unlike men, adult women sometimes contracted to be apprentices.[70] Where male apprenticeships normally last from five to seven years, and rarely less than three, those for females range from approximately two years to less than a month. A girl or woman learning dressmaking might spend two years as an apprentice, while a cooking apprentice might spend only a few weeks. The financial arrangements surrounding apprenticeship also vary. Female apprentices are much more likely than their male counterparts to make a cash payment for their training; male apprentices, in most cases, pay only with their labor. In lieu of a fixed payment at the beginning, many female apprentices instead make a monetary offering to their mistresses at the conclusion of their training. A male apprentice normally earns room and board, usually sleeping in either his master's compound or in the trading stall or shop, and the master is also expected to clothe the apprentice and to provide for his basic needs. On the other hand, a female apprenticed outside of her extended family would usually live with relatives. Upon the completion of his terms of service, the male apprentice would normally receive from his master a one-time cash grant with which to establish himself in business. Former apprentices, particularly males, might also be expected to purchase some of their inventory from or through former masters.[71] The ability of apprenticeship arrangements to operate without initial cash outlays contributed to their ability to function relatively normally if not immediately after the war, then certainly by the mid-1970s, and in many cases much earlier.

## "DOWN A STEP": SEX WORK, HUMILITY, AND ECONOMIC IMPERATIVES

The precipitous rise in commercial sex work among Igbo women is one of the most striking changes in social relations between Igbos and non-Igbos in post-war Kano. The selling of sexual services by Igbo women is something that many Igbo and non-Igbo men remember as a distinctly post-war phenomenon, one that emerged in 1970 and expanded during the early years of the decade. By the early 1980s, the visible presence of Igbo sex workers had diminished, probably in response to the rising influence of town and divisional unions, and a return to some degree of economic normalcy within the larger Igbo community. Not surprisingly, this aspect of social and economic life is very difficult to uncover in detail. In part this is because the stigma attached to it within the Igbo community has understandably led those who participated in it to wish to remain unknown. That Igbo sex workers appear to have had a largely non-Igbo clientele complicates the matter, since both Igbos and non-Igbos perceive that fact as emblematic of the diminished position of the Igbo community as a whole. It showed that "They had been taken down a step."[72] Members of the community spoke on the subject reluctantly, and treated it as an unfortunate consequence of the war. The Igbo men willing to discuss the matter reported that the women who participated have, by and large, left Kano to begin new lives elsewhere, often through marriage. Most non-Igbos who spoke on the subject acknowledge this, but suggested that some women who engaged in sex work remained in Kano, but had distanced themselves from that chapter of their lives.

In pre-war Kano, tight controls over women's behavior coalesced to structure the social networks of Igbo women in ways that made them, in general, inaccessible to members of other ethnic groups. The system of town unions helped to identify and sanction such "inappropriate behavior" as violent crime and drug abuse that might reflect poorly on the community. Offenders could expect their town or clan unions to sanction them, though more severe cases and those involving members of different unions might rise to the attention of the Kano Ibo Union. The same networks regulated the conduct of women and girls before the war. For example, a community-wide dress code governed attire for married women, who were required to cover their hair in public. According to a post-war community leader who lived in Kano before the war, "Wearing trousers and mini-skirts exposed our women to gossip by other tribes," and, along with other types of apparel deemed "provocative," was widely condemned.[73] Public social venues for women were largely limited to supervised situations such as church and school activities, and events involving community members like weddings, naming ceremonies, and town union meetings. Market transactions, though not formally supervised, were, theoretically, conducted in public view, and collective scrutiny enforced an informal code of decorum that limited contact between men and women to business. One intended consequence of these restrictions was to make it extremely difficult for Igbo commercial sex workers to operate in Kano. While there were Igbo women doing commercial sex work there before the war, they were very few, and were subject to summary expulsion if the community learned of their presence, which it considered an embarrassment.

Sex workers in Sabon Gari before the war included southern and Middle Belt women, and a number of Hausa *karuwai* [singular = *karuwa*, often mistranslated as "prostitute," see note] living along Weatherhead, Sani Giwa, Abadie, Odutola, and Sanyaolu streets in the southwestern portion of Sabon Gari.[74] These southern and Middle Belt women tended to reside in groups of half a dozen or fewer, in houses or in certain hotels. There were a few Igbos among them, some of whom masqueraded as Mid-Westerners or other southerners to avoid the attention of the unions.[75] The few Igbo women who participated in the trade, if detected, operated in the face of opposition from the network of unions. Union members dealt with suspected or known sex workers with techniques similar to those used to humiliate others who "could bring sharp criticism to the community." In most cases the matter was brought to the attention of the Ibo Union by members of the appropriate town, clan, or division union, who would then be sanctioned to put pressure on the woman to leave Kano. According to a post-war community leader, before the war "when an Igbo woman came to prostitution, we did what we could to get them out of town. We could get some boys to [verbally and publicly] harass the woman. This—and gossip—would get her to leave town of her own volition."[76]

After the war, the community, fragmented by pre-war standards, and preoccupied with questions of economic survival and rehabilitation, did not organize against the sex workers, though as town unions re-emerged, membership for single women was contingent on them being "reputably lodged." Nonetheless, despite not systematically harassing the women, Igbo men remained aware of their presence. During the late 1970s Ogunnika found Igbo men particularly "embarrassed by the large number of Igbo women in prostitution."[77] He found that across ethnic lines, men "treat prostitutes from their own ethnic group harshly, whereas prostitutes from other groups are treated less harshly. Their aim is to discourage their own women from prostitution, but to acquiesce to this practice among women of other ethnic groups."[78] Ogunnika has described the tendency for most men in Kano to seek out prostitutes from ethnic groups other than their own; his post-war observation meshes precisely with the pre-war recollections of male informants.[79]

Resentment by non-Igbos about the pre-war inaccessibility of Igbo women, the absence of community controls, and the post-war economic crisis meant that conditions were ripe for Igbo women willing to perform sex work. Information from male informants suggests that during the early 1970s the portion of single and widowed Igbo women in Kano who partook to some extent in sex work was substantial. While they arrived more or less contemporaneous with the early wave of male migrants, they were fewer in number. A former police officer placed the ages of most between seventeen and twenty.[80] And, significantly, most were not full-time sex workers; rather they also held jobs as traders, clerical workers, or retail clerks. Similarly, most spent only a limited time as sex workers, at most several years. The conventional wisdom is that they were using the trade to accumulate capital for other business ventures or for relocation expenses. Some Kano Igbos suggested that most had traveled to Kano and other cities to earn money to support relatives at home, while others among them had associated themselves with Nigerian soldiers stationed in Igboland during the war, for which they were ostracized in their home communities and ultimately forced to leave.[81]

The entry of Igbo women into sex work had far-reaching economic consequences. Before 1975 most Igbo women conducted sex work much as pre-war southern sex workers in Sabon Gari had: They made contact with potential patrons at drinking establishments and used their living quarters for liaisons. This placed them in direct competition with other sex workers, and the comparatively high demand for the services of Igbo women drove down the prices others could charge. In 1970, for example, an encounter with a southern or Middle Belt sex worker in Sabon Gari would have cost, generally, about one shilling; other expenses might include cigarettes or alcoholic drinks, with a bottle of beer costing about two shillings six pence. Northern women who practiced *masu gaskiya* in the Fagge ward, most of them non-Hausa, charged similarly.[82] (In comparison, standard pay for a manual laborer at the time was two shillings six pence per half day.) Igbo sex workers were able to charge around two shillings for services comparable to the ones other Sabon Gari and Fagge sex workers provided at half that price. The unavailability of Igbo women to sex trade patrons before the war offers the best explanation of this phenomenon. Patrons were willing to pay more for what had previously been unattainable, and which reinforced their perceptions of broad changes in Nigeria's social order.

By the time Igbos were reestablishing a presence in Kano, two important patterns of change were underway, each of which helped to ease the entry of Igbo women into the sex trade there. With the creation of new states, federal funds flowed into new state capitals, which then attracted entrepreneurial and administrative talent back to its home area. In the North this had the biggest effects on Kaduna and Kano, which saw outflows. Among those who responded to the expanding opportunities in the new state capitals were sex workers, and anecdotal evidence suggests that Jos in particular drew away a large share of Kano's Middle Belt sex workers.[83] At the same time, enforcement of anti-prostitution laws decreased after the Nigeria Police Force absorbed the country's Native Authority police forces between 1968 and 1971. In Kano it had been the NA police who had enforced those laws, and in absence of the force, sex workers could operate with little interference from authorities.

For Igbo sex workers, the scrutiny to avoid seems to have been that of other Igbos, and one way of doing that was to avoid Igbo landlords in favor of caretakers, most of whom were Hausa. At the same time, the increasing Igbo population in Sabon Gari brought with it a rise in the number of households containing women and children, which put market pressure on landlords to get rid of "undesirable" tenants. This explains in part why, according to Ogunnika, by 1973 Hausa landlords in Sabon Gari charged sex workers up to ten times as much rent as other tenants.[84] These higher rents, in turn, served to push the sex trade into hotels during the second half of the decade. In the hotels, managers or owners, both male and female, made money selling drinks and accommodation and their presence often provided the women with some protection against violence and non-payment. Meanwhile, the sex workers themselves controlled their trade, negotiating with customers and handling the money.

The shift to hotel-based work also triggered a more rigid financial calculus in the relationship between the provider and the patron, regardless of ethnicity. In the words of one man, "Before the war, the assumption was that if she does well, she'll get something in return. After the war it was more like 'I live in a hotel, I pay hotel bills, and I have to get paid.'"[85] As the trade moved into hotels and became increasingly professionalized, the number of part-time Igbo sex workers in Kano appears to have decreased markedly. At the same time, rents for sex workers rose and certain hotels became known as centers of an increasingly impersonal sex trade. Hausa *karuwai* based in Sabon Gari, particularly older ones, adapted to the new conditions by joining the move to hotels. There they began to provide services similar to those their non-Hausa counterparts offered, and at similar prices. While a minority of *karuwai* continued to practice much as they had before, most were forced to modify their practices as Hausa "men were being snatched away by more progressive" sex workers.[86] By the end of the decade, most sex work in Sabon Gari appears to have been conducted out of such hotels, and the amount of influence the hotel owners could exert over the women's activities had begun to expand, though to what extent is not clear.

If the presence of Igbo women in sex work signified that Igbos had been taken "down a step," there were other indicators as well. One expatriate recalled on several occasions seeing Hausa patrons of Sabon Gari drinking establishments tauntingly offer Igbos small sums of money if they would drink *kunu*, a millet-based gruel. While *kunu* was a regular part of many Hausas' diets, many Igbos had treated it with disdain before the war. In the months that followed the war, however, many accepted both the food and the money they were offered to consume it, to the amusement of non-Igbo onlookers.[87]

Almost without exception, both Hausa and Igbo share the belief that post-war Igbos in the North adopted humbler dispositions than Igbos had before the war, particularly when compared to the period of the Ironsi regime. As migrants who had been in Kano at the time point out, memories of 1966 and the role Igbo hubris had played in motivating that year's violence were strong among those who had lived through the disturbances. Furthermore, the defeat of Biafra, the economic privation most returnees faced, and the new political landscape contributed to a situation in which they hardly appeared threatening. In 1966 the specter of unification had led many in Kano to view the city's Igbos as the vanguard of Ironsi's invading army, as harbingers of Igbo plans to dominate the country. Now, they arrived as citizens of East Central State, outsiders in Kano present at the sufferance of the new state government. These factors helped to create a psychological space in which *Kanawa* could, with a mixture of admiration and surprise, acknowledge that the war had lasted much longer than anyone had predicted, and had been marked by tenacious Biafran resistance in the face of a vastly superior military force. This generated a reluctant but nonetheless powerful respect for the former Biafrans.[88] For *Kanawa* and other Northerners, personal interactions with Igbos played out in the space between feelings of political and economic security and grudging respect.

### "THEY'VE BEEN TELLING US YOU'RE ALL DEAD": RECONNECTING

Upon their return, many Igbos with roots in Kano were greeted with surprise that they were alive; first-time arrivals reported similar comments expressing surprise that there were any survivors from Biafra at all. Immanuel Irozuru, an Igbo who had grown up in and around Kano and who had unusually strong social connections to the Hausa community, reported his Hausa friends surprised to find him alive upon his return in April 1970. They believed that very few Igbos had survived the war.[89] A federal employee who returned in February said that people in Kano had the impression that there were no survivors.[90] And Chief Ohaeri, who arrived in early 1971, remembered being told "They've been telling us you're all dead. They've been lying to us."[91] In mid-1971 U.M. Nnadi was rehired by the factory where he had worked before the war. At that time Igbos made up only one percent of workers in large-scale industry in Kano. His co-workers, who included Hausas, Middle Belters and a few southerners, had also heard that there had been few Biafran survivors. This, Nnadi said, contributed to their kind treatment of him: "When your friends would see you in a tattered condition, they didn't mock you."[92] An early impetus for such rumors was the protracted struggle during September and October 1967 in and around Asaba and Onitsha between Biafran forces and Nigerian soldiers under the command of Colonel Murtala Muhammad. Murtala had strong ties to Kano, and rumors circulating there exaggerated Biafran casualties to the point of claiming that "all the Igbos had been killed."[93] Subsequently, similar rumors spread in Kano from boastful soldiers on leave, those stationed in the city, and wounded treated at the city's orthopedic hospital.

While most able-bodied men within Biafra experienced some sort of military or paramilitary service, migrants reported that in Kano there was very little stigma attached to their service.[94] Ogbogu's 1973 interviews revealed similar patterns. She wrote that most of the Hausa she interviewed were willing to treat the war as a conflict between governments.[95] A number of former Biafran officers and soldiers discussed their service with Hausa and other Northern friends upon their return. Irozuru, who was wounded in action, described an all-night discussion with working class and white collar Hausa friends shortly after his arrival. "They had lots of questions. They asked me: 'Did I fight?' I told them yes, I fought. They asked me if I was forced to join the army. I told them: 'No, I joined by choice.' They asked me how we managed to live. I told them about the hardship, the struggle."[96] *Eze* O.T. Nnadi, a first-time post-war migrant, had directed refugee camps during the war. He recounted similar discussions in the homes of western-educated Hausa elites.

> They asked me: "Did everyone in Biafra support Ojukwu?" I told them, yes. They asked me did I; I told them yes. They asked me why. I told them we were being killed—"We ran home, you attacked us. Ojukwu was persuaded to fight, mostly by university students. They forced Ojukwu to secede." And I told them that it was my country, right or wrong. "When your country goes to war, you have to fight, but that now I'm back. We didn't want fragmentation, but . . . " They were happy. They said I was honest.[97]

And D.O. Nnadi, among the first wave of civil servants recruited in 1970, recalled that no one asked about his service as an officer in the Biafran Army; rather, "people tried to reassure you in the office."[98]

Even as the curiosity the early returnees encountered waned, the mood of acceptance continued. A Kano-born engineer who returned there in 1974 said he felt "lovely. People were embracing you. They wanted you to feel at home. The war was over. People had seen the folly of such a senseless war. They would go out of their way to make you see that the war was not their fault but rather because of Ojukwu. It didn't matter much to them where an Igbo came from. They were more concerned with your character."[99] And Humphrey Umeh, who was wounded in action fighting for Biafra, arrived in Kano for the first time in 1975.

> I was prepared for being reminded of my rebel status—it never came up. We identify each other here; we know who is from where. It didn't matter in the end how much you disguised yourself, you'd be able in the end to tell where you come from—at least it's possible to exclude areas you couldn't possibly have come from. Here I was dealt with quite decently. I did detect, occasionally, certain signs of, even, patronage—bending over backward to accommodate you, like someone who was, say, a little handicapped in one particular way or another and needed to be assisted. If you made somebody angry without knowing it then, and he turned around to be nasty to you and discovered it was you [and] he could tell roughly where you came from, he would forebear, and would not go on with the quarreling.[100]

Interestingly, the only examples of open hostility to Igbos reported were directed at women. Hausa youth threw water and stones at Mrs. Caroline Jideonwo near her home in Gwagwarwa, a low-income, ethnically mixed area, in 1972. They taunted her with shouts of "*Inyamiri banza*" ("worthless Igbo"). In another case, Mrs. Victoria Uwaoma, a Sabon Gari restauranteur, was taunted with shouts in Hausa to "go home" and Mrs. Florence Duru also recalled cold words in the Sabon Gari market.[101] That such incidents stand out as exceptions reflects how the forbearance of *Kanawa* helped to ease the post-war meeting of communities.

## CONCLUSION

Post-war ethnicity operated in a new context. It was one of states instead of regions, an environment without political parties, and most importantly one in which the war had in large part fixed—at least for the moment—the place of the Igbo in Nigeria's political and economic order.

Still, within that context, Igbos, like other Nigerians, exploited the resources available to them. Ethnicity was one such resource. If belief that their ethnic group was not welcome in Nigeria had helped to unite Igbos behind the Biafran cause, then the shared experience of the war and post-war marginalization provided Igbos with a common vocabulary that they could draw upon in rebuilding their lives. If there were widely held beliefs about their ingenuity, tenacity, reliability, and commercial acumen, then they would exploit those beliefs. And if they were, as outsiders in the North, largely excluded from local patronage networks, then by way of compensation, they would take advantage of the infrastructure their concentric identities offered them. In this sense, it was Igbos themselves who transformed poison into medicine, by taking elements of an identity that offered stigma and converting them into instruments of uplift. Moreover, they did so without the compass of a pan-ethnic organization like the Igbo State Union, or a political core like the NCNC, both of which had been so closely tied to the penetration of Igbo ethnicity in the 1940s and 1950s. In that sense, the violence of 1966 and the war itself had become indispensable ingredients in the glue that held Igbo identity together. The process of post-war reconstruction would likewise become part of that glue.

Equally important was the fact that, by and large, Kano's Igbos were able to economically rehabilitate themselves. They did not make demands on state resources or create the impression that they were taking jobs away from Kano people. Indeed, even Igbo federal employees had to fit around other Nigerians, as evidenced when Malam Aminu Kano reminded Nigerians that rehired Igbo federal Posts and Telegraphs employees filled only vacant positions, and were not displacing current workers.[102] As we have seen, what institutional assistance Igbos received originated largely within their own extended community. The set of institutions that were the most important—and most closed to non-Igbos—was the system of town unions, which began to function almost immediately in some cases. By 1975 most Igbos in Kano were in some way affiliated with a union. This development, and the creation of the Igbo Community Association as a successor organization to the pre-war Kano Ibo Union are addressed in the following chapter, which focuses on changes in the relationships between Igbo migrants with both their host community and their home communities in the post-war period.

## NOTES

1. There were, for example, large Hausa populations in the North-East, North-West, North-Central, and Benue-Plateau States. The Igbo minority in the Mid-West

State meant that the strict association of the ECS with Igbos was not accurate, though in practice this tended to be overlooked outside of the Mid-West.

2. Paden noted in 1973 several Hausa attitudes that facilitated reconciliation. See Paden, *Religion and Political Culture in Kano*, 357.

3. Based on claims of property listed in the *Kano State Gazette* and FN 3A: Interview with Alhaji Uba Adamu, 13 November 1993, Kano.

4. Other such trucks appeared in Maiduguri, where more than a dozen arrived each week to haul fish from Lake Chad to the south. Observers reported that the Igbo drivers paid up to £500 per load, and often paid local traders in advance for loads the following week. USNA POL 18/2509/A-16: 7, 9/25 March 1971. The Kano observation was that of a bank manager, and the Maiduguri one that of the North-East State Community Development Commissioner.

5. FN 6: Interview with Mr. Felix Agwuenu, 1 April 1994, Kano.

6. "Kabilar Ibo Fiye da 800 a Kano" [Igbos in Kano Exceed 800], *Gaskiya Ta Fi Kwabo*, 3 August 1970. Cited in Paden, *Religion and Political Culture*, 356. Early in 1971, the state Permanent Secretary for Local Government gave a figure of between 600 and 700 Igbos "officially known" to reside in greater Kano. That other Igbos, less visible to officials, were present is clear. USNA POL 18/2509/A-16, 6, 25 March 1971.

7. Paden, *Religion and Political Culture*, 356.

8. USNA POL 15/ 2506/A-31, 12, 21 May 1971. Igbos appeared on road crews around Sokoto, Keffi, and Garkinda, and in villages like Lafia, Kagoro, Saminaka, Zonkwa, and Karu, where Igbo teachers were welcomed. USNA POL 15/2506/A-22, 9, 2 April 1972; USNA POL 18/2516/A-59, 5, 6 August 1971.

9. The A.G. Leventis retail chain saw its sales staff in the North shift from being nearly totally Igbo to overwhelmingly Yoruba. According to the company's Northern states director, the company initially replaced its Igbo staff in Kano with Hausa Muslims, but turned to Yorubas in large part because management found the Muslims' prayer schedule disruptive. Barclay's Bank executives estimated that in 1966 half of their staff in the North had been Igbos, and that those employees had been replaced by Northern Yorubas. USNA POL 18/2509/A-16, 2, 25 March 1971.

10. The decree, number 46 of 1970, identified broad categories of former employees subject to such penalties on the grounds that they had engaged in "hostile and subversive act[s]"; application of the decree, however, seems to have been largely political. See Federal Military Government of Nigeria, *Official Gazette* 57, No. 46 Part A (Lagos: Government Printing Office, 13 August 1970).

11. The best treatment of conditions in Igboland is Axel Harneit-Sievers, et al., *A Social History of the Nigerian Civil War: Perspectives from Below* (Hamburg: Lit Verlag, 1997).

12. 1971 ECS Administrator Ukpabi Asika described the ECS as overcrowded to a crowd in Jos in 1971, and encouraged Igbos to continue making inroads in other parts of the federation. USNA POL 18/2510/A-108, 14 December 1971.

13. Harneit-Sievers, "'No Victors, No Vanquished'?," 4.

14. "New Confidence Grows Among Nigerian Civil War Ruins," *Times*, 29 April 1970, 12.

15. The Biafran Army appears to have had officers who followed the same pattern.

16. The most common items smuggled out of Biafra included hemp/marijuana and distilled palm wine; salt, cigarettes, and food top the list of items brought into Biafra. The trade on the Nigerian side appears to have been more evenly divided between male and female agents, though the highly visible Hausa traders were men. FN 15: Interview with Mr. K.J. Asika, 12 February 1994, Kano; FN 90D: Interview with Mr. Humphrey S.C. Umeh, 20 June 1994. See also Harneit-Sievers, et al., *Social History*, 143–7.

17. Bridget Bloom, "Report from Iboland," *West Africa*, 24 January 1970, 95.

18. Chief D.O. Adinuso kept the car on jacks during the war. FN 4: Interview with Chief D.O. Adinuso, 1 July 1994, Kano.

19. *West Africa*, 24 January 1970, 95. See also Harneit-Sievers, et al., *Social History*, 174.

20. Sydney Emezue in Harneit-Sievers, et al., *Social History*, 148, 154.

21. Harneit-Sievers, et al., *Social History*, 178.

22. Harneit-Sievers, "'No Victors, No Vanquished'?," 4.

23. "£14m. for East-Central State," *West Africa*, 6 June 1970, 625. The money deposited was but a fraction of the total Biafran currency in circulation; according to the report, an estimated £200 million had circulated within Biafra.

24. Chinua Achebe, *The Trouble with Nigeria* (London: Heinemann, 1983), 46.

25. Minister of Finance Obafemi Awolowo—who, in many eyes reneged on a May 1967 promise to take the Western Region out of Nigeria if the East seceded—was seen as the mastermind of the plan, and this contributed to the perception that the flat redemption was punitive. His failure to lead the West to secede and his orchestration of the currency exchange led many to the conclusion that he had created situations whereby Yoruba Nigerians would be the main beneficiaries from Igbo misfortunes.

26. FN 42B: Interview with Mr. Emanuel Irozuru, 8 September 1994, Kano.

27. Harneit-Sievers, "'No Victors, No Vanquished'?," 5.

28. FN 4: Interview with Chief D.O. Adinuso, 1 July 1994, Kano.

29. For example, one trader was unable to redeem an account in Port Harcourt because of powerful anti-Igbo sentiment there. (FN 33: Interview with Chief Patrick Enendu, 1 May 1994, Kano.) Another reported three-to-four day waits at the bank where his account was held. (FN 19: Interview with Malam Ali Chuks, 15 November 1993, Kano.)

30. V.I. Bello, "The Intentions, Implementation Process and Problems with the Nigerian Enterprises Promotion Decree (No. 4) 1972," in Nigerian Economics Society, *Nigeria's Indigenization Policy: Proceedings of the November 1974 Symposium Organized by the Nigerian Economic Society on the Subject "Indigenisation: What Have We Achieved?"* (Ibadan: Department of Economics, University of Ibadan, 1974), 7. See also Nicholas Balabkins, *Indigenization and Economic Development: The Nigerian Experience* (London: Jai Press, 1982), and A.O. Sanda, *The Challenge of Nigeria's Indigenization* (Ibadan: Nigerian Institute of Social and Economic Research, 1982).

31. Okwudiba Nnoli, *Ethnicity and Development in Nigeria*, 143–4.

32. Wayne Nafziger, *The Economics of Political Instability*, 178.

33. FN 90B: Interview with Mr. Humphrey S.C. Umeh, 25 January 1994.

34. FN 12: Interview with Chief W.O. Anunobi, 7 August 1994, Kano.

35. FN 90B: Interview with Mr. Humphrey S.C. Umeh, 25 January 1994.

36. FN 90B: Interview with Mr. Humphrey S.C. Umeh, 25 January 1994.

37. FN 90B: Interview with Mr. Humphrey S.C. Umeh, 25 January 1994.

38. FN 90B: Interview with Mr. Humphrey S.C. Umeh, 25 January 1994.

39 See also Harneit-Sievers, et al., *Social History*, 171–2.

40. FN 90D: Interview with Mr. Humphrey S.C. Umeh, 20 June 1994. "Sannu" is a standard Hausa greeting. "One Nigeria" was a key phrase in federal wartime rhetoric which Harneit-Sievers called "the magic formula" to verbally "confirm that a person would neither resist nor flee" and had accepted federal terms. See *Social History*, 166.

41. FN 12: Interview with Chief W.O. Anunobi, 7 August 1994, Kano.

42. "Combating Nigeria's crime wave," *West Africa*, 8 August 1970, 896.

43. FN 26: Interview with Police Inspector Rilwanu Dutse (rtd.), 9 August 1994, Kano.

44. FN 76: Interview with Mr. Robert Onuora, 31 March 1994, Kano.

45. FN-Anonymous.

46. FN 6: Interview with Mr. Felix Agwuenu, 1 April 1994, Kano.

47. *Kano State Statistical Yearbook* (Kano: Military Governor's Office: 1972, 1974).

48. Audu Bako, *Policy Statement, 1 April 1968* (Kano: Information Division, Military Government Office, 1968), 4.

49. HCB ADM/1/28, 35, Intelligence Report, January 1970.

50. Kano State Public Service Commission, *Annual Report of the Public Service Commission of the Kano State of Nigeria for the Period 1st April, 1970 to 31st March, 1971* (Kano: Government Printer, 1971), 3.

51. There were 670 out-of-state workers in 1968 (29 percent), 1,163 in 1970 (28 percent), and 2,147 in 1974 (24 percent). Statistics from 1970, 1974, and 1977 editions of *Kano State Statistical Yearbook* (Kano: Military Governor's Office).

52. *Annual Report of the Public Service Commission*, 3.

53. FN 61: Interview with Mr. D.O. Nnadi, 4 May 1994, Kano.

54. These numbers are likely slight undercounts. Available state records did not indicate state of origin or ethnic affiliation. Native speakers of Igbo selected names they felt "definitely Igbo," "probably Igbo" and "possibly Igbo" from official registries of state employees and also from contemporary telephone directories, which listed many public and private sector employees by position, in most cases regardless of telephone access. Care was taken to avoid dual counting of the same individual because of multiple listings or variant spellings. Names determined "probably" or "possibly" Igbo were cross-checked, when possible, with individuals with personal knowledge of the individuals in question. In the few cases where this was not possible, the names were not counted. As most Igbo names have denotative meanings and many have strong historical associations with particular places, this was a reasonably reliable method of identification. Obviously, it misses the small number of Igbo individuals who did not carry Igbo names, and runs the unlikely risk of including non-Igbos who may have used Igbo names. Single incidents of each were detected during cross-checking.

55. *Annual Report of the Public Service Commission*, 3. In 1970–71 Kano State hired 1001 public service officers, of whom 697 were from Kano. Kwara state provided 111, and expatriates numbered 89. North Central State (21), Benue-Plateau State (19), and East Central State (19) were the other significant providers.

56. Several Igbo informants, both civil servants and independent business people, argued that unlike traders, for whom risk is professionally inherent, government employees are less likely to accept assignments in areas associated with personal risk.

57. FN 29: Interview with Mr. Goddy Emeka-Ejiofor, 28 March 1994, Kano.

58. FN 33: Interview with Chief Patrick Enendu, 1 May 1994, Kano.

59. FN 66: Interview with Mr. Mambo Nyamasi, 27 February 1994, Kano; FN 70B: Interview with Chief Davis Ohaeri, 18 June 1994, Kano.

60. FN 6: Interview with Mr. Felix Agwuenu, 1 April 1994, Kano.

61. FN 90D: Interview with Mr. Humphrey S.C. Umeh, 20 June 1994.

62. FN 32B: Interview with Mr. J.C. Emodi, 26 May 1993, Kano; FN 37: Interview with Chief A. Ezetah, 15 May 1993, Kano; FN 42A: Interview with Mr. Emanuel Irozuru, 30 March 1994, Kano; FN 61: Interview with Mr. D.O. Nnadi, 4 May 1994, Kano.

63. FN-Anonymous.

64. FN 37: Interview with Chief A. Ezetah, 15 May 1993, Kano. Chief Ezetah recalled cash gifts of up to £10. Also FN 96A: Interview with Alhaji Tanko Yakasai, 3 January 1994, Kano.

65. This pattern may have been in operation when Nigerian observers noted that Igbos were most of the supervisors and three-quarters of the workforce involved in the renovation of a housing estate the New Nigerian Development Company owned in Kaduna, despite the fact that a Northerner held the contract. USNA POL 18/2516/A-59, 5, 6 August 1971.

66. For a discussion of the war's impact on Igbo capitalism in Igboland, see Tom Forrest, *The Advance of African Capital: The Growth of Nigerian Private Enterprise* (Charlottesville: University Press of Virginia, 1994), chapters six and seven.

67. I am grateful to Professor Alan Frishman for making available to me copies of the original responses of business operators from the East Central State, as well as those from Mid-West, South-East, and Rivers States. The questionnaires from which these were taken represent a random third of the approximately 4,250 responses the students gathered. Frishman later determined that the survey enumerated about one third of the small industries operating at the time. Responses indicated the ethnic affiliation and state of origin of the business operator, or where multiple employees were present, information for the manager. If one assumes that the rate of enumeration for Igbo businesses was the same as for the metropolitan area as a whole, then the 77 respondents who identified themselves as Igbo (eight from Mid-West State, the rest from East Central State) reflect approximately one-ninth of all Igbo small businesses, which places the total at just under 700. There are, however, insufficient grounds for either accepting or rejecting that assumption; the total, therefore, must be treated carefully. See Alan Frishman, *Small-Scale Industry in Metropolitan Kano, Nigeria: A Report for the World Bank* (June, 1979).

68. Snuff making (6 percent), haircutting (5 percent), dry cleaning (5 percent) and sign painting (5 percent) were the other types of work enumerated four or more times.

69. FN 70B: Interview with Chief Davis Ohaeri, 18 June 1994, Kano; and small business survey data (1973).

70. During the 1980s the spread of secondary education made it far more likely than before that a novice apprentice would have a secondary education.

71. Chief C.O. Anyaka, for example, was an apprentice trader of stationery in Kano for three years during the late 1950s. At the end of his term of service, his master utilized a formula common to single-apprentice operations to calculate how much he would contribute to Anyaka's incipient enterprise. Based on inventory and sales figures, his master calculated the increase in the total value of the business during Anyaka's tenure. Anyaka received one-third of the increase, which was about £150.

72. FN-Anonymous.

73. FN 33: Interview with Chief Patrick Enendu, 1 May 1994, Kano.

74. Under normal circumstances, the practice of *karuwanci* is characterized by a protracted series of non-sexual contacts prior to any initiation of a sexual relationship. Such relationships might continue for months or even years. And where Sabon Gari sex workers attracted patrons from a variety of backgrounds, *karuwai* tended to draw from within the broader Hausa community. The Hausa phrase for the more direct variety of commercial sex is *masu gaskiya*, literally, "having truth," but is perhaps more clearly expressed by the Pidgin equivalent "hit and go." The complex social space occupied by *karuwai* is discussed in Barbara Callaway, *Muslim Hausa Women in Nigeria* (Syracuse: Syracuse University Press, 1987), 42–4, and at length in Rene Pittin, *Marriage and Alternative Strategies: Career Patterns of Hausa Women in Katsina City* (Ph.D. dissertation, University of London, 1979). The term is most broadly applied to women outside male supervision, usually divorcees or widows. As used more restrictively here, it refers to the subset of these women whose primary income derives from providing companionship, usually but not always including sexual services, to men.

75. The testimony of a retired Hausa police inspector reflected what other male informants of various ethnic backgrounds suggested: The majority of non-Hausa sex workers in pre-war Sabon Gari (and Gwagwarawa) were, or at least presented themselves as, Mid-Westerners, or as Middle Belters, in particular ethnic Tivs. They commonly met with potential patrons in drinking establishments at prearranged times. FN 26: Interview with Police Inspector Rilwanu Dutse (rtd.), 9 August 1994, Kano and FN-Anonymous.

76. FN 33: Interview with Chief Patrick Enendu, 1 May 1994, Kano.

77. Z.O. Ogunnika, *Mechanisms of Tension Management in a Plural Society: A Study of Inter-Ethnic Relations in Kano City, Nigeria* (Ph.D. dissertation, New School for Social Research, 1982), 104. See also Z.O. Ogunnika, *Inter-ethnic Tension Management in Nigeria* (Lagos: Mufets, 1994).

78. Ogunnika, *Mechanisms*, 102.

79. For Ogunnika, this pattern is a manifestation of ethnic rivalry. He argued that besides the desire of male customers to discourage women of their own ethnic group

from the practice, such inter-ethnic liaisons are frequently a source of pride for the patron in his interactions with men of his own ethnic group. Ogunnika, *Mechanisms,* 102. See also *Inter-ethnic Tension Management,* 73–4.

80. FN 26: Interview with Police Inspector Rilwanu Dutse (rtd.), 9 August 1994, Kano.

81. See Harneit-Sievers, et al., *Social History.*

82. Hausa *karuwai* operated on a different scale. They generally received at least five shillings in cash when they engaged in sex. In addition, however, the patron would almost certainly have incurred other expenses in his previous meetings with her, possibly spending up to a pound.

83. The 1966–1970 slowdown of commercial sex in Sabon Gari-Kano combined with the creation of Benue-Plateau State, and concomitant increase in activity in Jos. This appears to have lured a portion of sex workers from that area closer to home. FN 53: Interview with Alhaji Sharu Audu Mili, 22 September 1994, Kano; FN-Anonymous.

84. Z.O. Ogunnika, *Inter-ethnic Tension Management,* 73.

85. FN-Anonymous.

86. FN 22: Interview with Malam A.U. Dan Asabe, 14 September 1994, Kano. Also FN 26: Interview with Police Inspector Rilwanu Dutse (rtd.), 9 August 1994, Kano; FN-Anonymous.

87. FN 55A: Interview with Mr. Robert Montgomery, 5 March 1994, Kano. While such exchanges were sometimes tense, he recalled no incidents where the threat of violence appeared.

88. Paden made a similar observation. In paraphrasing Hausa attitudes toward returning Igbos, he wrote "The Hausa respect courage, and the war gave them a greater respect for the Ibos." Paden, *Religion and Political Culture,* 357.

89. FN 42A: Interview with Mr. Emanuel Irozuru, 30 March 1994, Kano.

90. FN-Anonymous.

91. FN 70A: Interview with Chief Davis Ohaeri, 19 March 1994, Kano.

92. FN 63: Interview with Mr. U.M. Nnadi, 4 June 1994, Kano. For the ethnic makeup of Kano's industrial work force, see Lubeck, *Islam and Urban Labor,* 323.

93. FN 38: Interview with Alhaji Abdulrahman Howeidy, 18 April 1994, Kano. See also Emma Okocha, *Blood on the Niger: An Untold Story of the Nigerian Civil War* (Washington DC: USA Africa, 1994), 24–33. Okocha's study details the massacre of Mid-Western Igbo civilians at Asaba during the war by troops of the Second Division under the command of Colonel Muhammad.

94. Of the Igbo men interviewed for this study, the majority fought for Biafra; of the others, two spent the war working and studying overseas, and one served the Biafran government in Europe. Several others indirectly served in the war effort, and two older men farmed.

95. Ogbogu, "Ibo Reintegration in Kano After the War," 42. See also Paden, *Religion and Political Culture,* 357.

96. FN 42A: Interview with Mr. Emanuel Irozuru, 30 March 1994, Kano.

97. FN 62B: Interview with *Eze* O.T. Nnadi, 2 October 1994, Kano.

98. FN 61: Interview with Mr. D.O. Nnadi, 4 May 1994, Kano.

99. FN-Anonymous.

100. FN 90B: Interview with Mr. Humphrey S.C. Umeh, 25 January 1994, Kano.

101. FN 45: Interview with Mrs. Caroline Jideonwo, 7 September 1994, Kano; FN 93: Interview with Mrs. Victoria Uwaoma, 15 September 1994, Kano; FN 25: Interview with Mrs. Florence Duru, 2 September 1994, Kano.

102. USNA POL 15/2508/A-173, 13 and 14 May 1970. At the time, Malam Aminu, who was Federal Commissioner for Communications, claimed that 1,078 of the 1,795 former Posts and Telegraphs employees in the Eastern Region who sought reinstatement had been.

# 7

# REBUILDING COMMUNITY, 1970–1986

## INTRODUCTION

Ethnicity remained at the core of the lives of most Kano Igbos in the years following the war. As they gradually rebuilt a framework of community institutions, they did so around the same concentric ethnic and local identities that had proven most reliable in years past. As the networks that individuals created for themselves became increasingly stable and intertwined, community-wide institutions became both possible and necessary. Even where Igbos established individual ties beyond their ethnic community, rarely did those ties obviate the need or desire for strong ties to townspeople and, eventually, other Igbos in the broadest sense. In part this pattern follows from the conscious or unconscious realization that ethnic affiliations and labels continued to exert powerful influence at all levels of Nigerian society. In part, the pattern followed the path of least resistance: People simply did what worked. The return to a sense of normalcy for Kano's Igbos was closely tied to the level of connectedness in ethnic networks. Unlike the pre-war period, where community institutions had played major roles in the lives of most of Kano's Igbos, the years that followed the war were characterized by a high level of social fragmentation and self-reliance. The reemergence of such institutions, then, is an important measure of both continuity and change within the Igbo community.

The trickle of migrants was more or less continuous during the 1970s, and much of the population was highly mobile. Its members' economic circumstances varied widely; some arrived in 1970 with the means to open small businesses immediately, and others came a year or two later with only the clothes on their backs. Regardless, however, the energy and financial resources of most Igbos went to provide for themselves and their families in Kano or in Igboland, and to generate working capital. In this environment, rebuilding formal community institutions was, by necessity, a low priority. This meant that while Igbos arriving in Kano could sometime turn to relatives, townspeople, and acquaintances, they initially did so without the formal structures of town, clan, or division unions, and with no Kano Ibo Union to monitor their collective interests. However, as Kano's Igbos regained a sense of stability, the reestablishment of community institutions went hand-in-hand with a return to a sense of normalcy. The institutions they created are also a window on the changes that the expulsion and Civil War fostered. A recent history of the Civil War has addressed the delicate notion of a "return to normalcy" among former Biafrans, and correctly foregrounds its highly subjective nature.[1] Indeed, even today where the economic, sociological, and psychological impacts of the war are not immediately visible in Kano's Igbo community, they usually lurk just beneath the surface. As I apply the term, normalcy simply suggests the ability of Kano's Igbos to establish new rhythms of life as a community and to treat those rhythms as reasonably stable.

This chapter points to several elements that, when taken together, suggests that it was in the early to mid-1980s that these new rhythms emerged. Over the decade and a half that followed the war, new versions of old institutions appeared, each of which reflects on how Kano's Igbos saw themselves as individuals, as members of various groups and networks, and as part of a migrant community. The reunification of families and establishment of stable households came first, along with the gradual reappearance of apprenticeships. Then, through the mid-1970s, unions based on home communities in Igboland reappeared as migrants reconnected with one another and used old patterns to build new networks. Through the 1970s, one of the main activities of unions was to contribute funds to the reconstruction of towns and villages in Igboland. At the same time, Kano's Igbos, like Igbo migrants all over of Nigeria, chose to invest their personal wealth at home in Igboland rather than in their adopted cities. That began to change in the 1980s, as Igbos demonstrated a renewed sense of security by beginning to erect buildings in Kano, again reflecting national patterns. And, after a return to civilian politics in the late 1970s presented new opportunities and gave focus to existing concerns, Igbo leaders created a new umbrella organization for all of Kano's Igbos in 1983. This important step marked the first time since 1966 that the Igbo community asserted its presence in explicitly ethnic terms. This step, as much as any other, suggests that Kano's Igbos had, in a collective sense, regained a sense of confidence. Later, in 1986, the community took the added step of creating a chieftaincy position and appointing Kano's first Igbo "traditional ruler."

## THE REBIRTH OF TOWN UNIONS

As discussed in chapter one, town unions had been the cornerstone of pre-war Igbo community life. Maintaining them, however, required energy and money that early post-war migrants put to other uses. After arriving in Kano, most established some sort of church affiliation, and built social networks around neighbors, fellow traders, or co-workers. Informants, however, minimized the importance of those relationships, in part because such associations were voluntary, and carried little accountability. The niche that unions filled as mutual-aid societies and social organizations remained largely unfilled. Not surprisingly, unions were among the first institutions that migrants created for themselves. Many migrants were members of unions even before they were reunited with family members.

One such example is the 1973 organization of the Mbanasa United Front. Mbanasa is one of more than a half dozen clans in the former Orlu Division. Of the division's sixty-six towns, seven fell into Mbanasa.[2] Despite the large contingent of Orlu emigrants in Kano, the number from the seven Mbanasa towns remained small through the 1970s. These small numbers made individual town unions impractical, and as was often the case, the clan union served as a surrogate. As late as 1979 the union had fewer than twenty full members, several of whose wives were associated members.[3] Like many post-war unions, the Mbanasa union came into being as the result of a tragedy. The union formed in 1973 after the child of a Mbanasa man living in Kano died. The child's father approached the oldest Mbanasa native in Kano for assistance. The elder organized a collection, and the child was buried in Kano's Christian cemetery. The half-dozen Mbanasa natives the death brought together continued to meet regularly and formalized their association soon thereafter. The union did not address the admission of single women as full members until 1979 when a newly arrived trader approached the union. She eventually withdrew her application, but others followed and were accepted.[4] The same year that the Mbanasa United Front formed, the Orlu Wayfarers Association met for the first time at the home of Chief Agu Ezetah. The meeting was attended by twelve members ranging from an eighteen year old to a man in his seventies.[5] Before the war a similar organization, the Orlu Division Union, had been one of Kano's most visible Igbo organizations. The name change was to emphasize its role as a collective welfare association and to distance it from the Ironsi-era ban on "tribal" organizations, a ban which exempted collective welfare groups. And, abandoning the word "union" was in recognition of the pre-war politicization of the Ibo State Union.[6] The Wayfarers Association grew quickly, and claimed several hundred members by the end of the decade.

The functions of unions remained largely the same as they had been before the war. Given the wartime devastation of Igboland, however, their contributions to the construction of infrastructure there was a particularly important addition and has been studied elsewhere.[7] At the same time, the hardship of the post-war period meant that during the early and mid-1970s the union's role in helping new arrivals with shelter and employment expanded to an unprecedented level, even though the level of support members were able to offer newcomers was diminished. Still, those who could provide temporary accommodation to new arrivals—in one case nearly two dozen—did so. The number of town unions is impossible to document before the formation of the Igbo Community Association in 1983, at which point it registered more than 100.[8] Just as the vast majority of pre-war migrants appear to have been actively associated with at least one such union, so by the mid-to-late 1970s the system of unions was sufficiently reestablished that most were affiliated at some level.

Nonetheless, a small number of migrants did not belong to their local unions. This was not new. In pre-war Challawa, for example, most of the Igbo employees at the water pumping station maintained close ties to the union system in nearby Kano. However, one man, remembered by his former Hausa neighbors only by his Hausa nickname, did not join his home town union. According to those neighbors, the man, called "Mai Tumbi" because of his large stomach, broke ties with his town union and the Kano Ibo Union and instead associated mainly with Hausas. This left him outside of the support system unions offered. When he died in the early 1960s, Hausa neighbors and a few Igbo co-workers pooled their resources to pay for his burial. Unlike most Igbo adults who died away from home, his remains were buried in Kano's Christian cemetery, and not returned to his patrilineal home, Asaba.[9] After the war some migrants also chose not to associate themselves with their town or clan unions. One woman, for example, gave her desire for privacy as the reason for not joining.[10] Others delayed joining until they had the financial wherewithal to do so. A male informant who held a relatively prestigious professional position during the mid-1970s learned of the existence of his town union in a chance meeting with a distant relation in Sabon Gari market. For several months, however, he avoided making himself known to them since his fluency in written English, his professional standing, and regular salary would have likely exposed him to demands on his time and financial resources that he was not prepared to accept. Further, like many in his position, his living quarters were not up to the standard he felt his townspeople would have expected of him. Several months later, after shoring up his finances and moving his family from the one room they had occupied into "a proper house," he sought out union members, and became an active participant in the group's activities.[11] Still, not having a union affiliation could lead to difficulties for oneself or one's relatives. In order to avoid them, an informant, himself an active union member, regularly made dues payments and obligatory contributions to his union on behalf of a poorer relation. His relative did not attend the union's monthly meetings, and in most cases his failure to do so would have been sufficient to cancel his membership. His occupation, however, made his repeated absences plausible. The informant said that keeping his relative's membership current was in his own interest, since if he failed to do so, he alone would have been responsible should his relative become sick or injured, or "fall into the hands of the police." By making payments on his relative's behalf, he placed the relative—and by extension himself—in the position of remaining eligible for union assistance.[12]

## WOMEN'S NETWORKS

Many town unions provided a boost to the economic prospects of their women members. Igbo unions at all levels are characterized by a system of parallel membership between two branches. As a rule, the main branch is open to men, married and single, and unmarried women, all over the age of eighteen. The second branch, often called the women's wing, is reserved for the wives of male members. A woman who married within her town, clan, or divisional union would cease to be eligible for membership in the main branch but could join the women's wing. On the other hand, were she to marry outside of her home area, she would, generally, end her membership in her home union and become a member of the women's wing of her husband's union.[13] The creation of women's wings necessarily followed the arrival of significant numbers of women in Kano, though in some cases members downplayed the division between the two wings. For a while, in most cases the married women met together with the men and single women. By the late 1970s, though, the bifurcated system was largely functioning. Where the dual system operates, the functions of the women's organization are similar to those carried out by the main group, though frequently with an important exception. Where formal assistance from the main organization to members tends to be limited to times of crisis, women's wings often contribute money to members who are raising capital for business ventures. Since marriage often marked a reduction in ties between a woman and her home community, the grants-in-aid that women's wings provided simultaneously strengthened her ties to her new community and compensated, at least partially, for her loss of access to resources from home. Like single women and men, membership for married women was contingent on them being "reputably employed" on a full-time basis, including self-employment. Particularly after the war, the small amounts of capital unions provided were important for women in establishing themselves commercially.

The women's wing of the Orlu Wayfarer's Association in Kano was founded in 1977, four year's after the parent organization. The delay was largely the result of the preponderance of men in Kano's Orlu community through the mid-1970s. It was after urging by wives of Association members, most of them new arrivals, that the union established the women's wing. At its inception, the women's wing had close to 200 members, and represented a pool of knowledge and resources beyond what any of their respective town unions could provide.[14] Of that number, about a quarter had professional or clerical jobs, and most of the rest were full or part-time traders or food sellers. One woman was a partner with her husband in selling auto parts. In its first ten years the women's wing collected voluntary contributions from members, and assisted approximately twenty members, most with funds to secure a market stall, or to help purchase supplies and equipment for dressmaking or food selling. In the Orlu union, the recipient was not expected to repay the money, but rather to contribute financially to the activities of the union once her business began to generate a profit.[15]

The delay between the first wave of Igbo men and their decisions to bring their families reflects, in most cases, concerns about economic and physical security. In cases where the husbands were the first to take residence in Kano, it was often several years before wives and children joined them on a full-time basis, by which point the post-war euphoria had subsided.[16] Regaining one's feet economically meant not only generating an income, but also securing adequate housing. While many public service employees were able to do this quickly with government housing or housing allowances, most others spent several years in Kano before they felt willing and able to bring their families. Assessing physical safety remained tricky, as fears of communal violence lingered, and varied depending on one's wealth and area of residence. Despite the absence of any significant anti-Igbo protests or violence during the 1970s, feelings of vulnerability remained. One measure of this is the fact that most Igbos avoided speaking Igbo in Kano's streets or markets until the late 1970s. Still, most informants reported that by the time they had arranged housing, they were confident that their families were at least as safe in Kano as they were in Igboland or elsewhere, and those who came after 1972 made the decision to bring their families primarily on the basis of finances and housing.

Most adult Igbo women engaged in some form of income-generating activity, many as traders, though women were much more likely than men to offer goods or provide services primarily for consumption within the Sabon Gari community. And, since they tended to keep their entrepreneurial activities separate from those of the men in their households, this had the effect of curtailing Igbo women's contact with the Kano community beyond Sabon Gari. While the formal restrictions on women's activities so common before the war had been largely abandoned during the economic scramble of the early and mid-1970s, the social networks of most married women remained limited in ways similar to pre-war patterns. While all of the men interviewed reported having some degree of regular contact with *Kanawa* during the first five years of their arrival, only about half of the women had regular contact, and a third reported having none at all. Not surprisingly, the women were also much less likely than their husbands to speak more than rudimentary Hausa, and most of the exceptions had been born in the North.

Just as it was men's economic activities that helped to broaden their personal networks beyond Sabon Gari, so the few Igbo women whose professional lives, or those of their husbands, carried them into the broader community had opportunities that others did not. Mrs. Juliana Ubuonu arrived in 1971 as the wife of a fast-rising attorney. Though she spoke no Hausa and lived in the former GRA, she had more contact with *Kanawa* than most. And Mrs. Chinyere Okpara's work as a teacher brought her in contact with *Kanawa* whom she felt were generally appreciative of her efforts.[17]

Another example of a woman whose professional life opened up broad social networks is Mrs. Mary Kanuh. Mrs. Kanuh arrived in

Kano in 1974, accompanying her husband, who had been transferred to Kano from Lagos by the national radio service. Her initial impressions of Kano were negative, and were colored by the difficulty the Orlu Wayfarer's Association, the divisional union to which she and her husband belonged, was experiencing in recovering its union hall from caretakers (See chapter five). She recalled that discussion among union members frequently centered on that matter. Unlike most of the women in the union at the time, however, Mrs. Kanuh's work carried her into the larger community, and she built networks that extended beyond Sabon Gari. By day she worked as a primary school teacher inside the old city, teaching young *Kanawa*. By night she worked as a food seller in Unguwar Uku, an ethnically mixed, low-income area. It was her experience as a teacher of women's adult education classes in night school in 1975, however, that most expanded her contact with women from outside the Sabon Gari community. Most of her students were Hausa, and she began to learn the language to be more effective in the classroom. For economic reasons she retired from teaching in 1976 to pursue food selling full time. Her qualifications as a teacher, however, made her extremely valuable to civic organizations, and she continued her activities beyond the Igbo community through the National Council of Women's Societies, an umbrella organization for various associations. She also remained active in Igbo women's groups, and her associations beyond the Igbo community broadened her appeal as a leader. Kano's first post-war umbrella organization for all of its Igbos, the Igbo Community Association, came into being in 1983, and four years later Mrs. Kanuh became the founding vice president of its Women's Wing. Then, in 1994, she became the wing's president.[18]

## FROM INFORMAL TO FORMAL LEADERSHIP

Between 1970 and 1983, Igbo leadership above the level of Kano's town, clan, and divisional unions flowed through informal channels. As established figures from the pre-war period, Chiefs Felix Okonkwo, J.B. Egbe, and Agu Ezetah were, by consensus, leading members of a community that was rebuilding its institutions. Notwithstanding concerns over abandoned property, relations between Igbos and *Kanawa* were generally good, and the chiefs' roles appear to have been largely consultative, consisting of occasional visits to the Emir, the governor, and other local dignitaries. Chiefs Egbe and Ezetah described their exchanges with Kano's leaders as routine, but Igbo and Hausa informants agreed that having recognized leaders and established lines of communication was helpful in maintaining confidence between communities. Had there been a crisis that threatened to escalate into intercommunal conflict, the task of speaking for—or perhaps to—Kano's Igbos would likely have befallen them. Many Igbos said that the men also used their influence to intervene on behalf of Sabon Gari residents on mundane matters such as waste removal, water and electric service, and road maintenance, as well as disputes surrounding abandoned property.

Each of the three had leadership credentials from the pre-war period, and were well-known in the larger community.[19] Chief Okonkwo had been an NCNC field officer, head of the successful Northern Traders Corporation, and special member of the Northern Region House of Assembly. He was also a former Kano Ibo Union president, though after the war he divided his time between Kano and the south. Like Okonkwo, Chief Egbe was a former Kano Ibo Union president. His experience during the colonial period and the First Republic had connected him with Kano's traditional elite. In 1966 Chief Egbe had held the position of deputy *Wakilin Waje*, an administrative position within the emirate system to which he had been appointed in 1963 after being hired as a clerk in 1948. As deputy *Wakili*, Chief Egbe was responsible for much of the everyday operation of Waje's government, which included Sabon Gari. In that capacity, he had personal access to the Emir, and was, for *Kanawa*, Kano's most visible Igbo. Pre-war Sabon Gari residents recall Chief Egbe, turbaned and on horseback, riding to greet the Emir each Friday, and as an official participant in public festivities where the Emir presided. One said that "Chief Egbe was a very big shot in Sabon Gari. He was regarded as a miniature head-of-state. He was seen as someone who can get to any limits."[20] The administrative reforms that followed the creation of Kano State meant that Chief Egbe did not regain his pre-war position upon his return, and he became a full-time hotelier and businessman.[21] The third man, Chief Ezetah, a lawyer and the youngest of the three, had been the main force behind the reorganization of the Orlu Wayfarer's Association in the early 1970s. By the early 1980s, sentiment in the various unions was that the time had come to create an umbrella organization to fill the shoes of the long-disbanded Kano Ibo Union. Ezetah was central to organizing the new Igbo Community Association (ICA), and became its first president in 1983. He was joined by other community leaders, including Chief Patrick Enendu, a successful trader who became ICA vice president and later succeeded Ezetah as its president.[22]

The emergence of the ICA was the result of several factors. Advocates were encouraged by the successful formation of a similar organization in Kaduna's smaller Igbo community a few years earlier. Formalizing their association appeared a natural step for Kano's Igbos since, for several years, informal links between the various town unions had been increasing. Against that backdrop, the explosive *Maitatsine* uprising of 1980 hammered home concerns about collective security. While the riots, in which hundreds of Muslims died, did not involve Igbos, the disturbance was a stark reminder of the potential for violence that existed in as large and diverse a city as Kano.[23] Proponents of an umbrella union argued that its presence would help the Igbo community to control its members, if necessary by expelling criminals and other undesirables. This type of preventive action, they believed, would reduce the likelihood of unwanted attention for themselves, and help to prevent isolated incidents from escalating into intercommunal violence.[24]

The unbanning of political parties in 1978 and the return to civilian politics the following year presented a different set of challenges and opportunities. According to one community member, the relative inflexibility of military administration obviated the need for political advocacy. On the other hand, "Within civilian administration, there is more need for dialogue," and with that, a need for a single community voice.[25] The political calculus of Nigeria's Second Republic was, in many ways, as complicated as that of the First. The governing party in Lagos, the National Party of Nigeria (NPN) was, based on its membership and platform, the successor party to the old Northern Peoples Congress. In part to satisfy complex election rules that required parties to demonstrate support in a number of states, the NPN had reached out to Igbos, both by selecting an Igbo as running mate to the party's far Northern presidential candidate, and by allowing Ojukwu to return to Nigeria after a decade in exile. In Kano, however, the NPN enjoyed limited support among *Kanawa* (who, true to the patterns of the First Republic, rallied behind a left-leaning opposition party, the Peoples Redemption Party (PRP), successor to the NEPU mantle). With many voters in Igboland supporting the NPN and still more behind the Igbo-led Nigerian Peoples Party, a Kano-based Igbo organization was a step toward preventing political alienation by Kano's PRP government. Upon its creation, the leaders of the ICA presented themselves to the Local Authority for recognition. Despite the obvious parallel to the old Kano Ibo Union, the decision to change the name was taken carefully.[26] In short, there was little to gain and much to lose by invoking the words "Ibo Union," words tainted by the disasters of

1966 and the propaganda that surrounded it. Just as the Orlu Wayfarers Association had changed its name to distance itself from its prewar predecessor, so did the ICA. Still, like the old Kano Ibo Union, the ICA was organized around town unions, and each registered, dues-paying union was entitled to representation in the ICA. Through their town unions and those unions' representatives to the ICA ordinary Igbos would be represented.

It was out of the ICA that the next major community development emerged. In 1986 a group of about 100 prominent members of the ICA calling itself the *Eze* Cabinet[27] took the unprecedented step of selecting a "traditional ruler," or *Eze*, for Kano's Igbos.[28] In fact, the post is largely symbolic, and the *Eze* has no power to rule. Rather, the position of *Eze* was designed to embody the unity of the Igbo community in a single, highly visible personality, and indeed after coronation, each *Eze* has been presented to the Emir as the community's representative. His mandate also includes functioning as a direct conduit between officials in Kano and members of the Igbo community. Some Igbos have likened the role of the *Eze* to that filled by Chief Egbe before the war, and indeed, it was Chief Egbe who placed the red cap of office on the head of the third *Eze* during his installation in 1993. Political considerations similar to those behind the formation of the ICA entered into the decision to create the position. For example, between 1980 and 1982 informal representatives of the Igbo community protested to Kano State's first civilian Governor, Muhammad Rimi, over the state's appropriation of the Ibo Union Grammar School a decade earlier. As Chief Davis Ohaeri recalled, "Rimi advised us: 'Who do we pay compensation to if there is no traditional ruler?'" They drew inspiration from the success of the Orlu Wayfarers Association, which had used pledges of support for the PRP to enlist the Governor's assistance in securing the long-delayed release of the Orlu Division Hall from its wartime caretakers. According to Chief Ohaeri, who was president of the Orlu union at the time, "We approached [Governor Rimi] and told him 'How can we vote for you if we have this problem?'" In fact, Chief Ezetah had drawn on this same situation in making his case for creating the ICA.[29] Unfortunately, the same year that the ICA came into being, members of Nigeria's military again overthrew civilian rule. In a new political climate that was much less receptive to civilian advocacy groups, a "traditional ruler" made sense. In the end, however, the ICA and later the *Eze* suspended their search for compensation for the Ibo Union Grammar School.

## "WORTH MORE AT HOME":
## PROPERTY AND THE PERCEPTION OF SECURITY

Just as the growth of increasingly visible community institutions were signals of rising levels of confidence among Kano's Igbos, so also were changes in patterns of property ownership. One of the most important transformations between Igbos of the pre- and post-war periods was a reversal in attitudes toward owning property outside of Igboland. The dislocations of 1966 found many migrant Igbos forced to leave property and wealth behind, and return to Igboland with limited resources. Housing there, tight even before the dislocations, became even more scarce as hundreds of thousands of refugees poured in. In the words of a prominent Kano Igbo, "Before the war the Igbo man accepted the philosophy of one Nigeria wholeheartedly, and believed that anyone could live anywhere. He would build four, five, six houses here [in the North] without anything at home. Then, when he returned home [in 1966], people there, even relatives, mocked him."[30] Another expressed a similar sentiment: "People who owned entire streets up here didn't have a single block on top of another in the village. People laughed at them. They were seen as improvident and wasteful. Out of necessity they asked 'What am I entitled to?' because they were squatting, but it was the wrong time."[31]

One far-reaching result of that experience was that after the war Igbo migrants with the means took care to build for themselves housing in Igboland, usually in or near their home villages, even if they had no intention of occupying it at the time. "In the end you have no local standing anywhere except in the village, so the moment people made money, they started to build in the villages. The loss that people suffered by establishing themselves away from home told them that the place to do it was in the village."[32] For many this meant—and continues to mean—balancing the competing demands for working business capital and living expenses in Kano with demands for resources at home. As some migrant Igbos pointed out, capital invested in houses in Igboland—a large proportion of which remain fully or partially vacant—represents potential investment money lying dormant. On the other hand, as Harneit-Sievers has noted, the construction of such structures has made a substantial contribution to rural and semi-rural economies throughout Igboland.[33]

Nonetheless, population pressure and a high level of competition for the limited economic opportunities in Igboland continued to force migration during the three decades that followed the war, even as Igbos, made cautious and deferential by the war, began to regain their confidence. "It is clear from the way we are stacked up on top of each other at home that we will continue to migrate. It is also clear that we will continue to draw attention to ourselves by being aggressive and hard-driven. But the smallest Igbo man is worth more at home than he is here."[34]

Many Igbo and Hausa observers pointed out that it was not during the 1970s, but rather the 1980s that large numbers of Igbos began to construct new buildings in Kano. This is best understood as a three-stage process. First was the predictable period during which Igbos impoverished by the war regained their financial footings, and used their income to meet short-term needs. Second, as they began to generate surplus capital, the lessons of 1966 encouraged those who did not have structures in Igboland to build them. Then, with housing in Igboland available to them if necessary, Igbos with capital to invest made decisions based on economic considerations and lifestyle preferences: Where were they likely to get the best return on their investment, in terms of rents collected, appreciation, and/or additional business generated? For those who anticipated spending most of their time in places outside of Igboland, it made sense to invest at least some of their capital where they lived. In the case of Kano, the lack of any significant conflict between Igbo and Hausa, the rapid growth of the city's economy, and the creation of social infrastructure by Igbos were all encouraging. Notably, in the early 1980s a majority of the first Igbos to erect new structures were those who had first taken residence in Kano after the war. In part, however, this is because those who returned in the 1970s already owned property in Kano and used their money to repair what they already had. Still, there is a sentiment in the Igbo community that it took the confidence of younger, newer arrivals to push their more reluctant elders, concerned with their economic competitiveness and image in the eyes of the community, to begin building anew.

## CONCLUSION

During the late 1980s and particularly during the nineties many of the "Kano One," those who had been in Kano before the war, left, often for good. As younger Igbos arrived, often as dependents or apprentices, they joined an Igbo population with a sophisticated network of town unions, a local umbrella union, and a nascent "traditional" rulership, as well as an established presence in the local economy. Further, most arrived without the sense of urgency that followed the war, and the long period without intercommunal violence involving Igbos and *Kanawa* eased their transition and sense of safety. To a certain degree, they could take for granted their places within a fairly stable migrant community, and with it the sense of normalcy that the first generation of post-war residents had so laboriously forged. Rather than expend their energy creating town unions, or carving out economic niches, they instead became part of what they found in place. For all of these reasons, they had little need to adopt the stance of humility that had predominated during the 1970s, a stance which had been so important to the successful reintroduction of an Igbo community. Instead, the new arrivals were, as a group, assertive in ways that their immediate predecessors had not been. It is little surprise then, that by the mid-1990s some of the post-war goodwill between *Kanawa* and Igbo residents had been lost.

At the same time, however, members of the generation of Igbos who fought the war and who remember the humiliations and hardships of the immediate post-war period were still alive and living in Kano at century's end. As established elders, many occupied positions of leadership within the system of unions and associated bodies, with the effect that the process of generational change is as yet incomplete. The institutions that Igbos created during the seventies and eighties, however, appeared stable during the mid-1990s, and were part of the fabric of life for most of Kano's Igbo residents. In that sense, the community had achieved a level of stability that would have been difficult to foresee in the immediate post-war period. Challenges to normalcy, however, would persist, as the economic, political and ethno-religious calculus of the country continued to shift.

## NOTES

1. Harneit-Sievers, et al., *A Social History of the Nigerian Civil War*, See particularly chapter six by Jones O. Ahazuem.

2. In 1994, Mbanasa was part of Ideato Local Government Area of Imo State.

3. During the early 1980s several of the seven Mbanasa towns formed their own unions in Kano. FN 90A: Interview with Mr. Humphrey S.C. Umeh, 10 October 1993.

4. FN 90D: Interview with Mr. Humphrey S.C. Umeh, 20 June 1994.

5. FN 12: Interview with Chief W.O. Anunobi, 7 August 1994, Kano.

6. FN 70B: Interview with Chief Davis Ohaeri, 18 June 1994, Kano.

7. Egboh has detailed the role of town unions in the development of infrastructure in Igboland, including their central role in post-war reconstruction. Edmund O. Egboh, *Community Development Efforts in Igboland* (Onitsha: Etukokwu Press, 1987).

8. In 1993 there were 161 town unions represented in the ICA, substantially more than the approximately 100 in the Ibo Union of 1966.

9. FN 81: Interview with Alhaji "Likita" Nahiru Ringim, Alhaji Garba Tsoho, Alhaji Suleman Musa Garko, Alhaji Bala Isiyaku, 5 June 1994, Challawa.

10. FN-Anonymous.

11. FN-Anonymous.

12. FN-Anonymous.

13. One informant maintained membership in her home divisional (Orlu) union after marrying and joining the women's wing of her husband's divisional union (Owerri); her case, however, appears unusual. FN 74: Interview with Mrs. Chinyere Okpara, 20 August 1994, Kano.

14. This number remained, more or less, constant through the late 1970s and early eighties. Membership reached a peak in 1991 at about 250. In 1994, the number had dropped to about 180 members. FN 48: Interview with Mrs. Mary Kanuh, 15 March 1994, Kano.

15. FN 48: Interview with Mrs. Mary Kanuh, 15 March 1994, Kano; also FN 70B: Interview with Chief Davis Ohaeri, 18 June 1994, Kano; FN 90D: Interview with Mr. Humphrey S.C. Umeh, 20 June 1994.

16. Of the 27 Igbo women who migrated or re-migrated to Kano during the 1970s interviewed during the course of this study, 25 said they joined or accompanied their husbands. Of those, two reported that the decision to move to Kano was made jointly; in the other cases the husbands made the decision.

17. FN 86: Interview with Mrs. Juliana Ubuonu, 26 August 1994, Kano; FN 74: Interview with Mrs. Chinyere Okpara, 20 August 1994, Kano.

18. FN 48: Interview with Mrs. Mary Kanuh, 15 March 1994, Kano.

19. Chiefs Ezetah and Okonkwo are also discussed in chapter six.

20. FN 35: Interview with Mr. Donatus Ezemwata, 16 April 1994, Kano.

21. FN 3D: Interview with Alhaji Uba Adamu, 18 April 1994, Kano; FN 4: Interview with Chief D.O. Adinuso, 1 July 1994, Kano; FN 33: Interview with Chief Patrick Enendu, 1 May 1994, Kano; FN 38: Interview with Alhaji Abdulrahman Howeidy, 18 April 1994, Kano.

22. FN 33: Interview with Chief Patrick Enendu, 1 May 1994, Kano; FN 37: Interview with Chief A. Ezetah, 15 May 1993, Kano.

23. The violent confrontation between followers of Muslim cleric Malam Marwa Maitatsine and authorities in Kano is detailed in Nasir B. Zahardeen, *The Maitatsine Saga* (Zaria: Hudahuda Publishers, 1988). See also Mervyn Hiskett, "The Maitatsine Riots in Kano, 1980: An Assessment," *Journal of Religion in Africa* 17, 3 (1987), and Elizabeth Isichei, "The Maitatsine Risings in Nigeria 1980–85: A Revolt of the Disinherited," *Journal of Religion in Africa* 17, 3 (1987).

24. FN 12: Interview with Chief W.O. Anunobi, 7 August 1994, Kano.

25. FN 6: Interview with Mr. Felix Agwuenu, 1 April 1994, Kano.

26. FN 6: Interview with Mr. Felix Agwuenu, 1 April 1994, Kano.

27. Generally speaking, the *Eze* Cabinet was and is made up of men upon whom the title of "chief" has been conferred by previous members of the council; few carried the title from home. Within Igbo society, the granting chieftaincy titles away from home is a post-war development, and expanded greatly during the 1970s and 1980s. Economic or political influence in one's home or emigrant community, free-born ancestry, and personal connections are important for acquiring the title. For a discussion of chieftaincy titles in Igbo society, see Harneit-Sievers, "Igbo 'Tradi-

tional Rulers': Chieftaincy and the State in Southeastern Nigeria," *Afrika Spectrum* (Hamburg) 33, 1 (1998).

28. The title itself was imported from Igboland, where it took on connotations of chieftaincy during the colonial period. The first *Eze* in Kano was Godwin Nwalusi, who held the title during 1986–1987 before his death by illness; the second, *Eze* Obi Okonkwo (no relation to Chief Felix Okonkwo), held the title between 1987 and 1990 before he was murdered by a former apprentice for reasons apparently unrelated to his ICA activities. Kano's third *Eze*, lawyer O.T. Nnadi was installed in 1993.

29. FN 70B: Interview with Chief Davis Ohaeri, 18 June 1994, Kano.

30. FN 33: Interview with Chief Patrick Enendu, 1 May 1994, Kano.

31. FN 90B: Interview with Mr. Humphrey S.C. Umeh, 25 January 1994.

32. FN 90B: Interview with Mr. Humphrey S.C. Umeh, 25 January 1994. This sentiment is very widespread. Throughout the 1990s it was unusual to find an Igbo who had invested in residential or commercial property in Kano without first building at least a house in the home village. "If you see an Igbo owning something here, you know he is worth twice as much at home" was a common refrain.

33. Harneit-Sievers, "No Victor, No Vanquished?," 12.

34. FN 90C: Interview with Mr. Humphrey S.C. Umeh, 18 May 1994.

# CONCLUSION: RELIGION AND ETHNICITY AT CENTURY'S END

## ETHNICITY AND INTERCOMMUNAL VIOLENCE IN THE 1990s

The links between ethnicity and intercommunal violence attracted a great deal of attention during the 1990s, in very large part because of events in Yugoslavia and surrounding territories, and in Rwanda. The Rwandan genocide of 1994 is, for Africanists and other students of postcolonial ethnicity, a natural historical magnet, a phenomenon that demands analysis and comparison.[1] The most compelling similarity between Nigeria's anti-Igbo violence and the genocide in Rwanda is the operation of ideas inherited from colonizers. In each case the arrival of the colonizer was accompanied by an ossification of ethnic categories and labels. Similarly, in each country the colonizer's departure created opportunities for indigenous political elites to exploit ethnic loyalties, prejudices, and stereotypes. And in both countries competition for control of the state led to carefully designed intercommunal violence in which ethnicity functioned as part of more complex political equations: In Nigeria, Igbo ethnicity was juxtaposed not with other ethnic identites, but rather with Northern regional identity, and then, to varying degrees, subregional and state identities. Similarly, in Rwanda, Tutsi ethnicity was but the thin edge of a wedge; Hutu who opposed the ruling party were also systematically targeted during the genocide of 1994.

Equally important, however, are the differences between the two countries' respective descents into catastrophic bloodshed. At least four fundamental differences in the conditions for intercommunal violence are immediately apparent. First of all, Nigeria's population in 1966 was approximately eight times that of Rwanda before the genocide (just over seven million), and its land area thirteen times that of tiny Rwanda. More important, by any conceivable measure, the degree of cultural pluralism in Nigeria was and is far greater than in Rwanda. Because of Nigeria's greater size and diversity, the political calculus of both colonial and independent Nigeria has been complex in ways absent in Rwanda. A second difference is the power of foreign influence, both African and European, in the respective cases. While foreign agendas, particularly British, were present in Nigeria during its crisis years, Rwanda appears to have been affected more directly by its larger African neighbors, to say nothing of French and Belgian influences. On a more qualitative note, the conditions of initial contact between many of Nigeria's groups were tied directly to the colonial project, unlike Rwanda, where Hutu, Tutsi, and Twa had long coexisted in a complex and evolving system of categorization and group membership. As a result, the links of genetic and marital kinship and multigenerational propinquity that one finds so frequently in the Rwandan setting only rarely if ever apply in the relationship between Nigeria's Igbos and Hausas. Finally, an environment of competition between adherents of Islam on one hand and Christianity on the other has imbued the Nigerian situation with a religious dimension largely absent in Rwanda.

It is on this final note, that of the complications that Nigeria's religious pluralism presents to our understanding of ethnicity, power, and violence there, that I wish to conclude. In the years since the Civil War, religious tensions in Nigeria have escalated, and remain high. Religious issues and religious constituencies have proven more durable than ethnic ones in the face of the political fragmentation inherent in smaller states. Religious divisions also have proven resistant to the inhibiting effects of military rule. Throughout the late 1970s and early 1980s the country debated the place of Islamic law in its judicial system, and as the new Christian century dawned with a southern Christian at the helm of the Nigerian state, a renewed debate over Islamic law arrived with it.

## KANO FROM THE 1960s TO THE 1990s

In the last decade religion appears, in many ways, to have supplanted ethnicity as the defining fault line between Kano's Igbo and Hausa communities. The frontier between Hausa Muslims and Igbo Christians has long been one on which religion and ethnicity have been intimately entangled. Nonetheless, Nigeria's national conversations have increasingly turned on questions of religion, and with that change relations on the ground in Kano have shifted perceptibly. As we will see, two incidents, one in 1991 and the other in 1995, reinforce this point, as do recent protests by Christians over the state government's decision to elevate the status of Islamic law. Through a broader lens, however, recent developments fit into the narrative of continuity and change discussed thus far.

The Igbos who rebuilt a community in Kano had been changed by the riots of 1966 and the experience of fighting and losing the Civil War, processes in which ethnicity functioned as a carefully directed social and political toxin. The Kano of 1966 had defended Northernization policies designed to limit the ability of southerners to gain economic and political footholds in the region. When threatened with administrative unification, anti-Igbo riots had made it clear that Northern power brokers and aspiring elites intended to retain control of the region. The coup that toppled Ironsi's government two months later showed that they had succeeded, and after that the violent expulsion of Igbos from the North completed Northerners' assertion of control. Igbo property and their niches in local economies found their way into the hands of other Nigerians, often those of local elites. The creation of states, each free to preferentially hire and promote its own citizens, meant that Igbos represented little of the threat that they had been perceived to pose in 1966. Further, the federal government was in the hands of a popular Middle Belt leader, and Igbos held few top positions in his administration, the civil service, parastatals, or the private sector. The monolithic Igbo monster that Northern leaders of the 1950s and 1960s had painted as so fierce had, for all practical purposes, lost its teeth.

Igbos found their way back to the North, but they came very differently than they had left. Individually and collectively impoverished, they slowly rebuilt their lives, in the process making few demands on state or local resources. More importantly, they returned outside of the real and imagined ethnic networks that had been so important in pre-war political discourses. The Kano that they returned to had changed fundamentally as well, so much so that in less than four years, local attitudes about Igbos' role in the political and economic life had practically reversed themselves. In the process these ideas had become part of an imperfect but still transformative attempt to restore confidence between communities. In this new context, Igbo ethnicity could be visible without being provocative. Further, the country's economy was about to swell with petrodollars, which would contribute to a national mood of optimism that was conducive to the conditional re-integration Igbos experienced. Kano, after 1968 the capital of Nigeria's most populous state, saw its economy expand as well. Optimism in the state flowed from this, and from a sense of political autonomy unprecedented in colonial or independent Nigeria. In this climate, it was fairly easy for Igbos to find places for themselves, particularly after the federal government had circulated propaganda espousing the unity of Igbos and other Nigerians. To further ease their reentry, most Igbos adopted postures befitting their status as losers of the war, while at the same time displaying much of the same acquisitiveness and ambition that had been held against them in the past. Given Igbos' relative impotence in the post-war political economy, however, Northerners did not feel threatened, and generally welcomed them—and the skills and trade they brought with them.

In metropolitan Kano, where the economy had grown fast enough during the 1970s to accommodate a doubling in population to more than a million, the 1990s saw industrial employment level off, then shrink. Nationally, Nigeria's economy, which reached a peak during the early 1980s, stagnated during the late 1980s, and through the early 1990s most Nigerians saw their standards of living in steady decline. At the same time, Igbo national political aspirations, long submerged, began to bubble toward the surface. Nationally, Igbos began to complain publicly that they were second-class citizens.[2] That sense of assertiveness manifested itself in Kano as well. In the view of some of Kano's younger Igbos, most "Kano Two" (Igbos who first migrated after the war) have been at the forefront of this new boldness. As they became established during the late 1980s, they began to buy property in Sabon Gari from Hausa landlords who had purchased it after the war. As Sabon Gari's population grew and its market became saturated, commercial and residential buildings there also commanded premium rents. As a result, Igbo entrepreneurs began to purchase property in other parts of the metropolis, much of it in predominantly Muslim areas. In the words of one Igbo, "During the seventies everyone was trying to find their feet. The Igbo man was still sober. He had not had the opportunity to exhibit the arrogance of the eighties. The Igbos couldn't exhibit what makes the other tribes hate them."[3] In his opinion, by the late 1980s, that had changed.

While the changes between the pre- and post-war periods are easy to identify, the continuities are just as important. The cultural differences between Igbos and Hausas, so heavily vaunted before the war, were every bit as great afterward. Most Igbos still identified as Christians, most still wore western dress, and many spoke English and drank alcohol. On whole, they continued to have more formal western education than their Hausa hosts. In time, as part of their individual and collective rebuilding efforts, they recreated the town unions that had been so much a part of pre-war life, and most again centered their social networks on other Igbos. Again they repatriated much of their earnings to Igboland, if anything at a higher rate than before. In the new context, however, these practices did not cause alarm among *Kanawa*. And given the new political dispensation, there was little cause for agitators to target them as before.

## RELIGION AND ETHNICITY ENTWINED

An end to civilian politics in 1966, the purging of high-ranking Igbos from the military, and the break up of Nigeria's regions began a transformation in the relationship between ethnicity and political constituencies. By creating smaller and smaller states—twelve in 1968, a figure which had grown to thirty-six in 2000—it has become more difficult to give political focus to large ethnic constituencies, since the homelands of the large ethnic groups are divided between several states. While ethnic politics persisted during Nigeria's second attempt at democratic government, the Second Republic of 1979–1983, there were no large-scale crises to rival those of 1966–1967. Indeed, not until 1993 would Nigeria again face the possibility of intercommunal violence on so large a scale. When it did appear possible, again it was national politics that threatened to light the fuse. In June of that year, M.K.O. Abiola, a southern Yoruba Muslim, was apparently elected president of Nigeria with a majority that extended far beyond Yorubaland. After a Northern-led military government annulled his apparent election, many Abiola supporters, most of them Western Yoruba, rose against the government.[4] In Lagos and other parts of Western Nigeria, often-violent protests lasted for months, and contributed to the ouster of General Ibrahim Babangida, and the rise to power of General Sani Abacha, another Northerner. As a result of the controversy surrounding the annulment, and Abiola's death in 1998, during the second half of the 1990s most discussions of ethnic politics in Nigeria turned on relations between Yorubas and Hausas, though many *Kanawa* were careful to distinguish between Western Yorubas and Northern Yoruba Muslims. The election in 1999 of former General Olusegun Obasanjo, a Yoruba Christian, as the first president of Nigeria's Third Republic has done little to quiet those discussions.

At the same time that Yorubas have come under increasing scrutiny from *Kanawa*, many Igbos harbor suspicions rooted in the crisis years and rekindled during the Abiola crisis. Of 1966, Nnoli has written

> The sad and painful fact about the killings was the indifference with which most non-Easterners treated the situation. None of the other ethnic groups saw the massacres as posing a serious national problem, or if they did, they were not courageous enough to say so. Each ethnic group retreated into a womb-like isolation as if indifference and the passage of time would make the whole problem go away. Nigeria seemed morally anesthetized.[5]

There is in these words, perhaps, a coded asterisk that points particularly at Yoruba in the West. Most Nigerians believe that in 1967 there was an agreement between Ojukwu and Obafemi Awolowo, the most prominent Yoruba political leader of his day, to the effect that if the East seceded from Nigeria, the West would go as well. When the West failed to do so, the explanation most popular among Igbos is that by remaining in Nigeria, Western Yorubas were able to claim for themselves many Igbo footholds in the economy. In today's conventional wisdom, the apparent prominence of Yorubas in banking, finance, and other parts of the private sector owes much to the absence of Igbos during the war, the loss of seniority they faced afterward, and the consequences of the post-war Indigenization Decree. If there was during the nineties an absence of sympathy for Western Yorubas among Kano's Igbos, the list of explanations must begin with this.

Despite increased attention by both groups to the Yoruba presence in the metropolis, the Igbo-Hausa relationship remained tense after religious issues led to intercommunal conflict involving members of the groups in 1991 and 1995. In each case, however, violence occurred without the explicit manipulation of ethnicity that was present in 1966. For that reason, I argue that we must treat each disturbance as a religious conflict that, because of circumstances and patterns of affiliation, unfolded mostly between two ethnic groups. The centrality of Islam to Hausa identity and *Kanawa's* often axiomatic association of Christianity with Igbos has meant past grievances, some long dormant, others lingering, were available for both sides to tap into, and almost inevitably surfaced. It also meant that some participants and observers, often fixated on overly simple conflict models, have seen a replay of past events. While the unresolved baggage of past conflicts was not in and of itself sufficient to lead to open controversy or violence, in moments of anger and tension, it reappeared, and became part of the new moment. Fortunately, unlike the crises of 1966, this happened without the benefit of elite agendas to focus those issues, recruit behind them, or provide rioters with the organizational infrastructure necessary for a massive escalation.

The riots themselves were fairly straightforward in their genesis. In October 1991 authorities gave permission to a German Christian evangelist to preach at a public racecourse in metropolitan Kano. Several weeks earlier a Muslim group had been denied permission to bring in a South African Muslim preacher, and the decision to allow the Christian minister access to public space angered many Muslims. "Aggressive publicity" by the Christian Association of Nigeria, much of it patently offensive to Muslims, escalated the situation.[6] On 14 October, mobs of Muslims, mostly made up of young boys and led by teenagers, roamed the city, searching for people they believed to be Christians. Some Igbos and other Christians witnessed these young people throwing stones at vehicles and pedestrans, and some described beatings and arson. Igbos themselves were not only the majority of Kano's Christians, but were also much better organized under an ethnic umbrella than were the city's Christians around religion. While other Christians responded variously, it was Igbos who organized themselves to fortify parts of Sabon Gari. They armed themselves, some with machetes, shotguns, or pistols, others with more sophisticated firearms. A large proportion of the Igbo community's adult men had military experience from the Civil War and were able to quickly establish an informal command structure. The idea, a number reported, was to avoid a replay of the 1966 massacre, which most continue to describe as genocide. Igbos from other parts of the city made their way to Sabon Gari, or to police and military barracks, some with help from soldiers and police. Others took shelter with Muslim neighbors, or locked themselves in their houses and hoped for the best. And at least once military authorities met with Igbo representatives at the edge of Sabon Gari to reassure them that soldiers were present to restore order and keep the peace. Falola reported an official casualty count of a dozen, but witnesses placed it in the hundreds.[7] Further, buildings and scores of private and commercial vehicles were severely damaged or destroyed along the southern edges of Sabon Gari. When the violence ended, the state government hauled the vehicle carcasses to a dump site near Shagari Quarters, south of the city, where they were stacked layers deep. Despite inquiries by individuals and community groups and official promises, there was no compensation for losses.[8]

The second outbreak of violence had an equally identifiable catalyst. In December of 1995, members of Kano's small but growing

Shi'ite Muslim community stormed a prison and decapitated an Igbo man, apparently with acquiescence from the guards. The man was being held in protective custody after reportedly desecrating a copy of the Qur'an in his home. Amid a sense that local authorities were afraid of the Shi'ites, Kano's Christians mobilized, and again eyes fell upon the well-organized Igbo community. Again Igbos from outlying areas fled to Sabon Gari, as did many non-Igbo Christians. This time, however, authorities recognized the danger and immediately used soldiers and police to control the situation. As a result, unlike 1991 there was no overt marshaling of forces in Sabon Gari, though many Igbos laid in supplies of food and water, or sent their families south in preparation for an escalation that, fortunately, did not come. It would be naive to suggest that ethnic chauvinism did not play a role in each disturbance. Clearly it did, on both sides. Still, in these cases ethnicity was simply a chisel. Religious agendas provided the driving force, as had political goals and fears in 1966.

Interestingly, anecdotal evidence suggests that this more recent violence has motivated some of the Igbos who invested in property outside of Sabon Gari during the eighties and early nineties to redirect their energy toward Sabon Gari, in some cases selling their holdings outside of the ward. Rents in Sabon Gari increased rapidly, particularly after 1995, and in 1998 were several times higher than in adjacent wards, despite virtual residential and commercial saturation in all of them. Igbos, and to a lesser degree other Christians, appeared willing to pay for the relative security of Sabon Gari and what I have heard Igbos and non-Igbos refer to as "Igbo civil defence." One Igbo informant sold a relatively spacious house he had built in an ethnically mixed area after the 1991 violence and moved his family into cramped, expensive quarters in Sabon Gari.[9] The same sense of uncertainty that drove him there has had the effect of driving some less affluent Igbos into less secure parts of greater Kano as they are simply priced out of Sabon Gari.

As this book goes to press the relationship between Igbo and Hausa in Kano is poised on the cusp of still more rapid change, and it is national debates on religion that are driving that change. As many of Nigeria's Northern states have granted official status to Islamic law (*shari'a*), tensions between *shari'a* advocates and its mostly Christian opponents have escalated. Some have theorized that the move toward *shari'a* in the North is in fact a thinly veiled attempt by the Northern states that embrace it to separate themselves from southern Nigeria legally if not physically. It is unclear whether the move toward *shari'a* is a response to political resurgence in southern Nigeria that began with Abiola's apparent election. It seems unlikely that any conflict with origins in religious rivalry can avoid linkage, deliberate or accidental, with lingering notions of North and south in Nigeria. The declining popularity in the North of President Obasanjo has raised the stakes even higher. In Northern cities where Igbos constitute the largest southern presence, the ghosts of 1966 are never far, and any perception of North-south rivalry is likely to rapidly take on ethnic overtones.

One reason for this is the fact that Igbo elites have taken an increasingly active stance in national debates on religion and politics. Among the many southern and Middle Belt leaders to weigh in against any new status for *shari'a,* the Igbo leadership forum *Ohaneze Ndi Igbo* in March 2000 voiced its support for turning Nigeria from a republic into a confederation, though it later softened its position. A few weeks later, a group calling itself Movement for the Actualisation of a Sovereign State of Biafra carried out a demonstration in Lagos.[10] Resurrecting either the idea of Igbo secession or the name "Biafra" would have been virtually unthinkable—or at least publicly unspeakable—before the renewed *shari'a* debate. That debate, however, set off incidents of intercommunal violence across Nigeria, most notably in Kaduna in the North and Aba in Igboland in 1999. That violence, in turn, appears to have lifted those taboos. In addition, there was protracted and ethnically focused fighting between Yorubas and Hausas in Yorubaland and Kano the same year, and other incidents since.[11] All of this speaks to the need for a national de-escalation. Unless national debates on the relationship between ethnicity and political power, and between religion and the state, move forward in a civil manner, it seems unrealistic not to expect periodic outbreaks of intercommunal violence. Given Nigeria's precarious economic status, the temptations to appeal to violence may simply be too great to resist as leaders faced with withering resources search for ways to first attract and then satisfy constituents and clients.

## WHICH WAY FORWARD?

One can only imagine the long-term consequences of Kano State's decision in 2000 to embrace *shari'a,* particularly if the state government should make non-Muslims subject to its dictates in all or part of their public lives. In any case, it seems likely that the state's commercial life will be radically transformed as markets, banks, factories, and even the transportation grid adjust. Even harder to project is how the imposition of *shari'a* will impact the long-term willingness of non-

Muslims to remain in Kano, or maintain business interests there. Further, if religiously charged violence should again strike Kano, the simple rule of numbers suggests that Kano's Igbos will, as a group, find it impossible to avoid becoming involved. At one extreme, if one can for a moment step away from the pessimism and alarm of Nigeria's Christians, one can perhaps imagine a situation in which the ramifications of *shari'a* for non-Muslims are limited, and non-Muslims are able to continue most or all of their commercial and professional activities, living as non-Muslims in a Muslim society that accepts their presence. In this scenario they will be able to live in enclaves much like the old Sabon Gari in which those parts of their lifestyle that are unIslamic are allowed to go on beyond the gaze of those who would be offended. And, while their interactions with Muslims and conduct in public arenas would be subject to *shari'a*, their dealings with one another would be subject to civil law, much as has been the case in the past. At the other extreme, so many Muslim and Christian leaders have invested themselves in confrontational positions that either a more drastic resolution or a protracted struggle appears likely. Without straining, one can hear echoes of the words Sultan Atiƙu told British representatives during their initial occupation of Hausaland, words whose sentiments threaten to drown out more moderate voices: "I do not consent that any one of you should ever dwell with us. Between us and you there are no dealings except those between Muslims and unbelievers: war as [God] Almighty has enjoined on us."[12] In the absence of a military threat, however, the range of possible relationships between Muslims and non-Muslims is great, and need not entail warfare, or indeed, violence in any form. Unfortunately, present-day religious discourse in Nigeria has few moderating influences, and, in any case, the *shari'a* debate has become entangled with a host of other economic and political issues.

## POISON AND MEDICINE REVISITED

Were we speaking of religious identities through the metaphor of poison and medicine, I suspect that it would be the toxic possibilities of religion that would require the most elaboration for a majority of readers. Few would question, at least in the abstract, assertions that in religious affiliations individuals could find the security of community, the comfort of shared symbolic systems, the validation of common beliefs, or a network of support in times of adversity. That religious affilations can—with equal ease, one could argue—be used to facilitate intercommunal violence, foster socially destructive intolerance, or justify oppression are not new ideas, yet would have to be argued more vigorously than the more comfortable aspects of religion.

Africanist arguments about ethnicity have tended to move in the other direction, and to gravitate toward ethnicity's less attractive face. Ethnicity in Africa has been, to various African and Western scholars, at various times, an unfortunate residue of Africa's precolonial past, an impediment to economic and political "progress," or to "modern" ideas like class consciousness, nationalism, or gender solidarity. More recently, some scholars have treated ethnicity as a colonially constructed device for social and political division that African leaders have cynically exploited in order to serve their own selfish ends. I have argued that while there is a great deal of truth to some of these assertions, the same identities that can be harnessed to the unfortunate and often toxic motives of political opportunists (both colonial and post-colonial) can also be an important—perhaps, for the moment, indispensible—foundation for tangible and intangible social, economic, and political benefits. I suggest, then, that the malleability of form and flexibility of application that are inherent in ethnicity are precisely what makes the toxic and medicinal potentials of ethnicity virtually inseparable.

With a Christian Yoruba president unpopular among far Northern Muslims, religious rhetoric at new levels of stridency, a depressed economy, and recent outbreaks of violence justified along religious and ethnic lines, Nigeria appears to have arrived at a key moment. Writing of Rwanda, Mamdani postulates that, in reconfiguring the relationship between ethnicity, political identities, and the state, Rwandans must make a fundamental choice: They must choose between "political union" and "political divorce."[13] While Nigeria's crisis is less acute than that facing Rwanda after the genocide, a similar decision seems looming, and given Nigeria's inherent complexity, arriving at a meaningful consensus is a daunting task. The challenges facing Africa's most populous and ethnically diverse country include finding a workable balance between secular and religious law, addressing competition over national political power between different ethnic, religious, and regional constituencies, and making the national economy work for ordinary Nigerians. If Nigeria is to continue to exist as it is presently configured, perhaps its biggest challenge will be to address these issues without using ethnicity or a combination of ethnicity and religion to focus the basest emotions. At the same time, the persistence and seeming ubiquity of ethnic sentiments, sensitivities, and networks in Nigerian society suggests that, at least for the foreseeable future, ethnicity is a force with which the country must establish a functional relationship, one in which there is medicine as well as poison.

## NOTES

1. See, for example, Prunier, *The Rwanda Crisis: History of a Genocide*; Alain Destexhe, *Rwanda and Genocide in the Twentieth Century*, translated by Alison Marschner (New York: New York University Press, 1995); and Fergal Keane, *Season of Blood: A Rwandan Journey* (New York: Viking, 1995).

2. The best example of this sentiment is a 1999 manifesto issued by *Ohaneze Ndi Igbo*, a group comprising Igbo leaders of thought. The document presented a broad range of grievances, including demands for apologies and reparations for the deaths and trauma that occured during 1966 and the war, and for the post-war marginalization of Igbos. Oha-Na-Eze Ndi Igbo, *The Violations of Human and Civil Rights of* Ndi Igbo *in the Federation of Nigeria (1966–1999)*(n.p., 1999). The document is available in the electronic journal *West Africa Review* 2, 2 (2001). See http://www.westafricareview.com/war/vol2.2/ohaneze.pdf.

3. FN-Anonymous.

4. There is an argument that a disproportionate share of those supporters came from a fairly small section of Yorubaland.

5. Nnoli, *Ethnicity and Development in Nigeria*, 136.

6. Toyin Falola, *Violence in Nigeria: The Crisis of Religious Politics and Secular Ideologies* (Rochester: University of Rochester Press, 1998), 212. See also Osaghae, *Trends on Migrant Political Organizations in Nigeria*, 51.

7. Falola, *Violence in Nigeria*, 212; informal interviews.

8. Informal interviews.

9. FN-Anonymous.

10. See, for example, "Fear of Biafra," *Abuja Mirror*, May 31–June 6, 2000 (http://www.ndirect.co.uk/~n.today/mop165.htm, or http://www.kwenu.com/afamefune/abuja_mirror.htm).

11. In July 1999 a Hausa woman was killed in the Yoruba town of Sagamu, ostensibly for breaking a local taboo. Further violence in Sagamu was followed by retaliatory attacks on Yorubas living in Kano. See Remi Oyo, "Calm Returns to Strife-Torn Cities," *Inter Press Service*, 30 July 1999.

12. H.F. Blackwell, ed., *The Occupation of Hausaland, 1900–04: Being a Translation of Arabic Letters Found in the Home of the Wazir of Sokoto, Bohari, in 1903* (1927, reprint London: Frank Cass, 1969), 13–14. See also the excellent dissertation, Muhammad Sani Umar, *Muslims' Intellectual Responses to British Colonialism in Northern Nigeria, 1903–1945* (Ph.D. dissertation, Northwestern University, 1997).

13. Mahmood Mamdani, *When Victims Become Killers: Colonialism, Nativism, and the Genocide in Rwanda* (Princeton: Princeton University Press, 2001), 265.

# Appendix:
# The 1966 Disturbances

In addition to the incidents of violence recounted in chapters two and three, the following incidents have been recorded.

## THE MAY–JUNE 1966 DISTURBANCES

Most of the incidents that follow began as protests against the Unification Decree, and anti-Igbo violence is the main feature of some. The day after the first demonstrations in Kano, Kaduna, and Jos-Bukuru on 28 May, others took place in a number of other Northern cities, including serious outbreaks of violence in Sokoto, Katsina, Zaria, Gumel, Bauchi, and Gombe. Funtua, Gusau, and Jimeta also experienced disturbances. And in the days that followed, violence took place in Alkaleri, Jega, Jalingo, Kontagora, Kaura Namoda, Bida, Birnin Kebbi, and Numan.

### Sokoto, Birnin Kebbi, Jega, and Gusau

In Sokoto, street violence preceded political demonstrations. On 29 May rioters stoned the local Catholic church, burned vehicles parked outside it, and pillaged Igbo shops. Nigeria Police Force (NPF) officers fired on the rioters, killing one student. An estimated 500 Igbos sheltered in police barracks.[1] Following the attack on the church, the expatriate Catholic Bishop of Sokoto told United States diplomats that he had received advance notice of the attack. The next day primary and secondary school students led mobs that staged a demonstration in which they carried signs that craft school students had made in the school shop. More rioting ensued.[2] By that time, the number gathered at NPF barracks for protection had doubled to an estimated 1000.[3] When a mob attacked the church again on the 31st, observers claimed to recognize Native Authority employees leading the mob.[4] Nigeria Police contained the violence, and, by the first week of June had an estimated 1500 Igbos sheltered in NPF barracks.

Gusau also saw attacks on Igbos on 29 May.[5] Then, a mob attacked the Sudan Interior Mission church in Gusau on 31 May, and there was more fighting on 2 June.[6] After disturbances in Sokoto and Gusau subsided, fighting erupted briefly on Friday 3 June in nearby Kaura Namoda. The following day, Nigerian authorities estimated a dozen dead in Sokoto Province.[7] Fighting began in Birnin Kebbi on 6 June. And, in nearby Jega, Igbos arriving by truck were, reportedly, systematically killed, despite the intervention of the Emir of Birnin Kebbi.[8]

## Zaria

On the 29th Ahmadu Bello University (ABU) students staged a peaceful protest at the Institute of Administration outside of Zaria. The Institute was a cornerstone of the NPC's plans to Northernize the region's civil service. The same day, however, another crowd moved from old Zaria city to its Sabon Gari, a distance of about two miles. On the way they attacked cars, petrol stations, and some houses.[9] The following day attacks continued and soldiers ringed Sabon Gari to repel attackers, with help from NPF reinforcements from Kaduna.[10] The city was placed under a 7 P.M. to 7 A.M. curfew.[11] On 31 May mobs attacked churches in Zaria, and at ABU southern students gathered and refused to return to their quarters after "rural thugs," day laborers, and junior staff attacked southern staff on campus.[12] Violence ended on 1 June after soldiers fired on rioters, killing at least two civilians.[13]

## Bauchi and Gombe

Leaflets announcing anti-unification demonstrations appeared in Bauchi on 27 May, the day before the region's first organized protests.[14] The town remained relatively calm until Monday the 30th, however, when students circulated a notice in the market reading "We Northerners are Going Ahead to do anything . . . Dead or Alive We Must Stand Together."[15] Looting and destruction of shops broke out that same morning, and Igbos took shelter with the NPF.[16] The following day was quiet, but violence broke out again the morning of 2 June after some left the barracks and returned to their shops. Many Igbos then fled by road to Jos.[17]

Gombe was quiet until the afternoon of Friday, 3 June. The next day Igbos fled to the train station. The Emir of Gombe visited them there, urged them to return to their homes in Gombe, and assured them of their safety. However, on Sunday, 5 June, there was looting of Igbo shops, the Catholic church and mission school were burned, and mobs blocked roads out of town to prevent Igbos from fleeing. The local Catholic priest put the death total at fourteen. He also reported that local Native Authority (NA) police stood idly by, but that a contingent of NPF temporarily restored order. That night, however, there was looting in Gombe, and, the priest reported, "thugs" from Gombe traveled to Kaltungo, where they entered the Catholic mission and schools looking for injured Igbos.[18]

### Niger Province: Bida

Demonstrations in Bida took place on 3 June, and two days later there was looting of Igbo shops. On 6 June, observers reported that Igbo-managed stores and petrol stations were closed.[19]

### Adamawa Province: Jalingo, Numan, and Jimeta

There was fighting in Jimeta, near Yola, on 29 May. Then, a week later, on 5 June, fighting broke out in Jimeta for the second time, and for the first time in Jalingo and Numan. In each town the NPF fired on rioters, and on 6 June Nigeria Police killed three members of a mob that attacked Igbos they were escorting to safety.[20]

## THE SEPTEMBER-OCTOBER 1966 DISTURBANCES

Following the Radio Cotonou broadcast on 29 September, violence broke out in several Northern cities.

### Maiduguri

After the broadcasts, soldiers participated in riots in Maiduguri, which had been relatively quiet following the Unification Decree.[21] Violence continued there until 2 October, despite a curfew.[22] On 4

October, Nigeria Police paid for a plane to evacuate Igbos from Maiduguri and also from Yola.[23]

### Katsina

Katsina, where very few Igbos had returned after the June riots, was relatively quiet. The only reported violence was directed against an Idoma physician who was "run out of town," ostensibly for his past help to Igbos.[24]

### Gusau

Missionaries in Gusau told U.S. diplomats that Igbo children had been taken from hospital beds and had their heads "bashed against the wall" while nurses stood by helpless.[25]

### Zaria

Authorities in Zaria buried 186 bodies in a single mass grave after riots led to the evacuation of Eastern staff from ABU on the 29th and 30th.[26]

### Kainji Dam Area

Construction of the Kainji Dam employed a work force that included 600 Igbo skilled workers and 5,000 Northern laborers. On 29–30 September, authorities counted 50 bodies, all or most Igbo, at the local hospital, and observers reported another thirty outside.[27] The project's European contractors evacuated the remaining Igbos and their dependents by road.[28]

### Bauchi and Gombe

In Bauchi, the major city nearest the dam, fighting broke out 1 October. Authorities appear to have done little to intervene. That day a Ministry of Information sound truck drove through parts of the city with a message not to attack Yorubas and other "non-Ibos."[29] Likewise, the Emir reportedly told an expatriate that for him to intervene was to expose himself to danger from his subjects.[30] Later in the week civilians—or perhaps soldiers in mufti—blocked the road from Maiduguri. The NPF assisted Igbos, in this case by flying to the south evacuees who had arrived from Maiduguri.[31]

## Minna

There were killings in Minna on the 29th, and mobs sacked a hotel and a bank. Surviving railroad staff commandeered a three-car train and left with Igbos able to board it.[32]

## Jos and Bukuru

After attacks on Igbos by soldiers and civilians on 29 September, the 30th was quiet, while the traditional leader of the city's Hausas, the *Sarkin* Jos, met with NPF, Army, and Muslim leaders in an attempt to calm things. Fighting, however, resumed on 1 October.[33] The next day Nigeria Police protected Easterners as soldiers shot at them.[34] The fighting died down as surviving Igbos made their way out of town by train, road and even on foot. The arrival of 120 Igbos in Port Harcourt on a flight from Jos on 3 October, however, set off a search for Hausas there by Igbo mobs.[35]

## Kaduna

Violence erupted in Kaduna the night of 29 September, when mobs destroyed property and attacked Igbos.[36]

## Sardauna Province: Mubi

By 30 September, Igbos in Mubi, in Sardauna Province, had fled across the border into Cameroon.[37]

## Western Region: Abeokuta

In the Western city of Abeokuta, a series of unfounded rumors contributed to an attack on Igbos by twenty-five to thirty soldiers at the Aro train station on 29 September. Ten died, and the next day soldiers reportedly kidnapped three or four others, and robbed their homes. The rumors included local bomb threats, the destruction of the Offa Bridge, attacks on Hausa children in Minna, and the deaths of 100 Hausas on a northbound train.[38]

## NOTES

1. USNA POL 23-9/2529/A-122, 23 June 1966.

2. USNA POL 23-8/2529, 6 June 1966; USNA POL 23-9/2529, 9 June 1966.

3. USNA POL 23-8/2529, 30 May 1966; USNA POL 23-9/2529, 9 June 1966.

4. USNA POL 23-8/2529, 31 May 1966.

5. USNA POL 23-8/2529, 29 May 1966.

6. USNA POL 23-8/2529, 31 May 1966; USNA POL 23-8/2529, 2 June 1966.

7. USNA POL 23-9/2529/A-122, 23 June 1966.

8. USNA POL 23-9/2529, 9 June 1966.

9. USNA POL 23-8/2529, 29 May 1966.

10. USNA POL 23-8/2529, 30 May 1966.

11. USNA POL 23-8/2529, 31 May 1966.

12. USNA POL 23-8/2529, 31 May 1966; USNA POL 23-8/2529, 31 May 1966.

13. USNA POL 23-9/2529/A-118, 13 June 1966.

14. USNA POL 23-9/2529, 6 June 1966.

15. USNA POL 23-8/2529, 30 May 1966.

16. USNA POL 23-8/2529, 31 May 1966.

17. USNA POL 23-8/2529, 2 June 1966; USNA POL 23-9/2529/A-122, 23 June 1966.

18. USNA POL 23-8/2529/A-617, 12 June 1966; USNA POL 23-8/2529, 3 June 1966.

19. USNA POL 23-9/2529/A-122, 23 June 1966; USNA POL 23-9/2529, 7 June 1966.

20. USNA POL 23-9/2529/A-118, 13 June 1966; USNA POL 23-9/2529, 7 June 1966; USNA POL 23-9/2529/A-122, 23 June 1966.

21. USNA POL 23-9/2530, 29 September 1966.

22. USNA POL 23-9/2530, 30 September 1966.

23. USNA POL 23-9/2530, 4 October 1966.

24. USNA POL 23-9/2530, 5 October 1966.

25. USNA POL 15/2506/A-22, 9, 2 April 1971.

26. USNA POL 23-9/2530. 30 September 1966; USNA POL 23-8/2529/A-203, 2, 20 October 1966.

27. USNA POL 23-9/2530, 4 October 1966.

28. Report of the UK High Commission, by C.E. Dymond, 14 October, 1966, reproduced in USNA POL 23-9/2530/A-203, 3, 20 October 1966.

29. USNA POL 23-9/2530, 1 October 1966.

30. USNA POL 23-8/2530/A-203, 2, 20 October 1966.

31. USNA POL 23-9/2530/3, 4 October 1966.

32. USNA POL 23-9/2530, 30 September 1966.

33. USNA POL 23-9/2530, 30 September 1966, 5 October 1966.

34. USNA POL 23-9/2530, 5 October 1966.

35. USNA POL 23-9/2530, 3 October 1966.

36. USNA POL 23-9/2530, 30 September 1966.

37. USNA POL 23-9/2530, 30 September 1966.

38. USNA POL 23-9/2530, 5 October 1966.

# BIBLIOGRAPHY

## ARCHIVAL MATERIALS

### Kano State History and Culture Bureau (HCB)

| | |
|---|---|
| HCB 56/147. | Disturbances, Kano Province, 1963–1967. |
| HCB 115/R.527. | Nigeria Railway Corporation. |
| HCB 218/R.974. | Cabinet Office; Riots, Kano, 1966. |
| HCB 562/CER/3, Vol. III. | Plots in Sabon Gari, correspondence. |
| HCB 760/IMM 45. | Ministry for Local Government, Provincial Refugees. |
| HCB 817/LAN/28, Vol. III. | Ministry for Local Government; City and Sabon Gari Plots. |
| HCB 1429/SCH 221. | Ibo Union Grammar School. |
| HCB ADM/1/28. | Kazaure Intelligence Reports. |
| HCB K/SEC/A8. | Reports from Police and Other Sources. |
| HCB K/SEC/A26. | Reports from Kano Metropolitan Administration Area, 1971. |
| HCB K/SEC/38. | Local Authority Security Reports, Kano Township. |
| HCB K/SEC/39. | Kano Northern Division Intelligence Reports. |
| HCB K/SEC/147. | Disturbances, Kano Province, 1963–1967. |
| HCB R.56, Vol. III. | Monthly Intelligence Reports. |
| HCB R.62. | Intelligence Reports. |
| HCB R.227. | Coup d'Etat. |

## Nigeria National Archive-Kaduna (NAK)

### *Premier's Office, Third Collection, Kano Province (Kano Prof)*

NAK 3695/8133/S.I.        Ex-gratia payments, 1953 Riots.

NAK ASI/17.115.           Complaints, Eastern Region.

NAK ASI/72.421.           Complaints, Eastern Region.

NAK ASI/115.              Complaints, Eastern Region.

### *Premier's Office, Third Collection, Sokoto Province (Sokoto Prof)*

NAK 798/4789.             Ibo Union, Sokoto.

## United States National Archives II

### *Department of State, Record Group 59*

USNA POL 6. Nigeria.              Diplomatic dispatches.

USNA POL 15. Nigeria.             Diplomatic dispatches.

USNA POL 16. Biafra.              Diplomatic dispatches.

USNA POL 18. Nigeria.             Diplomatic dispatches.

USNA POL 27. Biafra-Nigeria.      Diplomatic dispatches.

USNA POL 23-8. Nigeria.           Diplomatic dispatches.

USNA POL 23-9. Nigeria.           Diplomatic dispatches.

## OFFICIAL AND SEMI-OFFICIAL PUBLICATIONS

Asika, Ukpabi. *No Victor, No Vanquished: Opinions 1967–68*. Apapa: East Central State Information Service, 1968.

Bako, Audu. *Policy Statement, 1 April 1968*. Kano: Information Division, Military Government Office, 1968.

Britain-Biafra Association. *Biafra: The Case for Independence*. London: BBA, 1968.

Current Issues Society. *The Nigerian Situation: Facts and Background*. Kaduna: Gaskiya Corporation, 1966.

Federal Ministry of Information (Nigeria). *Blueprint for Nigerian Unity*. Lagos: Government Printing Office, 1967.

———. *Nigeria Answers Questions*. Lagos: Government Printing Office, 1968.

———. *Nigeria: The Dream Empire of a Rebel?* Lagos: Government Printing Office, 1968.

———. *The Collapse of a Rebellion and the Prospects of Lasting Peace*. Lagos: Government Printing Office, 1968.

———. *Igbos in a United Nigeria*. Lagos: Government Printing Office, 1968.

———. *Nigeria: 12-State Structure: The Only Way Out*. Lagos: Government Printing Office, 1968.

Federal Republic of Nigeria. "Ending the Fighting," address by Gen. Yakubu Gowon, June 1968.

———. "National Reconciliation in Post-War Nigeria," address by Gen. Yakubu Gowon, 1968.

———. "Peace, Stability and Harmony in Post-war Nigeria," address by Gen. Yakubu Gowon, 1968.

*Kano State Gazette.* Kano: Ministry of Information, 1970–1975.

Kano State Public Service Commission. *Annual Report of the Public Service Commission of the Kano State of Nigeria for the Period 1st April, 1970 to 31st March, 1971.* Kano: Government Printer, 1971.

*Kano State Statistical Yearbook.* Kano: Military Governor's Office, 1972, 1974.

*Kano Telephone Directory and Quarters List.*

Mid-West Region. *The Nigerian Crisis and the Midwest Decision.* Benin City, 1968.

Military Government Office (Kano State). "Policy Statement Broadcast." Kano: Information Division, Kano State, 1968.

Ministry of Information, Biafra. *The Case of Biafra.* Enugu, 1968.

Ministry of Information, Eastern Nigeria. *The Problem of Nigerian Unity: The Case of Eastern Nigeria.* Enugu, 1966.

Ministry of Information, Northern Group of Provinces. *Nigeria: The Realities of Our Time.* Kaduna: Government Printer, 1967.

Nigeria. *The Northernization of the Civil Service: A Review of the Policy and Machinery.* By Sir Sydney Phillipson and S.O. Adebo. Lagos: Government Printer, 1954.

———. *1957 Annual Report of the Nigerianisation Officer.* Lagos: Federal Government Printer, 1958.

———. *Report of the Commission appointed to enquire into the fears of Minorities and the means of allaying them.* London: HMSO, 1958.

Northern Nigeria. *The Creation of States.* Kaduna: Government Printing Office, 1967.

Northern Regional Legislature (Nigeria). *Northern House of Assembly Debates.* Kaduna: Government Printing Office, 1953.

Northern Region (Nigeria). *Report on the Kano Disturbances, 16–19 May, 1953.* Kaduna: Government Printer, 1953.

*Official Gazette.* Lagos: Federal Military Government of Nigeria, 1970.

## NEWSPAPERS

*Abuja Mirror* (Abuja)
*Daily Comet* (Kano)
*Daily Mail* (Lagos)
*Daily Times* (Lagos)
*Gaskiya Ta Fi Kwabo* (Kaduna)
*Inter Press Service* (electronic)
*New Nigerian* (Kaduna)
*Nigerian Citizen* (Kaduna)
*Renaissance* (Enugu)
*Times* (London)

## MAGAZINES

*Drum*
*West Africa*

## OTHER PRIMARY MATERIALS

Armstrong, R.G. *The Issues at Stake*. Ibadan: Ibadan University Press, 1967.

Azikiwe, Nnamdi. *Zik: A Selection from the Speeches of Nnamdi Azikiwe*. Cambridge: Cambridge University Press, 1961.

Graham-Douglas, Dr. Nabo B. *Ojukwu's Rebellion and World Opinion*. Apapa: Nigerian National Press Limited, n.d. (1968).

Ibo State Union. *Memorandum to the Willinks Commission*. Port Harcourt: N.P.P. Press, 1958.

Oha-Na-Eze Ndi Igbo. *The Violations of Human and Civil Rights of* Ndi Igbo *in the Federation of Nigeria (1966–1999): A Call for Reparations and Appropriate Restitutions. A Petition to the Human Rights Violations Investigating Committee* (N.p., 1999). Reproduced electronically in *West Africa Review* 2, 2 (2001). http://www.westafricareview.com/war/vol2.2/ohaneze.pdf.

## PUBLISHED SECONDARY MATERIALS

Achebe, Chinua. *The Trouble with Nigeria*. London: Heinemann, 1983.

Adamu, Mahdi. *The Hausa Factor in West African History*. Zaria: Ahmadu Bello University Press, 1978.

Adejuyigbe, Omolade, et al., eds. *Creation of States in Nigeria: A Review of Rationale, Demands and Problems up to 1980*. Lagos: Federal Government Printer, 1982.

Ademoyega, Adewale. *Why We Struck*. Ibadan: Evans Brothers, 1981.

Afigbo, A.E. *The Warrant Chiefs: Indirect Rule in Southeastern Nigeria, 1891–1929*. London: Longman, 1972.

———. *Ropes of Sand: Studies in Igbo History and Culture*. London: Longman, 1981.

Ahanotu, Austin M. "The Role of Ethnic Unions in the Development of Southern Nigeria: 1916–1966." In *Studies in Southern Nigerian History*. B.I. Obichere, ed. London: Frank Cass, 1982.

Akpan, Ntieyong U. *The Struggle for Secession, 1966–70*. London: Frank Cass, 1972.

Aluko, Samuel A. "The Problem of Displaced Persons." In Christian Council of Nigeria, *Christian Concern in the Nigerian Civil War*. Ibadan: Daystar Press, 1969.

Amaaze, Victor Bong. "The 'Igbo Scare' in the British Cameroons, c. 1945–61." *Journal of African History*, 31, 2 (1990): 281–293.

Amadiume, Ifi. *Male Daughters, Female Husbands: Gender and Sex in an African Society*. London: Zed Books, 1987.

Amselle, Jean-Loup. *Logiques métisses: anthropologie de l'identite en Afrique et Ailleurs*. Paris: Editions Payot, 1990.

Anber, Paul. "Modernization and Political Disintegration: Nigeria and the Ibos." *Journal of Modern African Studies*, 5, 2 (1967): 163–179.

Anderson, Benedict. *Imagined Communities: Reflections on the Origin and Spread of Nationalism*. London: Verso Editions, 1983.

Anthony, Douglas, "'Islam Does Not Belong to Them': Ethnic and Religious Identities Among Male Igbo Converts in Hausaland." *Africa*, 70, 3 (2000): 422–441.

Armstrong, R.G. *The Issues at Stake: Nigeria, 1967*. Ibadan: University Press, 1967.

Balabkins, Nicholas. *Indigenization and Economic Development: The Nigerian Experience*. London: Jai Press, 1982.

Balogun, Ola. *The Tragic Years: Nigeria in Crisis, 1966–1970*. Benin City: Ethiope Publishing Corporation, 1973.

Barth, Fredrik, ed. *Ethnic Groups and Boundaries: The Social Origin of Cultural Difference*. London: George Allen and Unwin Press, 1969.

Basden, G.T. *Among the Ibos of Nigeria: An account of the Curious & Interesting Habits, Customs & Beliefs of a little Known African People by one who has for many years lived amongst them on close & intimate terms*. 1921. Reprint, London: Frank Cass, 1966.

Bell-Failkoff, Andrew. *Ethnic Cleansing*. New York: St. Martin's Griffin, 1999.

Berman, Bruce and John Lonsdale. *Unhappy Valley: Conflict in Kenya and Africa, Book Two: Violence and Ethnicity*. Athens: Ohio University Press, 1992.

Bichi, Abdu Yahya, ed. *Wakokin Yabon Soja*. Kano: Centre for the Study of Nigerian Langauges (Bayero University), 1989.

Blackwell, H.F., ed. *The Occupation of Hausaland, 1900–04: Being a Translation of Arabic Letters Found in the Home of the Wazir of Sokoto, Bohari, in 1903*. 1927. Reprint, London: Frank Cass, 1969.

Bozzoli, Belinda. *Women of Phokeng: Consciousness, Life Strategy, and Migrancy in South Africa, 1900–1983*. Portsmouth: Heinemann, 1991.

Brandler, J.L. *Out of Nigeria: Witness to a Giant's Toils*. London: Radcliffe Press, 1993

Brass, Paul. *Riots and Pogroms*. New York University Press, 1996.

Bravman, Bill. *Making Ethnic Ways: Communities and Their Transformations in Taita, Kenya, 1800–1950*. Portsmouth: Heinemann, 1998.

Buchanan, K.M. and J.C. Pugh. *Land and Peoples in Nigeria*. London: University of London Press, 1958.

Callaway, Barbara. *Muslim Hausa Women in Nigeria*. Syracuse: Syracuse University Press, 1987.

Cervenka, Zdenek. *The Nigerian War 1967–1970: History of the War, Selected Bibliography and Documents*. Frankfurt am Main: Bernard and Graef Verlag für Wehrwesen, 1971.

Cohen, Abner. *Custom and Politics in Urban Africa: A Study of Hausa Migrants in Yoruba Towns*. Berkeley: University of California Press, 1969.

Coleman, James S. "The Ibo and Yoruba Strands in Nigerian Nationalism." In *Nigeria: Modernization and the Politics of Communalism*. Robert Melson and Howard Wolpe, eds. East Lansing: Michigan State University Press, 1971.

Comaroff, John and Jean Comaroff. *Ethnography and the Historical Imagination*. Boulder: Westview Press, 1992.

de St. Jorre, John. *The Brothers War; Biafra and Nigeria.* Boston: Houghton Mifflin, 1972.

Destexhe, Alain. *Rwanda and Genocide in the Twentieth Century.* Translated by Alison Marschner. New York: New York University Press, 1995.

Diamond, Larry. "Class, Ethnicity and the Democratic State: Nigeria, 1950–1966." *Comparative Studies in Society and History,* 25, 3 (1983): 457–489.

————. *Class, Ethnicity and Democracy in Nigeria: The Failure of the First Republic.* London: Macmillan Press, 1988.

Eades, J.S. *Strangers and Traders: Yoruba Markets and the State in Northern Ghana.* Trenton: Africa World Press, 1994.

Egboh, Edmund O. *Community Development Efforts in Igboland.* Onitsha: Etukokwu Press, 1987.

Ekechi, Felix. *Tradition and Transformation in Eastern Nigeria: A Sociopolitical History of Owerri and Its Hinterland, 1902–1947.* Kent: Kent State University Press, 1989.

Equiano, Olaudah. *The Interesting Narrative of the Life of Olaudah Equiano.* In *The Classic Slave Narratives.* Henry Louis Gates, ed. New York: Mentor Books, 1987

Fafunwa, A. Babs. *History of Education in Nigeria.* London: George Allen and Unwin, 1974.

Falola, Toyin. *Violence in Nigeria: The Crisis of Religious Politics and Secular Ideologies.* Rochester: University of Rochester Press, 1998.

Forde, Daryll and G.I. Jones. *The Ibo and Ibibio-Speaking Peoples of South-Eastern Nigeria.* London: Oxford University Press, 1950.

Forrest, Tom. *The Advance of African Capital: The Growth of Nigerian Private Enterprise.* Charlottesville: University Press of Virginia, 1994.

Forsyth, Frederick. *The Making of an African Legend: The Biafra Story.* New York: Penguin, 1977.

Frishman, Alan. *Small-Scale Industry in Metropolitan Kano, Nigeria: A Report for the World Bank.* New York: Washington: World Bank, 1979.

Furniss, Graham. "Hausa Poetry on the Nigerian Civil War." *African Languages and Cultures,* 4, 1 (1991): 21–28.

Furnivall, J.S. *Colonial Policy and Practice: A Comparative Study of Burma and Netherlands India.* Cambridge: Cambridge University Press, 1948.

Gbulie, Ben. *Nigeria's Five Majors.* Onitsha: African Educational Publishers, 1980.

Glickman, Harvey, ed. *Ethnic Conflict and Democratization in Africa.* Atlanta: African Studies Association Press, 1995.

Graham-Davis, Nabo B. *Ojukwu's Rebellion and World Opinion.* Apapa: Nigerian National Press Limited, 1968.

Green, M.M. *Igbo Village Affairs.* 1947. Reprint. London: Frank Cass, 1964.

Harneit-Sievers, Jones O. Ahazuem, et al. *A Social History of the Nigerian Civil War: Perspectives from Below.* Hamburg: Lit Verlag, 1997.

————. "Igbo 'Traditional Rulers': Chieftaincy and the State in Southeastern Nigeria." *Afrika Spectrum* (Hamburg), 33, 1 (1998): 57–70.

Hiskett, Mervyn. *The Development of Islam in West Africa.* New York: Longman, 1984.

————. "The Maitatsine Riots in Kano, 1980: An Assessment." *Journal of Religion in Africa* 17, 3 (1987): 209–223.

————. *The Sword of Truth: The Life and Times of the Shehu Usman Dan Fodio.* 2nd ed. Evanston: Northwestern University Press, 1994.

Hobsbawm, Eric and Terence Ranger, eds. *The Invention of Tradition.* Cambridge: Cambridge University Press, 1983.

Horowitz, Donald. *Ethnic Groups in Conflict.* Berkeley: University of California Press, 1985.

Igbokwe, Joe. *Igbos: Twenty-Five Years After Biafra.* Lagos, n.p., 1995.

Ike, Akwaelumo. *The Origin of the Ibos.* Aba: Silent Prayer Home Press, 1951.

Ikejiani, Okechukwu and Odinchezo Ikejiani. *Nigeria: Political Imperatives.* Enugu: Fourth Dimension, 1986.

Isichei, Elizabeth. *A History of the Igbo People.* New York: St. Martin's Press, 1976.

————. "The Maitatsine Risings in Nigeria 1980–85: A Revolt of the Disinherited." *Journal of Religion in Africa,* 17, 3 (1987): 194–208.

Jaggar, Philip. *The Blacksmiths of Kano City: A Study in Tradition, Innovation and Entrepreneurship.* Cologne: Köppe Verlag, 1994.

Jones, G.I. "Dual Organisation in Ibo Social Structures." *Africa,* 19, 2 (1949): 150–6.

Keane, Fergal. *Season of Blood: A Rwandan Journey.* New York: Viking, 1995.

Kirk-Greene, Anthony Hamilton Millard. *Lugard and the Amalgamation of Nigeria.* London: Frank Cass, 1968.

————. *Conflict and Crisis in Nigeria; a Documentary Sourcebook.* London: Oxford University Press, 1971.

————. *The Genesis of the Nigerian Civil War and the Theory of Fear.* Uppsala: The Scandinavian Institute of African Studies, 1975.

Kofele-Kale, Ndiva. *Tribesmen and Patriots: Political Culture in a Poly-Ethnic African State.* Washington: University Press of America, 1981.

Kukah, Matthew Hassan. *Religion, Politics and Power in Northern Nigeria.* Ibadan: Spectrum Books Limited, 1993.

Kuper, Hilda, ed. *Urbanization and Migration in West Africa.* Los Angeles: University of California Press, 1965.

Kuper, Leo and M.G. Smith. *Pluralism in Africa.* Berkeley: University of California Press, 1969.

Laitin, David. *Hegemony and Culture: Politics and Religious Change Among the Yoruba.* Chicago: University of Chicago Press, 1986.

Last, D.M. *The Sokoto Caliphate.* London: Longman, 1967.

Lemarchand, René. *Burundi: Ethnic Conflict and Genocide.* Cambridge: Cambridge University Press, 1995.

Lonsdale, John. "The Moral Economy of Mau-Mau: Wealth, Poverty and Civic Virtue in Kikuyu Political Thought." In *Unhappy Valley: Conflict in Kenya and Africa, Book Two: Violence and Ethnicity.* Bruce Berman and John Lonsdale. Athens: Ohio University Press, 1992.

Lubeck, Paul. *Islam and Urban Labor in Northern Nigeria: The Making of a Muslim Working Class.* Cambridge: Cambridge University Press, 1986.

Madiebo, Alexander A. *The Nigerian Revolution and the Biafran War.* Enugu: Fourth Dimension Publishers, 1980.

Mahadi, Abdullahi, et al., eds. *Nigeria: The State of the Nation and the Way Forward*. Kaduna: Arewa House, 1994.

Mainasara, A.M. *The Five Majors: Why They Struck*. Zaria: Hudahuda Publishing, 1982.

Malkki, Liisa. *Purity and Exile: Violence, Memory and National Cosmology among Hutu Refugees in Tanzania*. Chicago: University of Chicago Press, 1995.

Mamdani, Mahmood. *Citizen and Subject: Contemporary Africa and the Legacy of Late Colonialism*. Princeton University Press, 1996.

———. *When Victims Become Killers: Colonialism, Nativism, and the Genocide in Rwanda*. Princeton: Princeton University Press, 2001.

Melson, Robert and Howard Wolpe, eds. *Nigeria: Modernization and the Politics of Communalism*. East Lansing: Michigan State University, 1971.

Miles, William F.S. *Hausaland Divided*. Ithaca: Cornell University Press, 1994.

Mosugu, S.E. *Abandoned Property Edicts in the Northern States*. Zaria: Nigeria Institute of Administration, Ahmadu Bello University, 1972.

Muffett, D.J.M. *Let Truth Be Told: The Coups D'Etat of 1966*. Zaria: Hudahuda Publishing, 1982.

Muhammadu, Turi and Mohmammed Haruna. "The Civil War." In *Nigerian Government and Politics Under Military Rule 1966–79*. Oyeleye Oyediran, ed. New York: St. Martin's Press, 1979.

Nafziger, Wayne. "The Economic Impact of the Nigerian Civil War." *Journal of Modern African Studies*, 11, 4, (1973): 505–36.

———. *The Economics of Political Instability: The Biafran War*. Boulder, Colorado: Westview Press, 1983.

Newbury, Catharine. *The Cohesion of Oppression: Clientship and Ethnicity in Rwanda, 1860–1960*. New York: Columbia University Press, 1988.

———. "Ethnicity and the Politics of History in Rwanda." *Africa Today* 45, 1 (1998): 7–24.

Nigerian Economics Society. *Nigeria's Indigenisation Policy: Proceedings of the November 1974 Symposium Organized by the Nigerian Economic Society on the Subject "Indigenisation: What Have We Achieved?"* Ibadan: Department of Economics, University of Ibadan, 1974.

Nmoma, Veronica. "Ethnic Conflict, Constitutional Engineering and Democracy in Nigeria." In *Ethnic Conflict and Democratization in Africa*. Harvey Glickman, ed. Atlanta: African Studies Association Press, 1995.

Nnoli, Okwudiba. "The Dynamics of Ethnic Politics in Nigeria." *Journal of West African Studies*, 13–14 (1976).

———. *Ethnic Politics in Nigeria*. Enugu: Fourth Dimension Publishers, 1978.

———. *Ethnicity and Development in Nigeria*. Brookfield: Ashgate Publishing Company, 1995.

Nwankwo, Arthur A. and Samuel U. Ifejika. *Biafra: The Making of a Nation*. New York: Praeger, 1970.

Obasanjo, Olusegun. *My Command*. London: Heinemann, 1981.

Obiwu. *Igbos of Northern Nigeria*. Lagos: Torch Publications, 1996.

Ogunnika, Z.O. *Inter-ethnic Tension Management in Nigeria*. Lagos: Mufets, 1994.

Okocha, Emma. *Blood on the Niger: An Untold Story of the Nigerian Civil War*. Washington, DC: USA Africa, 1994.

Olukoshi, Adebayo O. "Bourgeois Social Movements and the Struggle for Democracy in Nigeria: An Inquiry into the 'Kaduna Mafia'." In *African Studies in Social Movements and Democracy,* Council for the Development of Social Science Research in Africa. Oxford: CODESRIA, 1995.

Onuora, Chukwuma. *The Role of Igbos Towards Nigerian Unity.* (1992).

Onwubu, Chukwuemeka. "Ethnic Identity, Political Integration and National Development: The Igbo Diaspora in Nigeria." *Journal of Modern African Studies,* 13, 4 (1975): 399–413.

Oriji, John N. *Traditions of Igbo Origin: A Study of Pre-Colonial Population Movements in Africa.* New York: Peter Lang, 1990.

Osaghae, Eghosa. *Trends in Migrant Political Organizations in Nigeria: The Igbo in Kano.* Ibadan: Institut Français de Recherche en Afrique, 1994.

————, *et al. Urban Violence in Nigeria.* Ibadan: Institut Français de Recherche en Afrique, 1994.

Otite, Onigu. *Ethnic Pluralism and Ethnicity in Nigeria.* Ibadan: Shaneson C.I. Limited, 1990.

Paden, John N. "Communal Competition, Conflict and Violence in Kano." In *Nigeria: Modernization and the Politics of Communalism.* Robert Melson and Howard Wolpe, eds. East Lansing: Michigan State University Press, 1971.

————. *Religion and Political Culture in Kano.* Berkeley: University of California Press, 1973.

————. *Ahmadu Bello, Sardauna of Sokoto: Values and Leadership in Nigeria.* Zaria: Hudahuda Publishing Co., 1986.

Perham, Margery. *Lugard, the Years of Authority 1889–1945.* London: Collins, 1960.

Plotnicov, Leonard. *Strangers to the City: Urban Man in Jos, Nigeria.* Pittsburgh: University of Pittsburgh, 1967.

Post, Kenneth and Michael Vickers, eds. *Structure and Conflict in Nigeria.* London: Heinemann, 1973.

Prunier, Gérard. *The Rwanda Crisis: History of a Genocide.* New York: Columbia University Press, 1995.

Reynolds, Jonathan. *The Time of Politics (Zamanin Siyasa): Islam and the Politics of Legitimacy in Northern Nigeria 1950–1966.* San Francisco: International Scholars Publications, 1999.

Roosens, Eugeen. *Creating Ethnicity: The Process of Ethnogenesis.* London: Sage Publications, 1989.

Sada, P.O. "Urbanism, Urban Structure and Migration in Nigeria." In *Problems of Migration in Nigeria: Proceedings of the Third National Seminar/Workshop on Problems of Migration in Nigeria.* O. Odumosu, et al., eds. Ibadan: Caxton Press, 1976.

Salamone, Frank. "Becoming Hausa: Ethnic Identity Change and Its Implications for the Study of Ethnic Pluralism and Stratification." *Africa,* 45, 4 (1975): 410–23.

————. "Ethnicity and the Nigerian Civil War." *L'Afrique et l'Adie modernes,* 111 (1976): 5–12.

————. "Ethnicity and Nigeria Since the End of the Civil War." *Dialectical Anthropology,* 22, 3–4 (1997): 303–333.

Sanda, Akinade Olumuyiwa. *The Challenge of Nigeria's Indigenization.* Ibadan: Nigerian Institute of Social and Economic Research, 1982.

Sklar, Richard and C.S. Whitaker. *African Politics and Problems in Development.* Boulder: Lynne Rienner, 1991.

Smock, Audrey. *Ibo Politics: The Role of Ethnic Unions in Eastern Nigeria.* Cambridge: Harvard University Press, 1971.

Spear, Thomas and Richard Waller, eds. *Becoming Maasai: Ethnicity and Identity in East Africa.* Athens: Ohio University Press, 1993.

Takaya, B.J. *The Middle Belt in Nigerian Politics.* Jos: ASA Publishers, 1991.

Takaya, B.J. and S.G. Tyoden. *The Kaduna Mafia.* Jos: Jos University Press, 1987.

Trevallion, B.A.W. *Metropolitan Kano: Report of the Twenty Year Development Plan, 1963–83.* Oxford: Pergamon Press, 1963.

Tyoden, Sonni Gwanle. *The Middle Belt in Nigerian Politics.* Jos: AHA Publishing House, 1993.

Uchendu, Victor. *The Igbo of Southeastern Nigeria.* New York: Holt, Reinhard and Wilson, 1965.

Ujo, A.A., ed. *Three Decades of the Nigerian Civil Service, 1960–1990.* Jos: Nigerian Political Science Association, 1990.

Usman, Yusufu Bala and George Amale Kwanashie, eds. *Inside Nigerian History 1950–1970. Proceedings of the Presidential Panel on Nigeria Since Independence History Project, 7–9 June 1995.* Zaria: Ahmadu Bello University Press, 1995.

van den Bersselaar, Dmitri. *In Search of Igbo Identity: Language, Culture and Politics in Nigeria, 1900–1966.* Leiden: University of Leiden Press, 1998.

Vail, Leroy, ed. *The Creation of Tribalism in Southern Africa.* Berkeley: University of California Press, 1989.

*Wakokin Yabon Soja.* Kano: Center for the Study of Nigerian Languages (Bayero University-Kano), n.d.

Wallerstein, Immanuel. "Ethnicity and National Integration in West Africa." *Cahiers d'études Africaines* 3 (1960): 129–139.

Waugh, Auberon and Suzanne Cronje. *Biafra: Britain's Shame.* London: Joseph, 1969.

Whitaker, C.S. *The Politics of Tradition: Continuity and Change in Northern Nigeria, 1946–1966.* Princeton University Press, 1970.

Yakasai, Tanko. "The Fall of the First Republic and Nigeria's Survival of the Crisis and the Civil War of 1966–1970." In *Inside Nigerian History 1950–1970. Proceedings of the Presidential Panel on Nigeria Since Independence History Project, 7–9 June 1995.* Yusufu Bala Usman and George Amale Kwanashie, eds. Zaria: Ahmadu Bello University Press, 1995.

Yahaya, A.D. "Experiences in the Northern States." In *Nigerian Public Administration 1960–1980: Perspectives and Prospects.* 'Lapido Adamolekun, ed. Ibadan: Heinemann Educational Publishers, 1985.

Young, Crawford. *The Politics of Cultural Pluralism.* Madison: University of Wisconsin Press, 1976.

———. "Nationalism, Ethnicity and Class in Africa: A Retrospective." *Cahiers d'études Africaines*, 26, 3 (1986): 421–495.

————. *The Rising Tide of Cultural Pluralism: The Nation State at Bay.* Madison: University of Wisconsin Press, 1993.

Zahardeen, Nasir B. *The Maitatsine Saga.* Zaria: Hudahuda Publishers, 1988.

Zukerman, M.E. "Nigerian Crisis: Economic Impact on the North." *Journal of Modern African Studies,* 8, 1 (1970): 37–54.

## UNPUBLISHED SECONDARY SOURCES

Allyn, David E. *The Sabon Gari System in Northern Nigeria, 1911–1940.* Ph.D. dissertation, UCLA, 1976.

Bako, Ahmed. *A Socio-Economic History of Sabon Gari Kano, 1913–1989.* Ph.D. dissertation, Bayero University-Kano, 1990.

Elegalam, Charles C. *The Causes and Consequences of Igbo Migration to Northern Nigeria, 1900–1966.* Ph.D. dissertation, Howard University, 1988.

Frishman, A. *The Spatial Growth and Residential Location of Kano Nigeria.* Ph.D. dissertation, Northwestern University, 1977.

Harneit-Sievers, Axel. "'No Victors, No Vanquished'? Reconstruction and Reintegration after the Nigerian Civil War." Unpublished paper, 1994.

Lacey, Linda. *Urban Migration in Developing Countries: A Case Study of Three Cities in Nigeria.* Ph.D. dissertation, Cornell University, 1981.

Ogbogu, Patricia. "Ibo Reintegration in Kano After the War." Undergraduate thesis, Ahmadu Bello University, 1973.

Ogunnika, Z.O. *Mechanisms of Tension Management in a Plural Society: A Study of Inter-Ethnic Relations in Kano City, Nigeria.* Ph.D. dissertation, New School for Social Research, 1982.

Paden, John N. *The Influence of Religious Elites on Political Culture and Community Integration in Kano, Nigeria.* Ph.D. dissertation, Harvard University, 1968.

Pittin, Rene. *Marriage and Alternative Strategies: Career Patterns of Hausa Women in Katsina City.* Ph.D. dissertation, University of London, 1979.

Umar, Muhammad Sani. *Muslims' Intellectual Responses to British Colonialism in Northern Nigeria, 1903–1945.* Ph.D. dissertation, Northwestern University, 1997.

## LIST OF INTERVIEWS

1. *Eze* Patrick Ibeakamma Acholonu, *Igwe* of Orlu, 20 September 1994, Orlu.

2. Alhaji Dauda Adamu, *Mai Unguwar* (Ward Head) Yakasai "A" Ward, 8 September 1994, Kano.

3A. Alhaji Uba Adamu, 13 November 1993, Kano.

3B. Alhaji Uba Adamu, 17 November 1993, Kano.

3C. Alhaji Uba Adamu, 1 December 1993, Kano.

3D. Alhaji Uba Adamu, 18 April 1994, Kano.

4.   Chief D.O. Adinuso, 1 July 1994, Kano.

5.   Alhaji Ado, *Mai Unguwar* (Ward Head) Ja'oji "A" Ward, 25 September 1994, Kano.

6.   Mr. Felix Agwuenu, 1 April 1994, Kano.

7.   Mrs. Ajegu, 19 August 1994, Kano.

8.   Mr. C. Ajezu, 25 March 1994, Kano.

9.   Mrs. Martha Ajezu, 15 September 1994, Kano.

10.  Malam Ali, *Mai Unguwar* (Ward Head) Takalmawa Ward, 19 September 1994, Kano.

11.  Mrs. Rose Anunobi, 20 August 1994, Kano.

12.  Chief W.O. Anunobi, 7 August 1994, Kano.

13.  Chief C.O. Anyaka, 5 July 1994, Kano.

14.  Malam Muhammad Anyanwu, 14–15 September 1994, Kano.

15.  Mr. K.J. Asika, 12 February 1994, Kano.

16.  Alhaji Sani Bala, 8 August 1994, Kano.

17A. Alhaji Aminu Sharif Bappa, 1 October 1994, Kano.

17B. Alhaji Aminu Sharif Bappa, 10 July 1998, Kano.

18.  Alhaji Bala Bello, *Mai Unguwar* (Ward Head) Unguwar Gini Ward, 22 August 1994, Kano.

19.  Malam Ali Chuks, 15 November 1993, Kano.

20.  Alhaji Magiyi Ciroma, *Wakilin Kudu*, 24 August 1994, Kano.

21.  Malam Yusuf Umar Dala, *Mai Unguwar* (Ward Head) Dala Ward, 20 July 1994, Kano.

22.  Malam A.U. Dan Asabe, 14 September 1994, Kano.

23.  Alhaji Usaini Dan Gumel, *Mai Unguwar* (Ward Head) Dukawa, 19 September 1994, Kano.

24.  Mr. Victor Dibiamaka, 15 December 1993, Kano.

25.  Mrs. Florence Duru, 2 September 1994, Kano.

26.  Police Inspector Rilwanu Dutse (rtd.), 9 August 1994, Kano.

27A. Chief J.B. Egbe, 27 December 1993, Kano.

27B. Chief J.B. Egbe, 30 September 1994, Kano.

28.  Mrs. M.A. Egboluche, 17 August 1994, Kano.

29.  Mr. Goddy Emeka-Ejiofor, 28 March 1994, Kano.

30.  Chief Jonathan Ekwolugo, 12 May 1994, Kano.

31.  Mrs. Bridget Emewalo, 4 September 1994, Kano.

32A. Mr. J.C. Emodi, 6 May 1993, Kano.

32B.  Mr. J.C. Emodi, 26 May 1993, Kano.

32C.  Mr. J.C. Emodi, 17 May 1994, Kano.

33.  Chief Patrick Enendu, 1 May 1994, Kano.

34.  Mr. Napoleon Ewuzie, 12 February 1994, Kano.

35.  Mr. Donatus Ezemwata, 16 April 1994, Kano.

36.  Mrs. Roseline Ezeoru, 29 August 1994, Kano.

37.  Chief A. Ezetah, 15 May 1993, Kano.

38.  Alhaji Abdulrahman Howeidy, 18 April 1994, Kano.

39.  Alhaji Baban Inna Ibrahim, *Mai Unguwar* (Ward Head) Yammuruci Ward, 21 September 1994, Kano.

40.  Alhaji Umaru Ibrahim, *Mai Unguwar* (Ward Head) Makwarari Ward, 20 September 1994, Kano.

41.  Mrs. Iheagwam, 11 September 1994, Kano.

42A.  Mr. Emanuel Irozuru, 30 March 1994, Kano.

42B.  Mr. Emanuel Irozuru, 8 September 1994, Kano.

43.  Alhaji Uba Isa, *Mai Unguwar* (Ward Head) Tudun Nufawa Ward, 18 September 1994, Kano.

44.  Mr. Yousuf M. Jaffar, 8 August 1994, Kano.

45.  Mrs. Caroline Jideonwo, 7 September 1994, Kano.

46.  Mrs. Charity John, 5 September 1994, Kano.

47.  Malam Isiyaku Kankurofi, 19 August 1994, Kano.

48.  Mrs. Mary Kanuh, 15 March 1994, Kano.

49.  Alhaji Shehu Usman Kazaure, 4 September 1994, Kano.

50.  Mr. Abdul R. Khatoun, 10 September 1994, Kano.

51.  Mr. Ogbiji Linus, 20 September 1994, Orlu.

52.  Mrs. Comfort Metu, 14 August 1994, Kano.

53.  Alhaji Sharu Audu Mili, *Mai Unguwar* (Ward Head) Sharifai Ward, 22 September 1994, Kano.

54.  Mrs. Agbonma Mmuo, 1 September 1994, Kano.

55A.  Mr. Robert Montgomery, 5 March 1994, Kano.

55B.  Mr. Robert Montgomery, 20 June 1994, Kano.

55C.  Mr. Robert Montgomery and Mrs. Maria Ojeh Montgomery, 22 June 1994, Kano.

56.  Alhaji Adamu Baba Muhammad, *Mai Unguwar* (Ward Head) Kofar Nassarawa Ward, and Malam Ibrahim Kuji, 24 August 1994, Kano.

57. Alhaji Dauda Muhammad, *Mai Unguwar* (Ward Head) Kofar Wambai Ward, 18 September 1994, Kano.

58. Alhaji Uba Muhammad, *Mai Unguwar* (Ward Head) Kofar Mata Ward, 18 September 1994, Kano.

59A. The Reverend Victor Musa, 14 April 1994, Kano.

59B. The Reverend Victor Musa, 26 April 1994, Kano.

60. Alhaji Sani Nababa, 1 October 1994, Kano.

61. Mr. D.O. Nnadi, 4 May 1994, Kano.

62A. Chief O.T. Nnadi, *Eze Ndi Igbo* (Chief of the Igbo People) of Kano, 6 June 1993, Kano.

62B. Chief O.T. Nnadi, *Eze Ndi Igbo* (Chief of the Igbo People) of Kano, 2 October 1994, Kano.

63. Mr. U.M. Nnadi, 4 June 1994, Kano.

64A. Chief Luke Nwode, 19 March 1994, Kano.

64B. Chief Luke Nwode, 7 April 1994, Kano.

65. Mrs. Teresa Nwode, 29 August 1994, Kano.

66. Mr. Mambo Nyamasi, 27 February 1994, Kano.

67. Mrs. Obi, 3 September 1994, Kano.

68. Mrs. V.N. Obionu, 26 August 1994, Kano.

69. Father John O'Brien, 11 March 1994, Kano.

70A. Chief Davis Ohaeri, 19 March 1994, Kano.

70B. Chief Davis Ohaeri, 18 June 1994, Kano.

71. Mrs. Uzoma Ojuku, 7 September 1994, Kano.

72. Mrs. Maria Okenwa, 16 September 1994, Kano.

73A. Malam Abdullahi Okere, 15 September 1994, Kano.

73B. Malam Abdullahi Okere, 30 September 1994, Kano.

74. Mrs. Chinyere Okpara, 20 August 1994, Kano.

75. Mrs. V.U. Okwuego, 24 August 1994, Kano.

76. Mr. Robert Onuora, 31 March 1994, Kano.

77A. Mr. Obed O. Onwochie, 14 June 1993, Kano.

77B. Mr. Obed O. Onwochie, 31 March 1994, Kano.

78. Mrs. Felicia Onwualu, 11 August 1994, Kano.

79A. Chief Michael Onyeador, 5 April 1994, Kano.

79B. Chief Michael Onyeador, 30 September 1994, Kano.

80. Mrs. Christiana Orakwe, 22 August 1994, Kano.

81. Alhaji "Likita" Nahiru Ringim, Alhaji Garba Tsoho, Alhaji Suleman Musa Garko, Alhaji Bala Isiyaku, 5 June 1994, Challawa.

82. Alhaji Abbas Sanusi, *Wamban Kano* (Senior Counselor to the Emir of Kano), 1 September 1994, Kano.

83. Professor Philip Shea, 16 November 1993, Kano.

84. Malam Sunusi, *Mai Unguwar* (Ward Head) Lolloki Ward, 17 September 1994, Kano.

85. Alhaji Talle, *Mai Unguwar* (Ward Head) Ja'oji "C" Ward, 23 September 1994, Kano.

86. Mrs. Juliana Ubuonu, 26 August 1994, Kano.

87. The Very Reverend Samuel Uche, 1 June 1994, Kano.

88. Malam Yunusa Ukatu, 14 February 1994, Kano.

89. Mrs. U. Ukoha, 30 August 1994, Kano.

90A. Mr. Humphrey S.C. Umeh, 10 October 1993, Kano.

90B. Mr. Humphrey S.C. Umeh, 25 January 1994, Kano.

90C. Mr. Humphrey S.C. Umeh, 18 May 1994, Kano.

90D. Mr. Humphrey S.C. Umeh, 20 June 1994, Kano.

90E. Mr. Humphrey S.C. Umeh, 5 July 1994, Kano.

91. Mr. Jesse Umeh, 25 June 1994, Kano.

92. Mrs. S.N.C. Umeh, 11 August 1994, Kano.

93. Mrs. Victoria Uwaoma, 15 September 1994, Kano.

94. Mrs. Veronica Uzokwe, 26 August 1994, Kano.

95. Alhaji Musa Ware, *Mai Unguwar* (Ward Head) Ja'oji "B" Ward, 25 September 1994, Kano.

96A. Alhaji Tanko Yakasai, 3 January 1994, Kano.

96B. Alhaji Tanko Yakasai, 17 January 1994, Kano.

97. Malam Zakari Ya'u, 5 April 1994, Kano.

98. Professor D. Murray Last, 5 November, 1995, Orlando, Florida (USA).

99. Professor Jean Boyd, 6 November 1995, Orlando, Florida (USA).

100. Alhaji Lawal Tudun Wada, 10 June 1998, Kano.

101. Alhaji Liman Ciroma, 4 July 1998, Kaduna.

# INDEX

**About the Author**

DOUGLAS A. ANTHONY is Assistant Professor of History at Franklin and Marshall College.